Air Fryer Cookbook UK

Simple, Affordable and Crunchy Air Fryer Recipes for Beginners

Helena Baxter

Copyright © 2022 by Helena Baxter

All rights reserved worldwide.

ISBN: 979-8427394048

No part of this book may be reproduced or transmitted in any form or by any means, electronic or mechanical, including photocopying, recording or by any information storage and retrieval system, without written permission from the publisher, except for the inclusion of brief quotations in a review.

Warning-Disclaimer

The purpose of this book is to educate and entertain. The author or publisher does not guarantee that anyone following the techniques, suggestions, tips, ideas, or strategies will become successful. The author and publisher shall have neither liability or responsibility to anyone with respect to any loss or damage caused, or alleged to be caused, directly or indirectly by the information contained in this book.

CONTENTS

INTRODUCTION **10**

HOW DOES THE AIR FRYER WORK? **10**

POULTRY **14**

1. Spice-Rubbed Jerk Chicken Wings 14
2. Chicken Kabobs with Salsa Verde 14
3. Portuguese Roasted Whole Chicken 15
4. Crunchy Drumsticks with Blue Cheese Sauce 15
5. Sesame Chicken Wings 15
6. Chicken Bites 16
7. Parmesan-Crusted Chicken Fingers 16
8. Shaking Tarragon Chicken Tenders 16
9. Chicken Breasts with Sweet Chili Adobo 17
10. Crispy Chicken with Parmesan 17
11. Chicken with Marinara Sauce 17
12. Sweet Chicken Breasts 17
13. Crispy Chicken Tenders with Hot Aioli 18
14. Lemony Roasted Chicken with Pancetta & Thyme 18
15. Sweet-Mustardy Thighs 18
16. Green Curry Hot Chicken Drumsticks 19
17. Homemade Chicken Nuggets 19
18. Chicken Stuffed with Sage and Garlic 19
19. Chicken Lollipop 20
20. Juicy Sweet Chili Chicken Fillets 20
21. Chicken Cheesy Divan Casserole 20
22. Chicken Breast with Prosciutto and Brie 21
23. Chicken Burgers 21
24. Spicy Chicken 21
25. Gorgeous Parmesan Chicken 22
26. Pineapple Chicken 22
27. Sweet Curried Chicken Cutlets 22
28. Juicy and Herby Chicken Thighs 23
29. Air Fried Chicken with Black Beans 23
30. Buffalo Chicken 23
31. Herby Chicken Schnitzel with Mozzarella 23
32. Quick and Crispy Chicken 24

33. Holiday Roasted Cornish Hen 24
34. Chicken with Rice 24
35. Mesmerizing Honey Chicken Drumsticks 25
36. Air Fried Chicken with Honey and Lemon 25
37. Spicy Honey Orange Chicken 25
38. Crunchy Chicken Fingers 26
39. Chicken Breasts with Tarragon 26
40. Cajun Chicken Tenders 26
41. Chicken with Cashew Nuts 27
42. Crunchy Coconut Chicken 27
43. Air Fried Southern Drumsticks 27
44. Fried Chicken Legs 28
45. Tom Yum Wings 28
46. Cordon Bleu Chicken 28
47. Chicken with Prunes 29
48. Rosemary Lemon Chicken 29
49. Greek-Style Chicken 29
50. Chicken Quarters with Broccoli and Rice 29
51. Asian-Style Chicken 30
52. Crumbed Sage Chicken Scallopini 30
53. Buttermilk Chicken Thighs 30
54. Sweet Garlicky Chicken Wings 31
55. KFC Like Chicken Tenders 31
56. Korean-Style Barbecued Satay 31
57. Chicken & Prawn Paste 32
58. Sticky Greek-Style Chicken Wings 32
59. Spicy Buffalo Chicken Wings 32
60. Crispy & Crunchy Mustard Chicken 32
61. Creamy Onion Chicken 33
62. Chicken Enchiladas 33
63. Graceful Mango Chicken 33
64. Chili Popcorn Chicken Bowl 34

65. Buttermilk Chicken 34
66. Creamy Asiago Chicken 34
67. Breaded Chicken Cutlets 35
68. Spicy Chicken Wings 35
69. Authentic Korean Chicken 35
70. Slightly Grilled Hawaiian Chicken 35
71. Awesome Candied Chicken 36
72. Coconut Chicken Bake 36
73. Lemon Pepper Chicken 36
74. Caprese Chicken With Balsamic Sauce 37
75. Sage And Chicken Escallops 37
76. Exquisite Coconut Chicken 37
77. Traditional Asian Sticky Chicken 37
78. Air Fried Cheese Chicken 38
79. Gingery Chicken Wings 38
80. Honey Chicken Drumsticks 38
81. Mustard and Maple Turkey Breast 39
82. Italian-Style Party Turkey Meatballs 39
83. Bacon-Wrapped Chicken Breasts 39
84. Turkey Cordon Bleu 40
85. Simple Panko Turkey 40
86. Thyme Turkey Nuggets 40
87. Awesome Sweet Turkey Bake 40

FISH AND SEAFOOD 42

88. Golden Cod Fish Nuggets 42
89. Crispy Salmon 42
90. Air Fried Tuna Sandwich 42
91. Fish & Chips 42
92. Crispy Fish Fingers 43
93. Hot Prawns 43
94. Grilled Barramundi in Lemon-Butter Sauce 43
95. Rich Crab Croquettes 44
96. Fried Catfish Fillets 44
97. Delicious Seafood Pie 45
98. Smoked Fish Quiche 45
99. Baby Octopus Hearty Salad 45
100. Greek-Style Salmon with Dill Sauce 46
101. Hot Crab Cakes 46
102. Crispy Prawn in Bacon Wraps 46
103. Frozen Sesame Fish Fillets 47
104. Full Baked Trout en Papillote with Herbs 47
105. Air Fried Dilly Trout 47
106. Air Fried Calamari 48
107. Breaded Scallops 48
108. Hot Salmon & Broccoli 48
109. Fish Tacos 48
110. Flatten Salmon Balls 49
111. Peppery and Lemony Haddock 49
112. Fish Finger Sandwich 49
113. Delicious Coconut Shrimp 50
114. Crab Cakes 50
115. Cajun-Rubbed Jumbo Shrimp 50
116. Soy Sauce Glazed Cod 50
117. Salmon Cakes 51
118. Pistachio Crusted Salmon 51
119. Favorite Shrimp Risotto 51
120. Tuna Patties 52
121. County Baked Crab Cakes 52
122. Chinese Garlic Shrimp 52
123. Beautiful Calamari Rings 52
124. Asian Shrimp Medley 53
125. Greek Style Fried Mussels 53
126. Panko Fish Nuggets 53
127. Lemony Salmon 54
128. Wild Alaskan Salmon with Parsley Sauce 54
129. A Worthy Sockeye Fish 54
130. Air-Fried Seafood 55
131. Lovely & Slightly "Blackened" Catfish 55
132. Crumbly Fishcakes 55
133. Cod Fennel Platter 55
134. Sautéed Shrimp 56
135. The Great Cat Fish 56
136. Quick and Easy Air Fried Salmon 56
137. A Bowl of Shrimp 56
138. Most-Authentic air fryer Fish & Cheese 57
139. The Great Air Fried Cod Fish 57
140. Parmesan Tilapia 57
141. Rosemary Garlic Prawns 57

142. Cajun Salmon with Lemon 58
143. Cod Cornflakes Nuggets 58
144. Authentic Alaskan Crab Legs 58
145. Herbed Garlic Lobster 58
146. Air Fried Fresh Broiled Tilapia 59
147. Original Trout Frittata 59

SNACKS AND SIDE DISHES 60

148. Rosemary Crispy Potatoes 60
149. Air-Fried Spiced Wings 60
150. Teriyaki Chicken Wings 60
151. Smoked Fish Balls 61
152. Spring Rolls 61
153. Prawn & Cabbage in Egg Rolls 61
154. Vanilla & Chocolate Cookies 62
155. Cauliflower with Buffalo Sauce 62
156. Crispy Chicken Nuggets 62
157. Crispy Squash 63
158. Air-Fried Chicken Tenders 63
159. Delicious Chicken Taquitos 63
160. Crispy Kale Chips 64
161. Herby Meatballs 64
162. Air-Fried Cheesy Broccoli with Garlic 64
163. Thyme & Garlic Sweet Potato Wedges 64
164. Air-Fried Pumpkin Seeds with Cardamom . 65
165. Chicken Wings with Alfredo Sauce 65
166. BBQ Chicken Pizza 65
167. Homemade Croquettes 66
168. Crispy Pepperoni Pizza 66
169. Air-Frier Baked Potatoes 66
170. Beef Meatballs 66
171. BBQ Chicken 67
172. Homemade Crispy Croutons 67
173. Air-Fried Chicken Breasts 67
174. Air-Fried Crispy Chicken Thighs 67
175. Whole Roasted Chicken 68
176. Air-Fried Chickpeas with Herbs 68
177. Classic French Fries 68
178. Air-Fried Brussels Sprouts 69
179. Garlicky Chips with Herbs 69
180. Cheesy Stuffed Mushrooms 69
181. Pita Pizzas 69
182. Spicy Fries 70
183. Mediterranean Bruschetta 70
184. Fried Agnolotti 70
185. Plums and Pancetta Bombs 70
186. Salmon Tarts 71
187. Parmesan Crusted Pickles 71
188. Breaded Mushrooms 71
189. Cheesy Sticks with Sweet Thai Sauce 71
190. Bacon-Wrapped Avocados 72
191. Hot Chicken Wingettes 72
192. Bacon & Chicken Wrapped Jalapenos 72
193. Mouth-Watering Salami Sticks 73
194. Carrot Crisps 73
195. Calamari with Olives 73
196. Sweet Mixed Nuts 74
197. Cheesy Onion Rings 74
198. Cheesy Sausage Balls 74
199. Crusted Coconut Shrimp 75
200. Quick Cheese Sticks 75
201. Spicy Cheese Lings 75
202. Radish Chips 76
203. Zucchini Parmesan Chips 76
204. Paprika Chicken Nuggets 76
205. Cool Chicken Croquettes 77
206. Herbed Croutons With Brie Cheese 77
207. Cheesy Bacon Fries 77
208. Chili Cheese Balls 78
209. Juicy Pickled Chips 78
210. Hearty Apple Chips 78
211. Appetizing Cod Fingers 79
212. Quick Rutabaga Chips 79
213. Macaroni Quiche 79
214. Pumpkin Wedges 79
215. Awesome Cheese Sticks 80
216. Elegant Carrot Cookies 80
217. Rice Pilaf with Cremini Mushrooms 80
218. Simple Cheesy Melty Mushrooms 81
219. Super Cabbage Canapes 81

220. Crispy Bacon with Butterbean Dip 81	229. Indian-Style Masala Cashew 84
221. Tender Eggplant Fries 81	230. Cheesy Cheddar Biscuits 84
222. Roasted Cashew Delight 82	231. Hearty Curly Fries 84
223. Rosemary Potato Chips 82	232. A Platter of French Fries 84
224. Almond French Beans 82	233. Bacon & Asparagus Spears 85
225. Spicy Cajun Shrimp 82	234. The Mini Cheese Scones 85
226. Roasted Brussels Sprouts 83	235. Tortilla Chips 85
227. Hearty Grilled Ham and Cheese 83	236. Salmon Croquettes 85
228. Simple Cheese Sandwich 83	

PORK, BEEF AND LAMB 87

237. Sweet Pork Tenderloins 87	267. The Ultimate Beef Chili 97
238. Pork and Apple Burger Patties 87	268. Roast Beef 97
239. Crispy Pork Chops 87	269. Peppercorn Meatloaf 97
240. Apple and Onion Topped Pork Chops 87	270. Liver Soufflé 98
241. The Simples and Yummiest Rib Eye Steak 88	271. Panko Beef Schnitzel 98
242. Pork Belly the Philippine Style 88	272. Beef Bulgogi 98
243. Honey Barbecue Pork Ribs 88	273. Beef Veggie Mix with Hoisin Sauce 98
244. The Crispiest Roast Pork 89	274. Simple Roast Beef with Herbs 99
245. Char Siew Pork Ribs 89	275. Beef & Tomato Meatballs 99
246. Zesty Breaded Chops 89	276. Mexican-Style Beef in Savoy Wraps 99
247. Bacon-Wrapped & Stuffed Pork Loins 90	277. Spicy Meatloaf with Tomato-Basil Sauce 100
248. Sausage Sticks Rolled in Bacon 90	278. Ginger-Garlic Beef Ribs with Hot Sauce 100
249. Roasted Pork Rack with Macadamia Nuts 91	279. Crispy Sweet and Spicy Beef Tenderloin 101
250. Aromatic Pork Chops 91	280. Chipotle Steak with Avocado-Lime Salsa 101
251. Tangy Pork Roast 91	281. Dreamy Beef Roast 101
252. Best Ever Pork Burgers 92	282. Crazy Beef Schnitzel 102
253. Spicy Tricolor Pork Kebabs 92	283. Burgundy Beef Dish 102
254. Pulled Pork Sliders with Bacon and Cheddar 93	284. Easy Homemade Beef Satay 102
255. Pork Chops with Mustardy-Sweet Marinade 93	285. Broccoli And Beef Dish 103
256. Sweet and Hot Ribs 93	286. Delicious Beef Rice 103
257. Spicy-Sweet Beef and Veggie Stir Fry 94	287. Yummy Worcestershire Beef Burgers 103
258. Meatloaf 94	288. Beer Dredged Corned Beef 104
259. Spice-Coated Steaks 94	289. Beef Stroganoff 104
260. Healthier Burgers 94	290. American Beef Roll 104
261. Air Fried Beef Empanada 95	291. Traditional Beef Meatballs 105
262. Beef Quesadillas 95	292. Original Rib Eye 105
263. Liver Muffins with Eggs 95	293. Honey & Pork Dish 105
264. Meatballs in Tomato Sauce 96	294. Mexican Pork And Rice 106
265. Thai Roasted Beef 96	295. Awesome Onion and Sausage Balls 106
266. Crunchy Beef Schnitzel 96	296. Juicy Double Cut Pork Chops 106

297. Sweet Pork Balls	106
298. Ultimate Ham Quiche Cups	107
299. Herbed Pork	107
300. Sweet & Tender Pork Chops	107
301. Special Crackling Pork Belly	108
302. The Butterbean Pork Ratatouille	108
303. The Feisty Air Fried Pigs in Blanket	108
304. Fruity Pear and Ham	108
305. Garlic & Bacon Platter	109
306. Ham & Cheese Sandwich	109
307. Savoury Apple Pork Bites	109
308. Crunchy Cashew Lamb Rack	110
309. Oregano & Thyme Lamb Chops	110
310. Lamb Meatballs	110
311. Lamb Steaks with Fresh Mint and Potatoes	110

VEGETABLES AND VEGETARIAN 112

312. Vegetable Croquettes	112
313. Crispy Air-Fried Tofu	112
314. Air-Fried Veggie Sushi	112
315. Roasted Balsamic Veggies	113
316. Corn Cakes	113
317. Air Fried Halloumi with Veggies	113
318. Vegetables Tacos	114
319. Tempura Veggies with Sesame Soy Sauce	114
320. Air-Fried Cauliflower	114
321. Polenta Fries	115
322. Air-Fried Falafel	115
323. Teriyaki Cauliflower	115
324. Sweet Potato French Fries	116
325. Spicy Mixed Veggie Bites	116
326. Brussels Sprouts with Garlic Aioli	116
327. Cheesy Stuffed Peppers	117
328. Cheesy Mushroom and Cauliflower Balls	117
329. Curried Cauliflower Florets	117
330. Roasted Rosemary Squash	118
331. Eggplant Gratin with Mozzarella Crust	118
332. Three Veg Bake	118
333. Easy Roast Winter Vegetable Delight	119
334. Potato, Eggplant, and Zucchini Chips	119
335. Stuffed Mushrooms with Bacon & Cheese	119
336. Tomato Sandwiches with Feta and Pesto	120
337. Italian Style Tofu	120
338. Two-Cheese Vegetable Frittata	120
339. Nutty Pumpkin with Blue Cheese	121
340. Chili Bean Burritos	121
341. Veggie Meatballs	121
342. Eggplant Cheeseburger	122
343. Cheesy Broccoli with Eggs	122
344. Air-Fried Sweet Potato	122
345. Crunchy Parmesan Zucchini	122
346. Spinach and Feta Crescent Triangles	123
347. Feta Cheese Triangles	123
348. Eggplant Caviar	123
349. Ratatouille	124
350. Cheesy Spinach Enchiladas	124
351. Chile Relleno	124
352. Cabbage Steaks	125
353. Cauliflower Rice with Tofu	125
354. Vegetable Spring Rolls	125
355. Crispy Ham Rolls	126
356. Pineapple Appetizer Ribs	126
357. Pasta with Roasted Veggies	126
358. Parsley-Loaded Mushrooms	126
359. Stuffed Mushrooms with Vegetables	127
360. Air Fried Vegetables with Garlic	127
361. Poblano and Tomato Stuffed Squash	127
362. Spicy Pepper, Sweet Potato Skewers	128
363. Grilled Tofu Sandwich	128
364. Quinoa and Veggie Stuffed Peppers	128
365. Tasty Baby Porcupine	128
366. Avocado Rolls	129
367. Vegetable Tortilla Pizza	129
368. Veggie Skewers	129
369. Paneer Cutlet	130
370. Simple Air Fried Ravioli	130
371. Crispy Nachos	130
372. Cheesy Muffins	131
373. Roasted Vegetable Salad	131

- 374. Quick Crispy Cheese Lings 131
- 375. Paneer Cheese Balls 131
- 376. Potato Filled Bread Rolls 132
- 377. Delicious Potato Pancakes 132
- 378. Drizzling Blooming Onion 132
- 379. Chickpeas & Spinach With Coconut 133
- 380. Low-Calorie Beets Dish 133
- 381. Parsnip & Potato Bake 133
- 382. Cool Mini Zucchini's 134
- 383. Roasted Brussels Sprouts & Pine Nuts 134
- 384. Baked Mediterranean Veggies 134
- 385. Indian Aloo Tikka 134
- 386. Extreme Zucchini Fries 135
- 387. Easy Fried Tomatoes 135
- 388. Zesty Pepper Bites 135
- 389. Cottage Cheese And Potatoes 136
- 390. Crispy & Tasty Tofu 136
- 391. Spiced Up Potato Wedges 136
- 392. Prawn Toast 136
- 393. Hearty Carrots 137
- 394. Surprising Quinoa Eggplant Rolls 137
- 395. Healthy Avocado Fries 137
- 396. Broccoli And Parmesan Dish 137
- 397. Quick Beetroot Chips 138
- 398. Curly Vegan Fries 138
- 399. Traditional Jacket Potatoes 138
- 400. Baked Green Beans 138
- 401. Feisty Baby Carrots 139
- 402. Elegant Garlic Mushroom 139
- 403. Mozzarella Cabbage with Blue cheese 139
- 404. Simple Brown Carrot Roast With Cumin 139

SWEETS AND DESSERTS 141

- 405. Air Fried Snickerdoodle Poppers 141
- 406. Moon Pie 141
- 407. Lemony Cheesecake 141
- 408. Baked Apples 141
- 409. Dark Chocolate Brownies 142
- 410. Chocolate and Raspberry Cake 142
- 411. Apple Caramel Relish 142
- 412. Chocolate and Peanut Butter Fondants 143
- 413. White chocolate Pudding 143
- 414. Lemon Curd 143
- 415. Almond Meringue Cookies 144
- 416. Chocolate Banana Sandwiches 144
- 417. Crème Brulee 144
- 418. The Most Chocolaty Fudge 145
- 419. White Chocolate Chip Cookies 145
- 420. White Filling Coconut and Oat Cookies 145
- 421. No Flour Lime Muffins 146
- 422. Mock Cherry Pie 146
- 423. Blueberry Muffins 146
- 424. Pineapple Cake 147
- 425. Lemon Glazed Muffins 147
- 426. Molten Lava Cake 147
- 427. Air Fried Doughnuts 147
- 428. Chocolate Soufflé 148
- 429. Cheat Apple Pie 148
- 430. Soft Buttermilk Biscuits 148
- 431. Orange Sponge Cake 149
- 432. Simple Coffee Cake 149
- 433. Banana Fritters 149
- 434. Berry Crumble 150
- 435. Baked Apples with Nuts 150
- 436. Pecan Pie 150
- 437. Delicious Apple Pie 150
- 438. Black & White Brownies 151
- 439. Hearty Apricot Crumbles 151
- 440. Hearty Banana Pastry 151
- 441. All-Star Banana Fritters 152
- 442. Almond Apples Treat 152

MORE AIR FRYER FAVORITES 153

443. Orange-Flavored Cupcakes 153
444. Blueberry Oat Bars 153
445. Potato and Spinach Omelet 153
446. Air-Fried Sourdough Sandwiches 154
447. Mango Bread 154
448. Greek-Style Frittata 154
449. Cheddar Hash Browns 155
450. Cherry and Almond Scones 155
451. French Toast with Vanilla Filling 155
452. Bacon & Egg Muffins 156
453. Banana and Hazelnut Muffins 156
454. Broccoli Cheese Quiche 156
455. Cinnamon French Toast Sticks 157
456. Sausage and Egg Casserole 157
457. Chili Hash Browns 157
458. Buttered Eggs in Hole 158
459. Breakfast Muffins with Walnuts 158
460. Paprika Rarebit 158
461. Breakfast Banana Bread 158
462. Ham and Cheese Mini Quiche 159
463. Chorizo Spanish Frittata 159
464. Zucchini Muffins 159
465. Onion and Cheese Omelet 160
466. The Simplest Grilled Cheese 160
467. Air Fried Shirred Eggs 160
468. Crustless Mediterranean Quiche 160
469. Prosciutto, Mozzarella and Egg in a Cup 161
470. Three Meat Cheesy Omelet 161
471. Raspberry and Vanilla Pancakes 161
472. Very Berry Breakfast Puffs 162
473. Sweet Bread Pudding with Raisins 162
474. Easy Air Fried Egg 162
475. Vanilla Toast 162
476. Flaxseed Porridge 163
477. Breakfast Sandwich 163
478. Sausage Frittata with Parmesan 163
479. Cinnamon Flavored Grilled Pineapples 164
480. Great Japanese Omelette 164
481. Blueberry Cream Cheese with French Toast 164
482. Clean Breakfast Sandwich 164
483. Bread Cups Omelette 165
484. Air Fried Turkey Calzone 165
485. Parsnip Hash Browns 165
486. Spicy Egg and Bacon Wraps 166
487. Mock Stir Fry 166
488. Exquisite German Pancake 166
489. Grilled Apple and Brie Sandwich 167
490. Turkey and Mushroom Sandwich 167
491. Garlicky Chicken on Green Bed 167
492. Baked Kale Omelet 167
493. Craving Cinnamon Toast 168
494. Toasted Herb and Garlic Bagel 168
495. Feta Breakfast 168
496. Cheesy Omelet 169
497. Caprese on Toast 169
498. Italian Sausage Patties 169
499. Mac and Cheese 169
500. Prosciutto and Mozzarella Bruschetta 170

INTRODUCTION

In a world where the fear of oil and fatty foods is increasing, it isn't easy to enjoy fried food without overthinking about your health. However, your days of being scared are over. You don't need to stay away from delicious fried food to be healthy. How? That's simple. Air fryers present a perfect and healthy way to prepare crisp and flavored meals.

The air fryer is one electric appliance your kitchen is already wishing you bring home. If you're wondering what an air fryer does, your oven presents a very close example. Generally, you can use air fryers to roast and bake food items. But that's not all you should know about air fryers. In this article, you'll get to see every vital piece of information about air fryers. And, should you be willing to buy one, here are all about what air fryers do.

HOW DOES THE AIR FRYER WORK?

The process of baking or cooking using air fryers is fairly simple. In case you missed it, air fryers do not actually fry foods. Most air fryers work by circulating heat through the appliance's heating element and a hot air fan. The device comes with an exhaust outlet that regulates the temperature and takes out excess hot air.

To produce perfect results, air fryers have time and temperature controls. You can easily adjust these controls to suit your food type and ingredients. When using an air fryer, most foods require a temperature ranging from (320 - 400)°F and about 8 to 25 minutes. Also, most foods need an oil coating to achieve brown layers and a crunchy feel.

The air fryer is an electric appliance and may not work without a power supply. So, to use the appliance, you'll need to power it up first. The appliances have baskets or pans where you place food for heating. To ensure even cooking, you may need to shake and toss food in the air fryer at intervals.

TYPES OF AIR FRYERS

If you're looking to buy an air fryer, there are four common types in the market. This section will tell you all you need to know about the different types of air fryers..

Your air fryer not only cuts down the amount of fat and oil you use, but it also reduces your daily calorie intake. When you use the air fryer, you'll be able to enjoy the foods you love while still eating a healthy diet. French fries when you're watching your weight? Absolutely! Eating healthy is all about consuming nutritious foods and still being able to enjoy those treats you love.

Basket Air Fryer

The first and most common type of air fryer is the basket air fryer. Basket air fryers have a deep basket in which you can put items you wish to fry. They also contain a high-power blower to throw heat around your food. Besides, the baskets usually have handles to allow you to toss and remove food items at intervals.

If you wish to cook meals with batters and coatings, basket air fryers are your top choice. Unlike other fryer types, they do not rip off your coating but maintains it while creating the Maillard effect you crave. Asides from the basket, these air fryers do not have many parts. So, you can be sure to use them for longer periods without risking damage.

Convection Oven Air Fryer

The convection oven air fryer comes as the closest option to basket fryers. If you wish to enjoy the benefits of both ovens and air fryers, convection models are a perfect choice. They combine conventional oven baking and heating features as well as hot air frying facilities. The convection oven model is famous for its countertop unit.

Most countertops units comprise of a bowl and a detachable lid. While some models use convection fans as the heating element in the lid, others have halogen bulbs serving the same function. Convection oven air fryers tend to have shorter life spans. Depending on the producer, they may also have designs that automatically turns your food over.

Paddle Air Fryers

Paddle Air Fryers are in a class of their own. What distinguishes them most is the stress-free cooking they afford you. Paddle air fryers turn your food over, so you only have to check them when they are done. Besides being convenient air fryers, paddle-type models can also make saucy meals, including risottos and curries.

Oil-less Turkey Fryers

There are other types of air frying appliances that aren't exactly like the rest. For oil-less turkey fryers, they are useful in making turkeys in a way similar to deep-frying. Most types of oil-less turkey fryers are more suitable for outdoor use. Electricity and propane are the two most common sources of power for this type of air fryers.

However, unlike the other three air fryer types, this model uses infrared heat in place of hot air. Notwithstanding, the result is still crisp and luscious turkey you'll enjoy.

BENEFITS OF USING THE AIR FRYER

The air fryer seems to be the next best thing in meal preparation. However, what does that mean for you and the average user? Here are some of the benefits you stand to gain by using air fryers.

- ### *Health Benefits*

One of the biggest plus sides of this appliance is that it provides the best escape from health challenges. Since you get to use a lot less oil than in deep frying, air fryers contain less fat. As a result, your chances of cholesterol, heart diseases, and inflammation reduce considerably. What's more? The absence of unhealthy oil and calories helps cut down on unnecessary weight gain.

- ### *Time*

While you may have to cook in batches given the size of this appliance, you still get to save time when using air fryers. Air fryers take about 8 to 25 minutes to complete your meals. Even within that short time, it doesn't compromise on the crisp and delicious nature of your food. When compared to other methods of frying, air fryers give you value for your money.

- ### *Safety*

You can be rest assured that you won't have to face oil spills or accidental splashes. If you follow manufacturer instructions, you can prevent burns, scalds, and fire accidents.

BEST FOODS FOR AIR FRYING

There's no doubt air fryers present one of the most healthy ways to make crisp and delicious meals. Yet, it's not suitable for every kind of food you dream of. If you want to get the best out of your air fryer, here are the meals you should try out with it.

1. French Fries
2. Poultry meat
3. Bananas
4. Shrimps
5. Pizza
6. Bacon
7. Fish
8. Steak
9. Doughnuts
10. Stuffed pepper

COMMON ERRORS TO AVOID WHEN USING THE AIR FRYER

There a common errors users make that damage their appliance or produce poorly cooked food. Here are some common mistakes and how you can avoid them.

Applying excess oil: All your fryer needs is two teaspoons of oil or moderate oil coating to work well. Using too much oil will leave your food improperly cooked.

Cooking wet food: Your appliance cannot get moisture off your food. So, to avoid damaging your fryer with dripping liquid put in crunchy or breaded food.

Cramping up your air fryer: You need to create a free room around your fryer. This space will make it work efficiently and release excess hot air without congestion

Cooking small food: Most fryers come with baskets or pans for placing your food. Food items smaller than French fries will probably slip off in the small space. When this happens, they may burn and let off smoke.

Leaving your air fryer dirty: Cleaning your appliance seems to be a no brainer. However, you may get tempted to ignore cleaning if there's no oil or dirt in the fryer. Doing this will harm your air fryer. Always clean with warm water and dishwashing liquid after every use.

Overcrowding your food: Always refuse the urge to stuff your fryer with food. The appliance cooks fast, so be patient enough to cook in batches. Cooking too much food at once will make the machine unable to spread heat across every side of the meal.

TIPS & TRICKS FOR BEST USE OF AIR FRYERS

Do you wish to give your appliance some royal treatment? Or do you wonder what you can do to avoid getting stuck with your machine? Here are ten effortless tips to better use and care for your appliance.

1. Before your first use, read the owner's manual carefully, so you don't miss out on anything.
2. Leave your air fryer to cool down before cleaning or storing.

3. Clean the exterior of your fryer with a moist cloth. Also, clean the interior with a sponge and hot water.

4. Wash the pans, baskets, and removable parts with dishwashing liquid and hot water. For your ease, you can also place them in the dishwasher as they are dishwasher safe. However, make sure they are dry before you put them back in the fryer.

5. Use rubber-tipped tongs in place of aluminum tongs to avoid scratching the tray and surfaces of your fryer.

6. If your food sticks hard to the fryer when cleaning, soak the pan or basket in soapy hot water. You will be able to remove them quickly.

7. Create at least four inches of room at the top and sides of your air fryer. Making space will allow it to function without overheating.

8. Inspect all plugs and cords before using your fryer. Keep your cables clean and check for damage always.

9. If you notice smoke, it may come from grease or food items that fell off the basket. Don't panic. Switch off the appliance and clean out the grease or take out food items.

10. Do you have a smelly air fryer? That's easy. Lingering food smell may be from odorous food. Clean and soak your basket or pan with soap and water. If the smell doesn't leave afterward, wipe the pan and air fryer with lemon juice. The smell should disappear when you rewash it.

POULTRY

1. Spice-Rubbed Jerk Chicken Wings

Total Time: 16 hrs 40 min | **Serves**: 4 | **Per serving**: Calories : 210; Carbs: 1g; Fat: 11g; Protein: 20g

INGREDIENTS

- 2 lb chicken wings
- 1 tbsp olive oil
- 3 cloves garlic, minced
- 1 tbsp chili powder
- ½ tbsp cinnamon powder
- ½ tsp allspice
- 1 habanero pepper, seeded
- 1 tbsp soy sauce
- ½ tbsp white pepper
- 60 ml red wine vinegar
- 3 tbsp lime juice
- 2 Scallions, chopped
- ½ tbsp grated ginger
- ½ tbsp chopped fresh thyme
- ⅓ tbsp sugar
- ½ tbsp salt

DIRECTIONS

In a bowl, add the olive oil, soy sauce, garlic, habanero pepper, allspice, cinnamon powder, cayenne pepper, white pepper, salt, sugar, thyme, ginger, scallions, lime juice, and red wine vinegar; mix well.

Add the chicken wings to the marinade mixture and coat it well with the mixture. Cover the bowl with cling film and refrigerate the chicken to marinate for 16 hours. Preheat the air fryer to 200 C. Remove the chicken from the fridge, drain all the liquid, and pat each wing dry using a paper towel.

Place half of the wings in the basket and cook for 16 minutes. Shake halfway through. Remove onto a serving platter and repeat the cooking process for the remaining wings. Serve with blue cheese dip or ranch dressing.

2. Chicken Kabobs with Salsa Verde

Total Time: 35 min | **Serves**: 3 | **Per serving**: Calories : 468; Carbs: 9.5g; Fat: 29g; Protein: 43g

INGREDIENTS

- 3 chicken breasts
- Salt to season
- 1 tbsp chili powder
- 60 ml maple syrup

For the Salsa Verde:
- 1 garlic clove
- 2 tbsp olive oil

- 120 ml soy sauce
- 2 red peppers
- 1 green pepper
- 7 mushrooms

- Zest and juice from 1 lime
- A pinch of salt

- 2 tbsp sesame seeds
- Cooking spray

- 1 tbsp fresh parsley, chopped

DIRECTIONS

Put the chicken breasts on a clean flat surface and cut them in 2-inch cubes with a knife. Add them to a bowl, along with the chili powder, salt, maple syrup, soy sauce, sesame seeds, and spray them with cooking spray. Toss to coat and set aside. Place the peppers on the chopping board. Use a knife to open, deseed and cut in cubes.

Likewise, cut the mushrooms in halves. Start stacking up the ingredients - stick 1 red pepper, then green, a chicken cube, and a mushroom half. Repeat the arrangement until the skewer is full. Repeat the process until all the ingredients are used. Preheat the air fryer to 170 C.

Brush the kabobs with soy sauce mixture and place them into the fryer basket. Grease with cooking spray and grill for 20 minutes; flip halfway through. Mix all salsa verde ingredients in your food processor and blend until you obtain a chunky paste. Remove the kabobs when ready and serve with a side of salsa verde.

3. Portuguese Roasted Whole Chicken

Total Time: 50 min | **Serves**: 4 | **Per serving**: Calories : 271; Carbs: 1g; Fat: 5.9g; Protein: 24.8g

INGREDIENTS

2 (½ lb) whole chicken, on the bone
Salt and pepper to season
1 tbsp chili powder
1 tbsp garlic powder
4 tbsp oregano
2 tbsp coriander powder
2 tbsp cumin powder
2 tbsp olive oil
4 tbsp paprika
1 lime, juiced

DIRECTIONS

In a bowl, pour the oregano, garlic powder, chili powder, ground coriander, paprika, cumin powder, pepper, salt, and olive oil. Mix well to create a rub for the chicken, and rub onto it. Refrigerate for 20 minutes.

Preheat the air fryer to 175 C. Remove the chicken from the refrigerator; place in the fryer basket and cook for 20 minutes. Use a skewer to poke the chicken to ensure that is clear of juices. If not, cook the chicken further for 5 to 10 minutes; let to rest for 10 minutes. After, drizzle the lime juice over and serve with green salad.

4. Crunchy Drumsticks with Blue Cheese Sauce

Total Time: 2 hrs 25 min | **Serves**: 4 | **Per serving**: Calories : 381; Carbs: 5g; Fat: 24.2g; Protein: 14.1g

INGREDIENTS

Drumsticks:
1 lb mini drumsticks
3 tbsp butter
3 tbsp paprika

Blue Cheese Sauce:
100g mayonnaise
220g crumbled blue cheese
240g sour cream
1 ½ tbsp garlic powder

2 tbsp powdered cumin
60g hot sauce
1 tbsp maple syrup

1 ½ tbsp onion powder
Salt and pepper to taste
1 ½ tbsp cayenne pepper
1 ½ tbsp white wine vinegar

2 tbsp onion powder
2 tbsp garlic powder

2 tbsp buttermilk
1 ½ Worcestershire sauce

DIRECTIONS

Start with the drumstick sauce; place a pan over medium heat on a stovetop. Melt the butter, and add the hot sauce, paprika, garlic, onion, maple syrup, and cumin; mix well. Cook the mixture for 5 minutes or until the sauce reduces. Turn off the heat and let cool. Put the drumsticks in a bowl, pour half of the sauce over, and mix it.

Save the remaining sauce for serving. Refrigerate the drumsticks for 2 hours. Make the blue cheese sauce: in a jug, add the sour cream, blue cheese, mayonnaise, garlic powder, onion powder, buttermilk, cayenne pepper, vinegar, Worcestershire sauce, pepper, and salt. Using a stick blender, blend the ingredients until they are well mixed with no large lumps. Adjust the salt and pepper taste as desired. Preheat the air fryer to 175 C.

Remove the drumsticks from the fridge and place them in the fryer basket; cook for 15 minutes. Turn the drumsticks with tongs every 5 minutes to ensure that they are evenly cooked. Remove the drumsticks to a serving bowl and pour the remaining sauce over. Serve with the blue cheese sauce and a side of celery sticks.

5. Sesame Chicken Wings

Total Time: 25 min | **Serves**: 4 | **Per serving**: Calories: 387; Carbs: 1.3g; Fat: 11.3g; Protein: 25.1g

INGREDIENTS

1 lb chicken wings
2 tbsp sesame oil
2 tbsp maple syrup
Salt and black pepper
3 tbsp sesame seeds

DIRECTIONS

In a bowl, add wings, oil, maple syrup, salt and pepper, and stir to coat well. In another bowl, add the sesame seeds and roll the wings in the seeds to coat thoroughly. Arrange the wings in an even layer inside your air fryer and cook for 12 minutes on 180 C, turning once halfway through.

6. Chicken Bites

Total Time: 25 min | **Serves**: 4 | **Per serving**: Calories: 415; Carbs: 3.2g; Fat: 32.1g; Protein: 4g

INGREDIENTS

2 chicken breasts, skinless, cut into 2 pieces each
1 egg, beaten
60g buttermilk
80g corn flakes, crushed
Salt and pepper to taste
Cooking spray

DIRECTIONS

In a bowl, whisk egg and buttermilk. Add in chicken pieces and stir to coat. On a plate, spread the cornflakes out and mix with salt and pepper. Coat the chicken pieces in the cornflakes. Spray the air fryer with cooking spray.

Arrange the chicken in an even layer in the air fryer; cook for 12 minutes at 180 C, turning once halfway through.

7. Parmesan-Crusted Chicken Fingers

Total Time: 1 hr 30 min | **Serves**: 2 | **Per serving**: Calories : 370; Carbs: 2g; Fat: 25g; Protein: 33g

INGREDIENTS

2 skinless and boneless chicken breasts, cut strips
1 tbsp salt
1 tbsp black pepper
2 cloves garlic, crushed
3 tbsp cornstarch
4 tbsp breadcrumbs, like flour bread
4 tbsp grated Parmesan cheese
2 eggs, beaten
Cooking spray

DIRECTIONS

Mix salt, garlic, and pepper in a bowl. Add the chicken and stir to coat. Marinate for an hour in the fridge.

Meanwhile, mix the breadcrumbs with cheese evenly; set aside. Remove the chicken from the fridge, lightly toss in cornstarch, dip in egg and coat them gently in the cheese mixture. Preheat the air fryer to 175 C.

Lightly spray the air fryer basket with cooking spray and place the chicken inside; cook for 15 minutes, until nice and crispy. Serve the chicken with a side of vegetable fries and cheese dip. Yum!

8. Shaking Tarragon Chicken Tenders

Total Time: 15min | **Serves**: 2 | **Per serving**: Calories : 230; Carbs: 0g; Fat: 5g; Protein: 18g

INGREDIENTS

2 chicken tenders
Salt and pepper to taste
½ tsp dried tarragon
1 tbsp butter

DIRECTIONS

Preheat the air fryer to 195 C. Lay a 12 X 12 inch cut of foil on a flat surface. Place the chicken breasts on the foil, sprinkle the tarragon on both, and share the butter onto both breasts. Sprinkle with salt and pepper.

Loosely wrap the foil around the breasts to enable airflow. Place the wrapped chicken in the basket and cook for 12 minutes. Remove the chicken and carefully unwrap the foil. Serve with the sauce extract and steamed veggies.

9. Chicken Breasts with Sweet Chili Adobo

Total Time: 20 min | **Serves**: 3 | **Per serving**: Calories : 164; Carbs: 0g; Fat: 6.4g; Protein: 24.8g

INGREDIENTS

3 chicken breasts
Salt to season
120 ml sweet chili sauce
3 tbsp turmeric

DIRECTIONS

Preheat the air fryer to 195 C. In a bowl, add the salt, sweet chili sauce, and turmeric; mix evenly with a spoon. Place the chicken breasts on a clean flat surface and with a brush, apply the turmeric sauce lightly on the chicken.

Place in the fryer basket and grill for 18 minutes; turn them halfway through. Serve with a side of steamed greens.

10. Crispy Chicken with Parmesan

Total Time: 30 min | **Serves**: 4 | **Per serving**: Calories: 210; Carbs: 0g; Fat: 8g; Protein: 20g

INGREDIENTS

Cooking spray
60g Italian breadcrumbs
2 tbsp grated Parmesan cheese
1 tablespoon butter, melted
4 chicken thighs
120 ml marinara sauce
60g grated Monterrey Jack cheese

DIRECTIONS

Spray the air fryer basket with cooking spray. In a bowl, mix the crumbs and Parmesan cheese. Pour the butter into another bowl. Brush the thighs with butter. Dip each one into the crumbs mixture, until well-coated.

Arrange two chicken thighs in the air fryer, and lightly spray with cooking oil. Cook for 5 minutes at 190 C. Flip over, top with a few tbsp marinara sauce and shredded Monterrey Jack cheese. Cook until no longer pink in the center, for 4 minutes. Repeat with the remaining thighs.

11. Chicken with Marinara Sauce

Total Time: 25 min | **Serves**: 2 | **Per serving**: Calories: 313; Carbs: 3.2g; Fat: 12.1g; Protein: 24g

INGREDIENTS

2 chicken breasts, skinless, beaten, ½-inch thick
1 egg, beaten
60g breadcrumbs
A pinch of salt and black pepper
2 tbsp marinara sauce
2 tbsp Grana Padano cheese, grated
2 slices mozzarella cheese

DIRECTIONS

Dip the breasts into the egg, then into the crumbs and arrange in the fryer; cook for 5 minutes at 200 C. Then, turn over and drizzle with marinara sauce, Grana Padano and mozzarella. Cook for 5 more minutes at 200 C.

12. Sweet Chicken Breasts

Total Time: 30min | **Serves**: 2/ **Per serving**: Calories: 321; Carbs: 0g; Fat: 13.7g; Protein: 35g

INGREDIENTS

2 tablespoons dijon mustard
1 tablespoon maple syrup
2 teaspoons minced fresh rosemary
¼ teaspoon salt
⅛ teaspoon black pepper
2 chicken breasts, boneless, skinless
Cooking spray

DIRECTIONS

In a bowl, mix mustard, maple syrup, rosemary, salt, and pepper. Rub mixture onto chicken breasts. Spray generously the air fryer basket generously with cooking spray. Arrange the breasts inside and cook for 20 minutes at 190 C, turning once halfway through.

13. Crispy Chicken Tenders with Hot Aioli

Total Time: 15 min | Serves: 4 | Per serving: Calories: 276; Carbs: 1.5g; Fat: 11.3g; Protein: 23g

INGREDIENTS

3 chicken breasts, skinless, cut into strips
4 tbsp olive oil
Aioli:
120g mayonnaise
120g breadcrumbs
Salt and pepper to taste
½ tbsp garlic powder

2 tbsp olive oil
½ tbsp ground chili

½ tbsp ground chili

DIRECTIONS

Mix breadcrumbs, salt, pepper, garlic powder and chili, and spread onto a plate. Spray the chicken with oil. Roll the strips in the breadcrumb mixture until well coated. Spray with a little bit of oil.

Arrange an even layer of strips into your air fryer and cook for 6 minutes at 180 C, turning once halfway through. To prepare the hot aioli: combine mayo with oil and ground chili. Serve hot.

14. Lemony Roasted Chicken with Pancetta & Thyme

Total Time: 60 min | Serves: 4 | Per serving: Calories: 264; Carbs: 1.2g; Fat: 8.1g; Protein: 22.5g

INGREDIENTS

1 small whole chicken
1 lemon
4 slices pancetta, roughly chopped
1 onion, chopped
1 sprig fresh thyme
Olive oil
Salt and black pepper

DIRECTIONS

In a bowl, mix pancetta, onion, thyme, salt, and black pepper. Pat dry the chicken with a dry paper towel. Insert the pancetta mixture into chicken's cavity and press tight.

Put in the whole lemon, and rub the top and sides of the chicken with salt and black pepper. Spray the air fryer's basket with olive oil and arrange the chicken inside. Cook for 30 minutes on 200 C, turning once halfway through.

15. Sweet-Mustardy Thighs

Total Time: 30 min | Serves: 4 | Per serving: Calories: 381; Carbs: 2.2g; Fat: 16.5g; Protein: 24.3g

INGREDIENTS

4 thighs, skin-on
3 tbsp honey
2 tbsp dijon mustard
½ tbsp garlic powder
Salt and pepper to taste

DIRECTIONS

In a bowl, mix honey, mustard, garlic, salt, and black pepper. Coat the thighs in the mixture and arrange them in your air fryer. Cook for 16 minutes at 200 C, turning once halfway through.

16. Green Curry Hot Chicken Drumsticks

Total Time: 25 min | **Serves**: 4 | **Per serving**: Calories: 342; Carbs: 1.7g; Fat: 18.6g; Protein: 21.3g

INGREDIENTS

4 chicken drumsticks, boneless, skinless
2 tbsp green curry paste
3 tbsp coconut cream
Salt and black pepper
½ jalapeño pepper, finely chopped
A handful fresh parsley, roughly chopped

DIRECTIONS

In a bowl, add drumsticks, paste, cream, salt, black pepper and jalapeno; coat the chicken well. Arrange the drumsticks in the air fryer and cook for 6 minutes at 200 C, flipping once halfway through. Serve with fresh cilantro.

17. Homemade Chicken Nuggets

Total Time: 15 min | **Serves**: 4 | **Per serving**: Calories: 264; Carbs: 6.2g; Fat: 21g; Protein: 14g

INGREDIENTS

2 chicken breasts, skinless, boneless, cut into nuggets
4 tbsp sour cream
60g breadcrumbs
½ tbsp garlic powder
½ tsp cayenne pepper
Salt and pepper to taste
Oil for spraying

DIRECTIONS

In a bowl, add sour cream and place the chicken. Stir well. Mix the breadcrumbs, garlic, cayenne, salt, and black pepper and scatter onto a plate. Roll up the chicken in the breadcrumbs to coat well. Grease the air with oil. Arrange the nuggets in an even layer and cook for 10 minutes on 180 C, turning once halfway through cooking.

18. Chicken Stuffed with Sage and Garlic

Total Time: 50 min | **Serves**: 2 | **Per serving**: Calories : 160; Carbs: 0g; Fat: 8g; Protein: 22g

INGREDIENTS

1 small chicken
1 ½ tbsp olive oil
Salt and pepper to season
120g breadcrumbs
20g chopped sage
20g chopped thyme
2 cloves garlic, crushed
1 brown onion, chopped
3 tbsp butter
2 eggs, beaten

DIRECTIONS

Rinse the chicken gently, pat dry with paper towel and remove any excess fat with a knife; set aside. On a stovetop, place a pan. Add the butter, garlic and onion and sauté to brown. Add the eggs, sage, thyme, pepper, and salt.

Mix well. Cook for 20 seconds and turn the heat off. Stuff the chicken with the mixture into the cavity. Then, tie the legs of the spatchcock with a butcher's twine and brush with olive oil. Rub the top and sides of the chicken generously with salt and pepper. Preheat the air fryer to 195 C.

Place the spatchcock into the fryer basket and roast for 25 minutes. Turn the chicken over and continue cooking for 10-15 minutes more; check throughout the cooking time to ensure it doesn't dry or overcooks. Remove onto a chopping board and wrap it with aluminum foil; let rest for 10 minutes. Serve with a side of steamed broccoli.

19. Chicken Lollipop

Total Time: 50 min | **Serves**: 3 | **Per serving**: Calories : 137; Carbs: 0g; Fat: 2.9g; Protein: 14.9g

INGREDIENTS

1 lb mini chicken drumsticks
½ tbsp soy sauce
1 tbsp lime juice
Salt and pepper to taste
1 tbsp cornstarch
½ tbsp minced garlic
½ tbsp chili powder
½ tbsp chopped coriander
½ tbsp garlic- ginger paste
1 tbsp vinegar
1 tbsp chili paste
½ tbsp beaten egg
1 tbsp paprika
1 tbsp flour
2 tbsp maple syrup

DIRECTIONS

Mix garlic ginger paste, chili powder, maple syrup, paprika powder, chopped coriander, plain vinegar, egg, garlic, and salt, in a bowl. Add the chicken drumsticks and toss to coat; Stir in cornstarch, flour, and lime juice.

Preheat the air fryer to 175 C. Remove each drumstick, shake off the excess marinade, and place in a single layer in the basket; cook for 5 minutes. Slide-out the basket, spray the chicken with cooking spray and continue to cook for 5 minutes. Remove onto a serving platter and serve with tomato dip and a side of steamed asparagus.

20. Juicy Sweet Chili Chicken Fillets

Total Time: 35 min | **Serves**: 3 | **Per serving**: Calories : 226; Carbs: 2g; Fat: 8g; Protein: 18.7g

INGREDIENTS

2 chicken fillets
Salt and pepper to taste
120g flour
3 eggs
120 ml apple cider vinegar
½ tbsp ginger paste
½ tbsp garlic paste
1 tbsp sugar
2 red chilies, minced
2 tbsp tomato puree
1 red pepper
1 green pepper
1 tbsp paprika
4 tbsp water
Cooking spray

DIRECTIONS

Preheat the air fryer to 175 C. Put the chicken breasts on a clean flat surface. Cut them in cubes. Pour the flour in a bowl, crack the eggs in, add the salt and pepper, whisk. Put the chicken in the flour mixture; mix to coat.

Place the chicken in the fryer's basket, spray with cooking spray, and fry for 8 minutes. Pull out the fryer basket, shake to toss, and spray again with cooking spray. Keep cooking for 7 minutes or until golden and crispy.

Remove the chicken to a plate. Put the red, yellow, and green peppers on a chopping board. Using a knife, cut open and deseed them; cut the flesh in long strips. In a bowl, add the water, apple cider vinegar, sugar, ginger and garlic puree, red chili, tomato puree, and smoked paprika; mix with a fork.

Place a skillet over medium heat on a stovetop and spray with cooking spray. Add the chicken and pepper strips. Stir and cook until the peppers are sweaty but still crunchy. Pour the chili mixture on the chicken, stir, and bring to simmer for 10 minutes; turn off the heat. Dish the chicken chili sauce into a serving bowl and serve.

21. Chicken Cheesy Divan Casserole

Total Time: 45 min | **Serves**: 3 | **Per serving**: Calories : 321; Carbs: 0g; Fat: 13.7g; Protein: 35g

INGREDIENTS

3 chicken breasts
Salt and pepper to taste
90g shredded Cheddar cheese
1 broccoli head
50g mushroom soup cream
20g croutons
Cooking spray

DIRECTIONS

Preheat the air fryer to 195 C. Place the chicken breasts on a clean flat surface and season with salt and pepper. Grease with cooking spray and place them in the fryer basket. Close the air fryer and cook for 13 minutes. Meanwhile, place the broccoli on the chopping board and use a knife to chop.

Remove them onto the chopping board, let cool, and cut into bite-size pieces. In a bowl, add the chicken, broccoli, cheddar cheese, and mushroom soup cream; mix well. Scoop the mixture into a 3 X 3 inches casserole dish, add the croutons on top and spray with cooking spray. Put the dish in the basket and cook for 10 minutes. Serve with a side of steamed greens.

22. Chicken Breast with Prosciutto and Brie

Total Time: 25 min | **Serves**: 2 | **Per serving**: Calories : 162; Carbs: 0g; Fat: 4g; Protein: 14g

INGREDIENTS

2 chicken breasts
1 tbsp olive oil
Salt and pepper to season
60g semi-dried tomatoes, sliced
80g brie cheese, halved
4 slices thin prosciutto

DIRECTIONS

Preheat the air fryer to 180 C. Put the chicken on a chopping board, and cut a small incision deep enough to make stuffing on both. Insert one slice of cheese and 4 to 5 tomato slices into each chicken.

Lay the prosciutto on the chopping board. Put the chicken on one side and roll the prosciutto over the chicken making sure that both ends of the prosciutto meet under the chicken.

Drizzle olive oil and sprinkle with salt and pepper. Place the chicken in the basket and cook for 10 minutes. Turn the breasts over and cook for another 5 minutes. Slice each chicken breast in half and serve with tomato salad.

23. Chicken Burgers

Total Time: 25 min | **Serves**: 4 | **Per serving**: Calories: 355; Carbs: 3.2g; Fat: 12.4g; Protein: 23.5g

INGREDIENTS

1 lb ground chicken
½ onion, chopped
2 garlic cloves, chopped
1 egg, beaten
60g breadcrumbs
½ tbsp ground cumin
½ tbsp paprika
½ tbsp coriander seeds, crushed
Salt and pepper to taste

DIRECTIONS

In a bowl, mix chicken, onion, garlic, egg, breadcrumbs, cumin, paprika, cilantro, salt, and black pepper, with hands; shape into 4 patties. Grease the air fryer with oil, and arrange the patties inside. Do not layer them. Cook in batches if needed. Cook for 10 minutes at 190 C, turning once halfway through.

24. Spicy Chicken

Total Time: 25 min | **Serves**: 4 | **Per serving**: Calories: 412; Carbs: 2.1g; Fat: 8.8g; Protein: 23.4g

INGREDIENTS

4 chicken thighs, boneless
2 garlic cloves, crushed
1 jalapeno pepper, finely chopped

4 tbsp chili sauce   Salt and black pepper

DIRECTIONS

In a bowl, add thighs, garlic, jalapeno, chili sauce, salt, and black pepper, and stir to coat. Arrange the thighs in an even layer inside your air fryer and cook for 12 minutes at 180 C, turning once halfway through. s

25. Gorgeous Parmesan Chicken

Total Time: 35 min | **Serves**: 2 | **Per serving**: Calories : 180; Carbs: 0g; Fat: 6g; Protein: 21g

INGREDIENTS

1 lb chicken wings
60g butter
30g grated Parmesan cheese
2 cloves garlic, minced
½ tbsp dried oregano
½ tbsp dried rosemary
Salt and pepper to season
¼ tsp paprika

DIRECTIONS

Preheat the air fryer to 185 C. Place the chicken on a plate and season with salt and pepper. Put the chicken in the fryer basket, close the air fryer, and fry for 5 minutes. Place a skillet over medium heat on a stovetop, add the butter, once melted add the garlic, stir and cook it for 1 minute.

Add the paprika, oregano, and rosemary to a bowl and mix them using a spoon. Add the mixture to the butter sauce. Stir and turn off the heat. Once the chicken breasts are ready, top them with the sauce, sprinkle with Parmesan cheese and cook in the air fryer for 5 minutes.

26. Pineapple Chicken

Total Time: 20 min | **Serves**: 2 | **Per serving**: Calories: 355; Carbs: 35g; Fat: 11g; Protein: 32g

INGREDIENTS

2 large chicken breasts, cubed
2 green bell peppers, sliced
½ onion, sliced
1 can drain pineapple chunks
120 ml barbecue sauce

DIRECTIONS

Preheat the air fryer to 185 C. Thread the green bell peppers, the chicken, the onions and the pineapple chunks on the skewers. Brush with barbecue sauce and fry for 20 minutes, until thoroughly cooked and slightly crispy.

27. Sweet Curried Chicken Cutlets

Total Time: 1 hr 35 min | **Serves**: 3 | **Per serving**: Calories : 170; Carbs: 0g; Fat: 3.5g; Protein: 22g

INGREDIENTS

2 chicken cutlets
1 tbsp mayonnaise
2 eggs
1 tbsp chili pepper
1 tbsp curry powder
1 tbsp sugar
1 tbsp soy sauce

DIRECTIONS

Put the chicken cutlets on a clean flat surface and use a knife to slice in diagonal pieces. Gently pound them to become thinner using a rolling pin. Place them in a bowl and add soy sauce, sugar, curry powder, and chili pepper.

Mix well and refrigerate for an hour; preheat the air fryer to 175 C. Remove the chicken and crack the eggs on. Add the mayonnaise and mix. Remove each chicken piece and shake well to remove as much liquid as possible.

Place them in the fryer basket and cook for 8 minutes. Flip and cook further for 6 minutes. Remove onto a serving platter and continue to cook with the remaining chicken. Serve with a side of steam greens.

28. Juicy and Herby Chicken Thighs

Total Time: 20 min | **Serves**: 2 | **Per serving**: Calories : 285; Carbs: 0g; Fat: 15g; Protein: 21g

INGREDIENTS

2 chicken thighs
200g tomatoes, quartered
4 cloves garlic, minced
½ tbsp dried tarragon
½ tbsp olive oil
¼ tsp red pepper flakes
Salt and pepper to taste

DIRECTIONS

Preheat the air fryer to 195 C. Add the tomatoes, red pepper flakes, tarragon, garlic, and olive oil to a medium bowl. Use a spoon to mix well. In a large ramekin, add the chicken and top with the tomato mixture.

Place the ramekin in the fryer basket and roast for 10 minutes. After baking, carefully remove the ramekin. Plate the chicken thighs, spoon the cooking juice over and serve.

29. Air Fried Chicken with Black Beans

Total Time: 18 min | **Serves**: 4 | **Per serving**: Calories: 368; Carbs: 56g; Fat: 8g; Protein: 45g

INGREDIENTS

4 boneless and skinless chicken breasts, cubed
1 can sweet corn
1 can black beans, rinsed and drained
140g red and green peppers, stripes, cooked
1 tbsp vegetable oil
2 tbsp chili powder

DIRECTIONS

Coat the chicken with salt, black pepper and a sprinkle of oil; cook for 15 minutes at 190 C. In a deep skillet, pour 1 tbsp. of oil and stir in the chili powder, the corn and the beans. Add a little bit of hot water and keep stirring for 3 more minutes. Transfer the corn, the beans and the chicken to a serving platter. Enjoy.

30. Buffalo Chicken

Total Time: 25 min | **Serves**: 4 | **Per serving**: Calories: 321; Carbs: 25.5g; Fat: 8.8g; Protein: 34.5g

INGREDIENTS

120g breadcrumbs
120g yogurt
1 lb chicken breasts cut into strips
1 tbsp ground cayenne
1 tbsp hot sauce
2 beaten eggs
1 tbsp sweet paprika
1 tbsp garlic powder

DIRECTIONS

Preheat the air fryer to 195 C. Whisk the eggs along with the hot sauce and yogurt. In a shallow bowl, combine the breadcrumbs, paprika, pepper, and garlic powder. Line a baking dish with parchment paper.

Dip the chicken in the egg/yogurt mixture first, and then coat with breadcrumbs. Arrange on the sheet and bake in the air fryer for 8 minutes. Flip the chicken over and bake for 8 more minutes on the other side.

31. Herby Chicken Schnitzel with Mozzarella

Total Time: 25 min | **Serves**: 2 | **Per serving**: Calories; 303; Carbs: 0.1g; Fat: 19.1g; Protein: 15.7g

INGREDIENTS

2 chicken breasts, skinless and boneless
2 eggs, cracked into a bowl
450 ml milk
4 tbsp tomato sauce
2 tbsp mixed herbs
450g mozzarella cheese
120g flour
100g shaved ham
120g breadcrumbs
Cooking spray

DIRECTIONS

Place the chicken breast between to plastic wraps and use a rolling pin to pound them to flatten out. Whisk the milk and eggs together, in a bowl. Pour the flour on a plate, the breadcrumbs in another dish, and start coating the chicken. Toss the chicken in flour, then in the egg mixture, and then in the breadcrumbs.

Preheat the air fryer to 175 C. Put the chicken in the fryer basket and cook for 10 minutes. Remove them onto a plate and top the chicken with the ham, tomato sauce, mozzarella cheese, and mixed herbs. Return the chicken to the fryer's basket and cook further for 5 minutes or until the mozzarella cheese melts. Serve with vegetable fries.

32. Quick and Crispy Chicken

Total Time: 15 min | **Serves**: 4 | **Per serving**: Calories: 218; Carbs: 25.3g; Fat: 8.5g; Protein: 29.5g

INGREDIENTS

8 chicken tenderloins
2 tbsp butter
2 oz breadcrumbs
1 large egg, whisked

DIRECTIONS

Preheat the air fryer to 190 C. Combine the butter and the breadcrumbs, in a bowl. Keep mixing and stirring until the mixture gets crumbly. Dip the chicken in the egg wash. Then dip the chicken in the crumbs mix.

Making sure it is evenly and fully covered; cook for 10 minutes. Serve the dish and enjoy its crispy taste!

33. Holiday Roasted Cornish Hen

Total Time: 14 hrs 20 min | **Serves**: 4 | **Per serving**: Calories 634; Carbs: 0g; Fat: 55.4g; Protein: 37.6g

INGREDIENTS

2 lb cornish hen
1 lemon, zested
¼ tbsp sugar
¼ tsp salt
1 tbsp chopped fresh rosemary
1 tbsp chopped fresh thyme
¼ tsp red pepper flakes
100 ml olive oil

DIRECTIONS

Place the hen on a chopping board with its back facing you, and use a knife to cut through from the top of the backbone to the bottom of the backbone, making 2 cuts; remove the backbone. Divide the hen into two lengthwise while cutting through the breastplate; set aside.

In a bowl, add the lemon zest, sugar, salt, rosemary, thyme, red pepper flakes, and olive oil; mix well. Add the hen pieces, coat all around with the spoon, and place in the refrigerator to marinate for 14 hours.

Preheat the air fryer to 195 C. After the marinating time, remove the hen pieces from the marinade and pat dry with a paper towel. Place in the fryer basket and roast for 16 minutes. Remove to a platter and serve with veggies.

34. Chicken with Rice

Total Time: 40 min | **Serves**: 4 | **Per serving**: Calories: 418; Carbs: 76 g; Fat: 21 g; Protein: 38 g

INGREDIENTS

- 4 chicken legs
- 200g rice
- 450 ml water
- 2 tomatoes, cubed
- 3 tbsp butter
- 1 tbsp tomato paste
- Salt and black pepper
- 1 onion
- 3 minced cloves garlic

DIRECTIONS

Rub the chicken legs with butter. Sprinkle with salt and pepper and fry in a preheated air fryer for 30 minutes at 190 C. Then, add small onion and a little bit of oil; keep stirring. Add the tomatoes, the tomato paste, and the garlic, and cook for 5 more minutes.

Meanwhile, in a pan, boil the rice in 2 cups of water for around 20 minutes. In a baking tray, place the rice and top it with the air fried chicken and cook in the air fryer for 5 minutes. Serve and enjoy!

35. Mesmerizing Honey Chicken Drumsticks

Total Time: 20 min | **Serves**: 3 | **Per serving**: Calories: 120; Carbs: 21g; Fat: 3g; Protein: 2g

INGREDIENTS

- 2 chicken drumsticks, skin removed
- 2 tbsp olive oil
- 2 tbsp honey
- ½ tbsp garlic, minced

DIRECTIONS

Preheat your air fryer to 200 C. Add garlic, oil and honey to a sealable zip bag. Add chicken and toss to coat; set aside for 30 minutes. Add the coated chicken to the air fryer basket, and cook for 15 minutes. Serve and enjoy!

36. Air Fried Chicken with Honey and Lemon

Total Time: 100 min | **Serves**: 6 | **Per serving**: Calories: 342; Carbs: 68g; Fat: 28g; Protein: 33g

INGREDIENTS

The Stuffing:
- 1 whole chicken, 3 lb
- 2 red and peeled onions
- 2 tbsp olive oil

The Marinade:
- 5 oz honey
- juice from 1 lemon

- 2 apricots
- 1 courgatte
- 1 apple

- 2 tbsp olive oil
- Salt and pepper

- 2 cloves finely chopped garlic
- Fresh chopped thyme
- Salt and pepper

DIRECTIONS

For the stuffing, chop all ingredients into tiny pieces. Transfer to a large bowl and add the olive oil. Season with salt and black pepper. Fill the cavity of the chicken with the stuffing, without packing it tightly.

Place the chicken in the air fryer and cook for 35 minutes at 170 C. Warm the honey and the lemon juice in a large pan; season with salt and pepper. Reduce the temperature of the air fryer to 160 C.

Brush the chicken with some of the honey-lemon marinade and return it to the fryer. Cook for another 70 minutes; brush the chicken every 20-25 minutes with the marinade. Garnish with parsley, and serve with potatoes.

37. Spicy Honey Orange Chicken

Total Time: 20 min | **Serves**: 4 | **Per serving**: Calories: 246; Carbs: 21g; Fat: 6g; Protein: 25g

INGREDIENTS

1 ½ pounds chicken breast, washed and sliced
Parsley to taste
100g coconut, shredded
90g breadcrumbs
2 whole eggs, beaten
70g flour
½ tsp pepper
Salt to taste
170g orange marmalade
1 tbsp red pepper flakes
90g honey
3 tbsp dijon mustard

DIRECTIONS

Preheat your air fryer to 200 C. In a mixing bowl, combine coconut, flour, salt, parsley and pepper. In another bowl, add the beaten eggs. Place breadcrumbs in a third bowl. Dredge chicken in egg mix, flour and finally in the breadcrumbs. Place the chicken in the air fryer cooking basket and bake for 15 minutes.

In a separate bowl, mix honey, orange marmalade, mustard and pepper flakes. Cover chicken with marmalade mixture and fry for 5 more minutes. Enjoy!

38. Crunchy Chicken Fingers

Total Time: 8 min | **Serves**: 2 | **Per serving**: Calories: 253; Carbs: 31g; Fat: 18g; Protein: 28g

INGREDIENTS

2 medium-sized chicken breasts, cut in stripes
3 tbsp Parmesan cheese
¼ tbsp fresh chives, chopped
40g breadcrumbs
1 egg white
2 tbsp plum sauce, optional
½ tbsp fresh thyme, chopped
½ tbsp black pepper
1 tbsp water

DIRECTIONS

Preheat the air fryer to 180 C. Mix the chives, Parmesan cheese, thyme, pepper and breadcrumbs. In another bowl, whisk the egg white and mix with the water. Dip the chicken strips into the egg mixture and the breadcrumb mixture. Place the strips in the air fryer basket and cook for 10 minutes. Serve with plum sauce.

39. Chicken Breasts with Tarragon

Total Time: 15 min | **Serves**: 3 | **Per serving**: Calories: 493; Carbs: 36.5g; Fat: 11g; Protein: 57.5g

INGREDIENTS

1 boneless and skinless chicken breast
½ tbsp butter
¼ tbsp kosher salt
½ tsp dried tarragon
¼ tbsp black and fresh ground pepper

DIRECTIONS

Preheat the air fryer to 190 C and place each chicken breast on a 12x12 inches foil wrap. Top the chicken with tarragon and butter; season with salt and pepper to taste. Wrap the foil around the chicken breast in a loose way to create a flow of air. Cook the in the air fryer for 15 minutes. Carefully unwrap the chicken and serve.

40. Cajun Chicken Tenders

Total Time: 25 min | **Serves**: 4 | **Per serving**: Calories: 253; Carbs: 16g; Fat: 11g; Protein: 23.5g

INGREDIENTS

3 lb chicken breast cut into slices
3 eggs
300g flour, divided
1 tbsp olive oil
½ tbsp plus
½ tbsp garlic powder, divided
1 tbsp salt
3 tbsp cajun seasoning, divided
60 ml milk

DIRECTIONS

Season the chicken with salt, pepper, ½ tbsp garlic powder and 2 tbsp Cajun seasoning.

Combine 2 cups flour, the rest of the Cajun seasoning and the rest of the garlic powder, in a bowl. In another bowl, whisk the eggs, milk, olive oil, and quarter cup flour. Preheat the air fryer to 185 C.

Line a baking sheet with parchment paper. Dip the chicken into the egg mixture first, and then into the flour mixture. Arrange on the sheet. If there isn't enough room, work in two batches. Cook for 12 to 15 minutes.

41. Chicken with Cashew Nuts

Total Time: 30 min | **Serves**: 4 | **Per serving**: Calories: 425; Carbs: 25g; Fat: 35g; Protein: 53g

INGREDIENTS

1 lb chicken cubes
2 tbsp soy sauce
1 tbsp cornflour
130g onion cubes
1 carrot, chopped
50g cashew nuts, fried
1 capsicum, cut
2 tbsp garlic, crushed
Salt and white pepper

DIRECTIONS

Marinate the chicken cubes with ½ tbsp of white pepper, ½ tsp salt, 2 tbsp soya sauce, and add 1 tbsp cornflour. Set aside for 25 minutes. Preheat the air fryer to 190 C and transfer the marinated chicken. Add the garlic, the onion, the capsicum, and the carrot; fry for 5-6 minutes. Roll it in the cashew nuts before serving.

42. Crunchy Coconut Chicken

Total Time: 22 min | **Serves**: 4 | **Per serving**: Calories: 651; Carbs: 21.6g; Fat: 47g; Protein: 66g

INGREDIENTS

150g coconut flakes
4 chicken breasts cut into strips
80g cornstarch
¼ tsp pepper
¼ tsp salt
3 eggs, beaten

DIRECTIONS

Preheat the air fryer to 175 C. Mix salt, pepper, and cornstarch in a small bowl. Line a baking sheet with parchment paper. Dip the chicken first in the cornstarch, then into the eggs, and finally, coat with coconut flakes. Arrange on the sheet and cook for 8 minutes. Flip the chicken over, and cook for 8 more minutes, until crispy.

43. Air Fried Southern Drumsticks

Total Time: 50 min | **Serves**: 4 | **Per serving**: Calories: 197; Carbs: 5.2g; Fat: 6g; Protein: 29.2g

INGREDIENTS

8 chicken drumsticks
2 tbsp oregano
2 tbsp thyme
2 oz oats
60 ml milk
¼ steamed cauliflower florets
1 egg
1 tbsp ground cayenne
Salt and pepper, to taste

DIRECTIONS

Preheat the air fryer to 175 C and season the drumsticks with salt and pepper; rub them with the milk. Place all the other ingredients, except the egg, in a food processor. Process until smooth. Dip each drumstick in the egg first, and then in the oat mixture. Arrange half of them on a baking mat inside the air fryer. Cook for 20 minutes. Repeat with the other batch.

44. Fried Chicken Legs

Total Time: 60 min | **Serves**: 5 | **Per serving**: Calories: 288; Carbs: 15g; Fat: 11g; Protein: 35g

INGREDIENTS

5 quarters chicken legs
2 lemons, halved
5 tbsp garlic powder
5 tbsp dried basil
5 tbsp oregano, dried
80 ml olive oil
Salt and black pepper

DIRECTIONS

Set the air fryer to 175 C. Place the chicken in a large deep bowl. Brush the chicken legs with a tbsp of olive oil.

Sprinkle with the lemon juice and arrange in the air fryer. In another bowl, combine basil, oregano, garlic powder, salt and pepper. Sprinkle the seasoning mixture on the chicken. Cook in the preheated air fryer for 50 minutes, shaking every 10-15 minutes.

45. Tom Yum Wings

Total Time: 4 hrs 20 min | **Serves**: 2 | **Per serving**: Calories: 287; Carbs: 20g; Fat: 7g; Protein: 26g

INGREDIENTS

8 chicken wings
1 tbsp water
2 tbsp potato starch
2 tbsp cornstarch
2 tbsp tom yum paste
½ tbsp baking powder

DIRECTIONS

Combine the tom yum paste and water, in a small bowl. Place the wings in a large bowl, add the tom yum mixture and coat well. Cover the bowl and refrigerate for 4 hours. Preheat the air fryer to 185 C.

Combine the baking powder, cornstarch and potato starch. Dip each wing in the starch mixture. Place on a lined baking dish in the air fryer and cook for 7 minutes. Flip over and cook for 5 to 7 minutes more.

46. Cordon Bleu Chicken

Total Time: 40 min | **Serves**: 4 | **Per serving**: Calories: 317; Carbs: 48g; Fat: 22g; Protein: 35g

INGREDIENTS

4 skinless and boneless chicken breasts
4 slices ham
4 slices Swiss cheese
3 tbsp all-purpose flour
4 tbsp butter
1 tbsp paprika
1 tbsp chicken bouillon granules
120 ml dry white wine
240g heavy whipping cream
1 tbsp cornstarch

DIRECTIONS

Preheat the air fryer to 190 C. Pound the chicken breasts and put a slice of ham on each of the chicken breasts. Fold the edges of the chicken over the filling and secure the edges with toothpicks. In a medium bowl, combine the paprika and the flour, and coat the chicken pieces. Fry the chicken for 20 minutes.

In a large skillet, heat the butter and add the bouillon and wine; reduce the heat to low. Remove the chicken from the air fryer and place it in the skillet. Let simmer for around 20-25 minutes.

47. Chicken with Prunes

Total Time: 55 min | **Serves:** 6 | **Per serving:** Calories: 288; Carbs: 44g; Fat: 18g; Protein: 39g

INGREDIENTS

- 1 whole chicken, 3 lb
- 90g pitted prunes
- 3 minced cloves of garlic
- 2 tbsp capers
- 2 bay leaves
- 2 tbsp red wine vinegar
- 2 tbsp olive oil
- 1 tbsp dried oregano
- 50g packed brown sugar
- 1 tbsp chopped and fresh parsley
- Salt and black pepper

DIRECTIONS

In a big and deep bowl, mix the prunes, the olives, capers, garlic, olive oil, bay leaves, oregano, vinegar, salt and pepper. Spread the mixture on the bottom of a baking tray, and place the chicken.

Preheat the air fryer to 180 C. Sprinkle a little bit of brown sugar on top of the chicken; cook for 55 minutes.

48. Rosemary Lemon Chicken

Total Time: 60 min | **Serves:** 2 | **Per serving:** Calories: 275; Carbs: 19g; Fat: 7.6g; Protein: 36g

INGREDIENTS

- 2 chicken breasts
- 1 tbsp minced ginger
- 2 rosemary sprigs
- ½ lemon, cut into wedges
- 1 tbsp soy sauce
- ½ tbsp olive oil
- 1 tbsp oyster sauce
- 3 tbsp brown sugar

DIRECTIONS

Add the ginger, soy sauce, and olive oil, in a bowl; add the chicken and coat well. Cover the bowl and refrigerate for 30 minutes. Preheat the air fryer to 185 C. Transfer the marinated chicken to a baking dish and cook inside the fryer for 6 minutes.

Mix the oyster sauce, rosemary and brown sugar, in a small bowl. Pour the sauce over the chicken. Arrange the lemon wedges in the dish. Return to the air fryer and cook for 13 more minutes.

49. Greek-Style Chicken

Total Time: 45 min | **Serves:** 6 | **Per serving:** Calories: 283; Carbs: 34g; Fat: 12g; Protein: 27g

INGREDIENTS

- 1 whole chicken, 3 lb, cut in pieces
- 3 chopped cloves of garlic
- 120 ml olive oil
- 120 ml white wine
- 1 tbsp fresh rosemary
- 1 tbsp chopped fresh oregano
- 1 tbsp fresh thyme
- Juice from 1 lemon
- Salt and black pepper, to taste

DIRECTIONS

In a large bowl, combine cloves of garlic, rosemary, thyme, olive oil, lemon juice, oregano, salt and pepper. Mix all ingredients very well and spread the mixture into a baking dish. Add the chicken and stir.

Preheat the air fryer to 190 C, and transfer in the chicken mixture. Sprinkle with wine and cook for 45 minutes.

50. Chicken Quarters with Broccoli and Rice

Total Time: 60 min | **Serves:** 3 | **Per serving:** Calories: 256; Carbs: 29g; Fat: 15g; Protein: 23g

INGREDIENTS

3 chicken leg quarters
1 package instant long grain rice
160g chopped broccoli
450 ml water
1 can condensed cream chicken soup
1 tbsp minced garlic

DIRECTIONS

Preheat the air fryer to 195 C, and place the chicken quarters in the air fryer. Season with salt, pepper and one tbsp of oil; cook for 30 minutes. In a large deep bowl, mix the rice, water, minced garlic, soup and broccoli. Combine the mixture very well.

Remove the chicken from the air fryer and place it on a platter to drain. Spread the rice mixture on the bottom of the dish and place the chicken on top of the rice. Cook again for 30 minutes.

51. Asian-Style Chicken

Total Time: 35 min | Serves: 4 | Per serving: Calories: 313; Carbs: 64g; Fat: 14g; Protein: 31g

INGREDIENTS

1 lb chicken, cut in stripes
2 tomatoes, cubed
3 green peppers, cut in stripes
1 tbsp cumin powder
1 large onion
2 tbsp oil
1 tbsp mustard
A pinch of ginger
A pinch of fresh and chopped coriander
Salt and black pepper

DIRECTIONS

Heat the oil in a deep pan. Add the mustard, the onion, the ginger, the cumin and the green chili peppers. Sauté the mixture for 2-3 minutes. Then, add the tomatoes, the coriander and salt and keep stirring.

Preheat the air fryer to 190 C. Coat the chicken with oil, salt and pepper and cook it for 25 minutes. Remove from the air fryer and pour the sauce over and around.

52. Crumbed Sage Chicken Scallopini

Total Time: 20 min | Serves: 4 | Per serving: Calories: 218; Carbs: 8.9g; Fat: 5.9g; Protein: 30.4g

INGREDIENTS

4 chicken breasts, skinless and boneless
3 oz breadcrumbs
2 tbsp grated Parmesan cheese
2 oz flour
2 eggs, beaten
1 tbsp fresh, chopped sage
Cooking spray

DIRECTIONS

Preheat the air fryer to 185 C. Place some plastic wrap underneath and on top of the chicken breasts. Using a rolling pin, beat the meat until it becomes really thin. In a bowl, combine the Parmesan cheese, sage and breadcrumbs.

Dip the chicken in the egg first, and then in the sage mixture. Spray with cooking oil and arrange tin the air fryer. Bake for 10-12 minutes, flipping once, until golden brown.

53. Buttermilk Chicken Thighs

Total Time: 4 hrs 40 min | Serves: 6 | Per serving: Calories: 322; Carbs: 36g; Fat: 4g; Protein: 33g

INGREDIENTS

1 ½ lb chicken thighs
1 tbsp cayenne pepper
3 tbsp salt divided

250g flour
2 tbsp black pepper
1 tbsp paprika
1 tbsp baking powder
500g buttermilk

DIRECTIONS

Rinse and pat dry the chicken thighs. Place the chicken thighs in a bowl. Add cayenne pepper, 2 tbsp of salt, black pepper and buttermilk, and stir to coat well. Refrigerate for 4 hours. Preheat the air fryer to 175 C.

In another bowl, mix the flour, paprika, 1 tbsp of salt, and baking powder. Dredge half of the chicken thighs, one at a time, in the flour, and then place on a lined dish. Cook for 10 minutes, flip over and cook for 8 more minutes. Repeat with the other batch.

54. Sweet Garlicky Chicken Wings

Total Time: 20 min | **Serves**: 4 | **Per serving**: Calories: 335; Carbs: 22g; Fat: 24g; Protein: 30g

INGREDIENTS

16 chicken wings
60g butter
90g honey
½ tbsp salt
4 garlic cloves, minced
100g potato starch

DIRECTIONS

Preheat the air fryer to 185 C. Rinse and pat dry the wings, and place them in a bowl. Add the starch to the bowl, and mix to coat the chicken. Place the chicken in a baking dish that has been previously coated with cooking oil.

Cook for 5 minutes in the air fryer. Whisk the rest of the ingredients together in a bowl. Pour the sauce over the wings and cook for another 10 minutes.

55. KFC Like Chicken Tenders

Total Time: 25 min | **Serves**: 4 | **Per serving**: Calories: 401; Carbs: 20g; Fat: 5g; Protein: 88g

INGREDIENTS

¾ pound chicken tenders
For Breading
2 whole eggs, beaten
60g seasoned breadcrumbs
60g all-purpose flour
1 tbsp black pepper
2 tbsp olive oil

DIRECTIONS

Preheat your air fryer to 170 C. Add breadcrumbs, eggs and flour in three separate bowls (individually). Mix breadcrumbs with oil and season with salt and pepper. Dredge the tenders into flour, eggs and into the crumbs.

Add chicken tenders in the air fryer and cook for 10 minutes. Increase to 195 C, and cook for 5 more minutes.

56. Korean-Style Barbecued Satay

Total Time: 4h 15 min | **Serves**: 4 | **Per serving**: Calories: 215; Carbs: 15g; Fat: 8g; Protein: 27g

INGREDIENTS

1 lb boneless and skinless chicken tenders
4 cloves garlic, chopped
4 scallions, chopped
2 tbsp sesame seeds, toasted
1 tbsp fresh ginger, grated
120 ml pineapple juice
120 ml soy sauce
80 ml sesame oil
A pinch of black pepper

DIRECTIONS

Skew each tender and trim any excess fat. Mix the other ingredients in one large bowl. Add the skewered chicken and place in the fridge for 4 to 24 hours. Preheat the air fryer to 185 C.

Using a paper towel, pat the chicken until it is completely dry. Fry for 10 minutes.

57. Chicken & Prawn Paste

Total Time: 30 min | **Serves**: 2 | **Per serving**: Calories: 110; Carbs: 7g; Fat: 5g; Protein: 7g

INGREDIENTS

8 chicken wings, washed and cut into small portions
½ tbsp sugar
2 tbsp cornflour
½ tbsp wine
1 tbsp shrimp paste
1 tbsp ginger
½ tbsp olive oil

DIRECTIONS

Preheat your air fryer to 180 C. In a bowl, mix oil, ginger, wine and sugar. Cover the chicken wings with the prepared marinade and top with flour. Add the floured chicken to shrimp paste and coat it.

Place the prepared chicken in your air fryer's cooking basket and cook for 20 minutes, until crispy on the outside.

58. Sticky Greek-Style Chicken Wings

Total Time: 25 min | **Serves**: 3 | **Per serving**: Calories: 420; Carbs: 13g; Fat: 11g; Protein: 65g

INGREDIENTS

1 pound chicken wings
1 tbsp coriander
Salt and pepper to taste
1 tbsp cashews cream
1 garlic clove, minced
1 tbsp yogurt
2 tbsp honey
½ tbsp vinegar
½ tbsp ginger, minced
½ tbsp garlic chili sauce

DIRECTIONS

Preheat the air fryer to 180 C. Season the wings with salt and pepper, and place them in the air fryer, and cook for 15 minutes. In a bowl, mix the remaining ingredients. Top the chicken with sauce and cook for 5 more minutes.

59. Spicy Buffalo Chicken Wings

Total Time: 35 min | **Serves**: 4 | **Per serving**: Calories: 464; Carbs: 10g; Fat: 21g; Protein: 19g

INGREDIENTS

4 pounds chicken wing
120 ml cayenne pepper sauce
120 ml coconut oil
1 tbsp Worcestershire sauce
1 tbsp kosher salt

DIRECTIONS

In a mixing cup, combine cayenne pepper sauce, coconut oil, Worcestershire sauce and salt; set aside. Pat the chicken dry and place in the air fryer cooking basket. Cook for 25 minutes at 190 C.

Increase the temperature to 200 C and cook for 5 more minutes. Transfer into a large sized mixing bowl and toss in the prepared sauce. Serve with celery sticks and enjoy!

60. Crispy & Crunchy Mustard Chicken

Total Time: 20 min | **Serves**: 4 | **Per serving**: Calories: 432; Carbs: 0g; Fat: 24g; Protein: 36g

INGREDIENTS

4 garlic cloves, minced
8 chicken slices
1 tbsp thyme leaves
120 ml dry wine
Salt as needed
130g dijon mustard
240g breadcrumbs
2 tbsp melted butter
1 tbsp lemon zest
2 tbsp olive oil

DIRECTIONS

Preheat your air fryer to 175 C. In a bowl, mix garlic, salt, cloves, breadcrumbs, pepper, oil, butter and lemon zest.

In another bowl, mix mustard and wine. Place chicken slices in the wine mixture and then in the crumb mixture. Place the prepared chicken in the air fryer cooking basket and cook for 15 minutes.

61. Creamy Onion Chicken

Total Time: 20 min | **Serves**: 4 | **Per serving**: Calories: 282; Carbs: 55g; Fat: 4g; Protein: 8g

INGREDIENTS

4 chicken breasts, cubed
180 ml onion soup mix
240g mushroom soup
120g cream

DIRECTIONS

Preheat your Fryer to 200 C. Add mushrooms, onion mix and cream in a frying pan. Heat on low heat for 1 minute. Pour the warm mixture over chicken slices and allow to sit for 25 minutes. Place the marinated chicken in the air fryer cooking basket and cook for 15 minutes. Serve with the remaining cream and enjoy!

62. Chicken Enchiladas

Total Time: 65 min | **Serves**: 6 | **Per serving**: Calories: 226; Carbs: 13g; Fat: 14g; Protein: 16g

INGREDIENTS

420g chicken breast, chopped
180g cheese, grated
130g salsa
1 can green chilies, chopped
12 flour tortillas
2 cans enchilada sauce

DIRECTIONS

Preheat your Fryer to 200 C. In a bowl, mix salsa and enchilada sauce. Toss in the chopped chicken to coat. Place the chicken on the tortillas and roll; top with cheese. Place the prepared tortillas in the air fryer cooking basket and cook for 60 minutes. Serve with guacamole

63. Graceful Mango Chicken

Total Time: 3 hrs 20 min | **Serves**: 2 | **Per serving**: Calories: 421; Carbs: 25g; Fat: 7g; Protein: 30g

INGREDIENTS

2 chicken breasts, cubed
1 large mango, sauce and cubed
1 medium avocado, sliced
1 red pepper, chopped
5 tbsp balsamic vinegar
15 tbsp olive oil
4 garlic cloves, minced
1 tbsp oregano
1 tbsp parsley, chopped
A pinch of mustard powder
Salt and pepper to taste

DIRECTIONS

In a bowl, mix whole mango, garlic, oil, and balsamic vinegar. Add the mixture to a blender and blend well. Pour the liquid over chicken cubes and soak for 3 hours. Take a pastry brush and rub the mixture over breasts as well.

Preheat your air fryer to 180 C. Place the chicken cubes in the cooking basket, and cook for 12 minutes. Add avocado, pork chops mango and pepper and toss well. Drizzle balsamic vinegar and garnish with chopped parsley.

64. Chili Popcorn Chicken Bowl

Total Time: 20 min | **Serves**: 4 | **Per serving**: Calories: 361; Carbs: 37g; Fat: 12g; Protein: 26g

INGREDIENTS

1 pound chicken tenders, cut into strips
50g panko breadcrumbs
1 egg
4 tbsp cornflour
1 tsp dried oregano
1 tsp chili powder
2 tbsp butter, melted
Salt and black pepper to taste

DIRECTIONS

Preheat your Fryer to 200 C.

In a bowl, combine the flour, oregano, salt, chili powder, and black pepper. In another bowl, beat the egg with some salt. In a third, pour the panko breadcrumbs.

Dip the chicken strips in the flour, then in the egg, and then coat with the breadcrumbs. Place in the air fryer basket. Drizzle the with the melted butter and cook for 12 minutes, flipping once halfway through. Serve in bowl.

65. Buttermilk Chicken

Total Time: 30 min | **Serves**: 4 | **Per serving**: Calories: 422; Carbs: 8g; Fat: 27g; Protein: 3g

INGREDIENTS

6 chicken drumsticks, skin on and bone in
500g buttermilk
2 tbsp salt
2 tbsp black pepper
1 tbsp cayenne pepper
250g all-purpose flour
1 tbsp baking powder
1 tbsp garlic powder
1 tbsp paprika
1 tbsp salt

DIRECTIONS

Rinse chicken thoroughly underwater and pat them dry; remove any fat residue. In a large bowl, mix paprika, black pepper and chicken. Toss well to coat the chicken evenly. Pour buttermilk over chicken and toss to coat.

Let the chicken chill overnight. Preheat your air fryer to 200 C. In another bowl, mix flour, paprika, pepper and salt. Roll the chicken in the seasoned flour. Place the chicken in the cooking basket in a single layer and cook for 10 minutes. Repeat the same steps for the other pieces.

66. Creamy Asiago Chicken

Total Time: 20 min | **Serves**: 4 | **Per serving**: Calories: 250; Carbs: 33g; Fat: 6g; Protein: 14g

INGREDIENTS

4 chicken breasts, cubed
1 tbsp garlic powder
230g mayonnaise
½ tsp pepper
100g soft cheese
½ tbsp salt
Chopped basil for garnish

DIRECTIONS

Preheat your air fryer to 190 C. In a bowl, mix cheese, mayonnaise, garlic powder and salt to form a marinade. Cover your chicken with the marinade. Place the marinated chicken in your air fryer's cooking basket and cook for 15 minutes. Serve with a garnish of chopped basil.

67. Breaded Chicken Cutlets

Total Time: 20 min | **Serves:** 4 | **Per serving:** Calories: 270; Carbs: 17g; Fat: 13g; Protein: 36g

INGREDIENTS

30g Parmesan cheese, grated
4 chicken cutlets
⅛ tbsp paprika
¼ tsp pepper
2 tbsp panko breadcrumbs
1 tbsp parsley
½ tbsp garlic powder
2 large eggs, beaten

DIRECTIONS

Preheat your air fryer to 200 C. In a bowl, mix Parmesan cheese, breadcrumbs, garlic powder, pepper, paprika and mash the mixture. Add eggs in a bowl. Dip the chicken cutlets in eggs, dredge them in cheese and panko mixture. Place the prepared cutlets in the cooking basket and cook for 15 minutes.

68. Spicy Chicken Wings

Total Time: 25 min | **Serves:** 2 | **Per serving:** Calories: 273; Carbs: 19g; Fat: 12g; Protein: 25g

INGREDIENTS

10 chicken wings
2 tbsp hot chili sauce
½ tbsp lime juice
½ tbsp honey
½ tbsp kosher salt
½ tbsp black pepper

DIRECTIONS

Preheat the air fryer to 175 C. Mix the lime juice, honey and chili sauce. Toss the mixture over the chicken wings.

Put the chicken wings in the air fryer basket and cook for 25 minutes. Shake the basket every 5 minutes.

69. Authentic Korean Chicken

Total Time: 15 min | **Serves:** 5 | **Per serving:** Calories: 413; Carbs: 20g; Fat: 5g; Protein: 48g

INGREDIENTS

1 pound chicken wings
8 oz flour
8 oz breadcrumbs
3 beaten eggs
4 tbsp Canola oil
Salt and pepper to taste
2 tbsp sesame seeds
2 tbsp Korean red pepper paste
1 tbsp apple cider vinegar
2 tbsp honey
1 tbsp soy sauce
Sesame seeds, to serve

DIRECTIONS

Separate the chicken wings into winglets and drummettes. In a bowl, mix salt, oil and pepper. Preheat your air fryer to a temperature of 175 C. Coat the chicken with beaten eggs followed by breadcrumbs and flour.

Place the chicken in your air fryer's cooking basket. Spray with a bit of oil and cook for 15 minutes.

Mix red pepper paste, apple cider vinegar, soy sauce, honey and ¼ cup of water in a saucepan and bring to a boil over medium heat. Transfer the chicken to sauce mixture and toss to coat. Garnish with sesame to enjoy!

70. Slightly Grilled Hawaiian Chicken

Total Time: 25 min | **Serves:** 2 | **Per serving:** Calories: 2102 Carbs: 14g; Fat: 3g; Protein: 29g

INGREDIENTS

4 chicken breasts, cubed
2 garlic clove, minced
100g ketchup

½ tbsp ginger, minced
120 ml soy sauce

2 tbsp sherry
120 ml pineapple juice

2 tbsp apple cider vinegar
110g brown sugar

DIRECTIONS

Preheat your air fryer to 180 C. In a bowl, mix in ketchup, pineapple juice, sugar, cider vinegar, ginger. Heat the sauce in a frying pan over low heat. Cover chicken with the soy sauce and sherry; pour the hot sauce on top. Set aside for 15 minutes to marinate. Place the chicken in the air fryer cooking basket and cook for 15 minutes.

71. Awesome Candied Chicken

Total Time: 20 min | **Serves**: 6 | **Per serving**: Calories: 175; Carbs: 3g; Fat: 1g; Protein: 0g

INGREDIENTS

30g flour
½ tbsp flour
5 chicken breasts, sliced
1 tbsp Worcestershire sauce

3 tbsp olive oil
20g onions, chopped
300g brown sugar
60g yellow mustard

200 ml water
100g ketchup

DIRECTIONS

Preheat your Fryer to 180 C. In a bowl, mix in flour, salt and pepper. Cover the chicken slices with flour mixture and drizzle oil over the chicken. In another bowl, mix brown sugar, water, ketchup, chopped onion, mustard, Worcestershire sauce and salt. Transfer chicken to marinade mixture; set aside for 10 minutes. Place the chicken in your air fryer's cooking basket and cook for 15 minutes.

72. Coconut Chicken Bake

Total Time: 20 min | **Serves**: 6 | **Per serving**: Calories: 175; Carbs: 3g; Fat: 1g; Protein: 0g

INGREDIENTS

2 large eggs, beaten
2 tbsp garlic powder
1 tbsp salt

½ tbsp ground black pepper
100g breadcrumbs
80g shredded coconut

1 pound chicken tenders
Cooking spray

DIRECTIONS

Preheat your fryer to 200 C. Spray a baking sheet with cooking spray. In a wide dish, whisk in garlic powder, eggs, pepper and salt. In another bowl, mix the breadcrumbs and coconut.

Dip your chicken tenders in egg, then in the coconut mix; shake off any excess. Place the prepared chicken tenders in your air fryer's cooking basket and cook for 12-14 minutes until golden brown.

73. Lemon Pepper Chicken

Total Time: 20 min | **Serves**: 2 | **Per serving**: Calories: 301; Carbs: 20g; Fat: 22g; Protein: 23g

INGREDIENTS

1 chicken breast
2 lemon, juiced and rind reserved

1 tbsp chicken seasoning
1 tbsp garlic puree

A handful of peppercorns
Salt and pepper to taste

DIRECTIONS

Preheat your fryer to 175 C. Place a silver foil sheet on a flat surface. Add all seasonings alongside the lemon rind. Lay the chicken breast onto a chopping board and trim any fat and little bones. Season each side with the pepper and salt. Rub the chicken seasoning on both sides well. Place on your silver foil sheet and rub. Seal tightly and flatten with a rolling pin. Place the breast in the basket and cook for 15 minutes. Serve hot.

74. Caprese Chicken With Balsamic Sauce

Total Time: 25 min | **Serves**: 6 | **Per serving**: Calories: 510; Carbs: 0g; Fat: 54g; Protein: 30g

INGREDIENTS

6 chicken breasts, cubed
6 basil leaves
60 ml balsamic vinegar
6 slices tomato
1 tbsp butter
6 slices mozzarella cheese

DIRECTIONS

Preheat your Fryer to 200 C and heat butter and balsamic vinegar in a frying pan over medium heat. Cover the chicken meat with the marinade. Place the chicken in the cooking basket and cook for 20 minutes. Cover the chicken with basil, tomato slices and cheese. Serve and enjoy!

75. Sage And Chicken Escallops

Total Time: 10 min | **Serves**: 6 | **Per serving**: Calories: 373; Carbs: 11g; Fat: 26g; Protein: 11g

INGREDIENTS

4 skinless chicken breast
2 ½ oz panko breadcrumbs
1 ounce Parmesan cheese, grated
6 sage leaves, chopped
1 ¼ ounce flour
2 beaten eggs

DIRECTIONS

Place the chicken breasts between a cling film, beat well using a rolling pin until a ½ cm thickness is achieved.

In a bowl, add Parmesan cheese, sage and breadcrumbs. Dredge the chicken into the seasoned flour and dredge into the egg. Finally, dredge into the breadcrumbs. Preheat your air fryer to 195 C. Spray both sides of chicken breasts with cooking spray and cook in the air fryer for 4 minutes, until golden.

76. Exquisite Coconut Chicken

Total Time: 25 min | **Serves**: 4 | **Per serving**: Calories: 421; Carbs: 11g; Fat: 26g; Protein: 36g

INGREDIENTS

3 chicken breasts, cubed
Oil as needed
300g coconut flakes
3 whole eggs, beaten
120g cornstarch
Salt to taste
1 tbsp cayenne pepper
Pepper to taste

DIRECTIONS

Preheat your air fryer to 175 C. In a bowl, mix salt, cornstarch, cayenne pepper, pepper. In another bowl, add beaten eggs and coconut flakes. Cover chicken with pepper mix. Dredge chicken in the egg mix. Cover chicken with oil. Place the prepared chicken in your air fryer's cooking basket and cook for 20 minutes.

77. Traditional Asian Sticky Chicken

Total Time: 25 min | **Serves**: 3 | **Per serving**: Calories: 244; Carbs: 10g; Fat: 5g; Protein: 37g

INGREDIENTS

1 pound chicken wingettes
1 tbsp coriander leaves, chopped
Salt and black pepper, to taste
1 tbsp roasted peanuts, chopped

½ tbsp apple cider vinegar
1 garlic clove, minced
½ tbsp chili sauce
1 ginger, minced

1 ½ tbsp soy sauce
2 ½ tbsp honey

DIRECTIONS

Preheat your air fryer to 180 C. Wash chicken wingettes thoroughly; season with salt and pepper. In a bowl, mix ginger, garlic, chili sauce, honey, soy sauce, cilantro, and vinegar. Cover chicken with honey sauce. Place the prepared chicken to your air fryer's cooking basket and cook for 20 minutes. Serve sprinkled with peanuts.

78. Air Fried Cheese Chicken

Total Time: 15 min | Serves: 6 | Per serving: Calories: 364; Carbs: 12; Fat: 12g; Protein: 33g

INGREDIENTS

2 pieces chicken breast (8 oz each), sliced in half
6 tbsp seasoned breadcrumbs

2 tbsp Parmesan cheese, grated
1 tbsp melted butter
100g mozzarella cheese, shredded

1 tbsp marinara sauce
Cooking spray as needed

DIRECTIONS

Preheat your air fryer to 195 C. Grease the cooking basket with Cooking spray. In a small bowl, mix breadcrumbs and Parmesan cheese. In another microwave proof bowl, add butter and melt in the microwave.

Brush the chicken pieces with butter and dredge into the breadcrumbs. Add chicken to the cooking basket and cook for 6 minutes. Turn over and top with marinara sauce and shredded mozzarella; cook for 3 more minutes.

79. Gingery Chicken Wings

Total Time: 25 min | Serves: 4 | Per serving: Calories: 358; Carbs: 1g; Fat: 31g; Protein: 18g

INGREDIENTS

8 chicken drumsticks
1 tbsp olive oil
1 tbsp sesame oil

4 tbsp honey
3 tbsp light soy sauce
2 crushed garlic clove

1 small knob fresh ginger, grated
1 small bunch coriander, chopped
2 tbsp sesame seeds, toasted

DIRECTIONS

Add all ingredients in a freezer bag, except sesame and coriander. Seal up and massage until the drumsticks are coated well. Preheat your air fryer to 200 C. Place the drumsticks in the cooking basket and cook for 10 minutes. Lower the temperature to 165 C and cook for 10 more minutes. Sprinkle with some sesame and coriander seeds.

80. Honey Chicken Drumsticks

Total Time: 20 min | Serves: 2 | Per serving: Calories: 172; Carbs: 11g; Fat: 7g; Protein: 15g

INGREDIENTS

2 chicken drumsticks, skin removed
2 tbsp olive oil

2 tbsp honey
½ tbsp garlic, minced

DIRECTIONS

Add the ingredients to a resealable bag; massage until well-coated. Allow the chicken to marinate for 30 minutes. Preheat your air fryer to 200 C. Add the chicken to the cooking basket and cook for 15 minutes, shaking once.

81. Mustard and Maple Turkey Breast

Total Time: 1 hr | **Serves**: 6 | **Per serving**: Calories: 529; Carbs: 77g; Fat: 20g; Protein: 13g

INGREDIENTS

5 lb of whole turkey breast
60g maple syrup
2 tbsp dijon mustard
½ tbsp smoked paprika
1 tbsp thyme
2 tbsp olive oil
½ tbsp sage
½ tbsp salt and black pepper
1 tbsp butter, melted

DIRECTIONS

Preheat the air fryer to 175 C and brush the turkey with the olive oil. Combine all herbs and seasoning, in a small bowl, and rub the turkey with the mixture. Air fry the turkey for 25 minutes. Flip the turkey on its side and continue to cook for 12 more minutes.

Now, turn on the opposite side, and again, cook for an additional 12 minutes. Whisk the butter, maple and mustard together in a small bowl. When done, brush the glaze all over the turkey. Return to the air fryer and cook for 5 more minutes, until nice and crispy.

82. Italian-Style Party Turkey Meatballs

Total Time: 40 min | **Serves**: 3 to 4 | **Per serving**: Calories : 145; Carbs: 1.9g; Fat: 5.7g; Protein: 15.4g

INGREDIENTS

1 lb ground turkey
1 egg
60g breadcrumbs
1 tbsp garlic powder
1 tbsp Italian seasoning
1 tbsp onion powder
30g Parmesan cheese
Salt and pepper to taste
Cooking spray

DIRECTIONS

Preheat the air fryer to 200 C. In a bowl, add the ground turkey, crack the egg onto it, add the breadcrumbs, garlic powder, onion powder, Italian seasoning, Parmesan cheese, salt, and pepper. Use your hands to mix them well. Spoon out portions and make bite-size balls out of the mixture.

Grease the fryer basket with cooking spray and add 10 turkey balls to the fryer's basket; cook for 12 minutes. Slide-out the fryer basket halfway through and shake. When ready, remove onto a serving platter and continue the cooking process for the remaining balls. Serve the turkey balls with marinara sauce and a side of noodles.

83. Bacon-Wrapped Chicken Breasts

Total Time: 20 min | **Serves**: 2 to 4 | **Per serving**: Calories : 297; Carbs: 0g; Fat: 28g; Protein: 7g

INGREDIENTS

2 chicken breasts
8 oz onion and chive cream cheese
1 tbsp butter
6 turkey bacon
Salt to taste
1 tbsp fresh parsley, chopped
juice from ½ lemon

DIRECTIONS

Preheat the air fryer to 195 C. Stretch out the bacon slightly and lay them on in 2 sets; 3 bacon strips together on each side. Place the chicken breast on each bacon set and use a knife to smear the cream cheese on both. Share the butter on top and sprinkle with salt. Wrap the bacon around the chicken and secure the ends into the wrap.

Place the wrapped chicken in the fryer's basket and cook for 14 minutes. Turn the chicken halfway through. Remove the chicken onto a serving platter and top with parsley and lemon juice. Serve with steamed greens.

84. Turkey Cordon Bleu

Total Time: 35 min | **Serves**: 4 | **Per serving**: Calories: 316; Carbs: 17g; Fat: 9 g; Protein: 37 g

INGREDIENTS

2 turkey breasts
1 ham slice
1 slice cheddar cheese
2 oz breadcrumbs
1 tbsp cream cheese
1 tbsp garlic powder
1 tbsp thyme
1 tbsp tarragon
1 egg, beaten
Salt and pepper, to taste

DIRECTIONS

Preheat the air fryer to 175 C. Cut the turkey in the middle, that way so you can add ingredients in the center. Season with salt, pepper, thyme and tarragon. Combine the cream cheese and garlic powder, in a small bowl.

Spread the mixture on the inside of the breasts. Place half cheddar slice and half ham slice in the center of each breast. Dip the cordon bleu in egg first, then sprinkle with breadcrumbs. Cook in the greased frying basket for 30 minutes, shaking once, until golden brown.

85. Simple Panko Turkey

Total Time: 25 min | **Serves**: 6 | **Per serving**: Calories: 286; Carbs: 6.6g; Fat: 18g; Protein: 24g

INGREDIENTS

6 turkey breasts, boneless and skinless
240g bread crumbs
1 tbsp salt
½ tsp cayenne pepper
½ tbsp black pepper
1 stick butter, melted

DIRECTIONS

In a bowl, combine the crumbs, half of the black pepper, cayenne pepper, and half of the salt. In another small bowl, combine the melted butter with salt and pepper. Don't add salt if you use salted butter.

Brush the butter mixture over the turkey breast. Coat the turkey with the panko mixture. Arrange them on a lined baking dish. Air fry for 15 minutes at 195 C. If the turkey breasts are thinner, cook only for 8 minutes.

86. Thyme Turkey Nuggets

Total Time: 20 min | **Serves**: 2 | **Per serving**: Calories: 423; Carbs: 50.9g; Fat: 8.6g; Protein: 34g

INGREDIENTS

8 oz turkey breast, boneless and skinless
1 egg, beaten
120g breadcrumbs
1 tbsp dried thyme
½ tbsp dried parsley
Salt and pepper, to taste

DIRECTIONS

Preheat the air fryer to 175 C. Mince the turkey in a food processor; transfer to a bowl. Stir in the thyme and parsley, and season with salt and pepper.

Take a nugget-sized piece of the turkey mixture and shape it into a ball, or another form. Dip in the breadcrumbs, then egg, then in the breadcrumbs again. Place the nuggets onto a prepared baking dish, and cook for 10 minutes.

87. Awesome Sweet Turkey Bake

Total Time: 50 min | **Serves**: 3 | **Per serving**: Calories : 290; Carbs: 3g; Fat: 23g; Protein: 16g

INGREDIENTS

- 1 lb turkey breasts
- Salt and pepper to season
- 180 ml chicken soup cream
- 60g mayonnaise
- 2 tbsp lemon juice
- 30g slivered almonds, chopped
- 30g breadcrumbs
- 2 tbsp chopped green onion
- 2 tbsp chopped pimentos
- 2 Boiled eggs, chopped
- 20g diced celery
- Cooking spray

DIRECTIONS

Preheat the air fryer to 195 C. Place the turkey breasts on a clean flat surface and season with salt and pepper.

Grease with cooking spray and place them in the fryer's basket; cook for 13 minutes. Remove turkey back onto the chopping board, let cool, and cut into dices. In a bowl, add the celery, chopped eggs, pimentos, green onions, slivered almonds, lemon juice, mayonnaise, diced turkey, and chicken soup cream and mix well.

Grease a casserole dish with cooking spray, scoop the turkey mixture into the bowl, sprinkle the breadcrumbs on it, and spray with cooking spray. Put the dish in the fryer basket, and bake the ingredients at 195 C for 20 minutes. Remove and serve with a side of steamed asparagus.

FISH AND SEAFOOD

88. Golden Cod Fish Nuggets

Total Time: 20 min | **Serves**: 4 | **Per serving**: Calories : 168; Carbs: 0.4g; Fat: 7.7g; Protein: 16.8g

INGREDIENTS

4 Cod fillets
2 tbsp olive oil
2 eggs, beaten
120g breadcrumbs
A pinch of salt
120g flour

DIRECTIONS

Preheat the air fryer to 195 C. Place the breadcrumbs, olive oil, and salt in a food processor and process until evenly combined. Pour the breadcrumb mixture into a bowl, the eggs into another bowl, and the flour into a third bowl. Toss the cod fillets in the flour, then in the eggs, and then in the breadcrumb mixture.

Place them in the fryer basket, close and cook for 9 minutes. At the 5-minute mark, quickly turn the chicken nuggets over. Once golden brown, remove onto a serving plate and serve with vegetable fries.

89. Crispy Salmon

Total Time: 18 min | **Serves**: 2 | **Per serving**: Calories : 318; Carbs: 3.3g; Fat: 22.5g; Protein: 24.6g

INGREDIENTS

2 salmon fillets
Cooking spray
Salt and ground black pepper, to taste

DIRECTIONS

Rinse and pat dry the fillets with a paper towel. Coat the fish generously on both sides, with cooking spray. Season with salt and freshly ground pepper. Arrange the fillets skin-side-down in the air fryer and cook for 10 minutes at 175 C turning once halfway through cooking. Serve with lemon wedges and steamed asparagus!

90. Air Fried Tuna Sandwich

Total Time: 10 min | **Serves**: 2 | **Per serving**: Calories: 310; Carbs: 1.2g; Fat: 29.1g; Protein: 4.3g

INGREDIENTS

4 slices of white bread
2 small tins of tuna, drained
½ onion, finely chopped
2 tbsp mayonnaise
250g mozzarella cheese, shredded
Cooking spray

DIRECTIONS

Lay the bread on a cutting board. In a bowl, mix tuna, onion, mayonnaise. Spoon the mixture over two bread slices.

Top with cheese and put the other piece of bread on top. Spray with oil each side and arrange the sandwiches into the air fryer. Cook at 180 C for 6 minutes, turning once halfway through cooking.

91. Fish & Chips

Total Time: 25 min | **Serves**: 4 | **Per serving**: Calories: 294; Carbs: 32.2g; Fat: 6.1g; Protein: 24g

INGREDIENTS

4 potatoes, cut into thin slices
Cooking spray
Salt and pepper to taste
4 white fish fillets
2 tbsp flour
1 egg, beaten
120g breadcrumbs
Salt and black pepper

DIRECTIONS

Spray the slices with olive oil and season with salt and black pepper. Place them in the air fryer, and cook for 20 minutes at 200 C.

Meanwhile, spread flour on a plate and coat the fish. Dip them in the egg, then into the crumbs and season with salt and black pepper. At the 10 minutes' mark, add the fish to the fryer and cook with the chips. Cook until crispy. Serve with lemon slices, mayo and ketchup.

92. Crispy Fish Fingers

Total Time: 20 min | **Serves**: 8 | **Per serving**: Calories: 310; Carbs: 5.2g; Fat: 11.3g; Protein: 21.5g

INGREDIENTS

2 white fish fillets, cut into 4 fingers each
1 egg, beaten
120g buttermilk
100g panko breadcrumbs
Salt and black pepper
Cooking spray

DIRECTIONS

In a bowl, mix egg and buttermilk. On a plate, mix and spread crumbs, salt, and black pepper. Dip each finger into the egg mixture, then roll it up in the crumbs, and spray with olive oil. Arrange them in the air fryer and cook for 10 minutes at 175 C, turning once halfway through. Serve with garlic mayo and lemon wedges.

93. Hot Prawns

Total Time: 12 min | **Serves**: 8 | **Per serving**: Calories: 114; Carbs: 2.2g; Fat: 2.1g; Protein: 14g

INGREDIENTS

8 prawns, cleaned
Salt and black pepper
½ tsp ground cayenne
½ tsp chili flakes
½ tsp ground cumin
½ tsp garlic powder
Cooking spray

DIRECTIONS

In a bowl, season the prawns with salt and black pepper. Sprinkle cayenne, flakes, cumin and garlic and stir to coat. Spray the air fryer's basket with oil and arrange the prawns in an even layer. Cook for 8 minutes at 175 C, turning once halfway through. Serve with fresh lettuce leaves or sweet chili/mayo sauce.

94. Grilled Barramundi in Lemon-Butter Sauce

Total Time: 25 min | **Serves**: 3 | **Per serving**: Calories : 155; Carbs: 0.8g; Fat: 4.3g; Protein: 25.3g

INGREDIENTS

3 (½ lb) barramundi fillets
2 lemons, juiced
Salt and pepper to taste
6 oz butter
240g chickened cream
100 ml white wine
2 bay leaves
15 black peppercorns
2 cloves garlic, minced
2 shallots, chopped

DIRECTIONS

Preheat the air fryer to 195 C. Place the barramundi fillets on a baking paper and put them in the fryer basket. Cook for 15 minutes. Remove to a serving platter without the paper.

Place a small pan over low heat on a stovetop. Add the garlic and shallots, and dry fry for 20 seconds. Add the wine, bay leaves, and peppercorns. Stir and allow the liquid to reduce by three quarters, and add the cream. Stir and let the sauce thicken into a dark cream color.

Add the butter, whisk it into the cream until it has fully melted. Add the lemon juice, pepper, and salt. Turn the heat off. Strain the sauce into a serving bowl. Pour the sauce over the fish and serve with a side of rice.

95. Rich Crab Croquettes

Total Time: 30 min | **Serves**: 4 | **Per serving**: Calories: 206; Carbs: 5.4g; Fat: 12.5g; Protein: 14g

INGREDIENTS

Filling:
1 ½ lb lump crab meat
3 egg whites, beaten
80g sour cream
80g mayonnaise

Breading:
180g breadcrumbs
2 tsp olive oil

1 ½ tbsp olive oil
1 red pepper, chopped finely
50g chopped red onion
2 ½ tbsp chopped celery

120g flour
4 eggs, beaten

½ tsp chopped tarragon
½ tsp chopped chives
1 tsp chopped parsley
1 tsp cayenne pepper

Salt to taste

DIRECTIONS

Place a skillet over medium heat on a stovetop, add 1 ½ tbsp olive oil, red pepper, onion, and celery. Sauté for 5 minutes or until sweaty and translucent. Turn off heat. Add the breadcrumbs, the remaining olive oil, and salt to a food processor. Blend to mix evenly; set aside. In 2 separate bowls, add the flour and 4 eggs respectively, set aside.

In a separate bowl, add the crabmeat, mayo, egg whites, sour cream, tarragon, chives, parsley, cayenne pepper, and the celery sauté and mix evenly. Form bite-sized balls from the mixture and place onto a plate.

Preheat the air fryer to 195 C. Dip each crab meatball (croquettes) in the egg mixture and press them in the breadcrumb mixture. Place the croquettes in the fryer basket, 12 to 15 at a time, avoid overcrowding.

Close the air fryer and cook for 10 minutes or until golden brown. Remove them and plate them. Serve the crab croquettes with tomato dipping sauce and a side of vegetable fries.

96. Fried Catfish Fillets

Total Time: 40 min | **Serves**: 2 | **Per serving**: Calories : 182; Carbs: 2g; Fat: 12.8g; Protein: 11.1g

INGREDIENTS

2 catfish fillets
3 tbsp breadcrumbs
1 tsp cayenne pepper

1 tsp dry fish seasoning, of choice
2 sprigs parsley, chopped
Salt to taste, optional

Cooking spray

DIRECTIONS

Preheat air fryer to 200 C. Pour all the dry ingredients, except the parsley, in a zipper bag. Pat dry and add the fish pieces. Close the bag and shake to coat the fish well. Do this with one fish piece at a time.

Lightly spray the fish with olive oil. Arrange them in the fryer basket, one at a time depending on the size of the fish. Close the air fryer and cook for 10 minutes. Flip the fish and cook further for 10 minutes. For extra crispiness, cook for 3 more minutes. Garnish with parsley and serve as a lunch accompaniment.

97. Delicious Seafood Pie

Total Time: 60 min | **Serves:** 3 | **Per serving:** Calories: 318; Carbs: 3.3g; Fat: 22.5g; Protein: 24.6g

INGREDIENTS

240 ml seafood marinara mix
1 lb russet potatoes, peeled and quartered
250 ml water
1 carrot, grated
½ head baby fennel, grated
1 bunch dill sprigs, chopped
1 sprig parsley, chopped
A handful of baby spinach
1 small tomato, diced
½ celery sticks, grated
2 tbsp butter
1 tbsp milk
60g grated Cheddar cheese
1 small red chili, minced
½ lemon, juiced
Salt and pepper to taste

DIRECTIONS

Add the potatoes to a pan, pour the water, and bring to a boil over medium heat on a stovetop. Use a fork to check that if they are soft and mash-able, after about 12 minutes. Drain the water and use a potato masher to mash. Add the butter, milk, salt, and pepper. Mash until smooth and well mixed; set aside.

In a bowl, add the celery, carrots, cheese, chili, fennel, parsley, lemon juice, seafood mix, dill, tomato, spinach, salt, and pepper; mix well.

Preheat the air fryer to 170 C. In a 6 inches casserole dish, add half of the carrots mixture and level. Top with half of the potato mixture and level. Place the dish in the air fryer and bake for 20 minutes until golden brown and the seafood is properly cooked. Remove the dish and add the remaining seafood mixture and level out.

Top with the remaining potato mash and level it too. Place the dish back to the fryer and cook for 20 minutes. Once ready, ensure that it's well cooked, and remove the dish. Slice the pie and serve with a green salad.

98. Smoked Fish Quiche

Total Time: 35 min | **Serves:** 5 | **Per serving:** Calories: 404; Carbs: 3.2g; Fat: 32.1g; Protein: 4g

INGREDIENTS

1 quiche pastry case
5 eggs, lightly beaten
4 tbsp heavy cream
30g finely chopped green onions
20g chopped parsley
1 tsp baking powder
Salt and black pepper
1 lb smoked fish
220g shredded mozzarella cheese

DIRECTIONS

In a bowl, whisk eggs, cream, scallions, parsley, baking powder, salt and black. Add in fish and cheese, stir to combine. Line the air fryer with baking paper. Pour the mixture into the pastry case and place it gently inside the air fryer. Cook for 25 minutes at 180 C. Check past 15 minutes, so it's not overcooked.

99. Baby Octopus Hearty Salad

Total Time: 50 min | **Serves:** 3 | **Per serving:** Calories : 299; Carbs: 3g; Fat: 20.8g; Protein: 17.3g

INGREDIENTS

1 lb baby octopus, cleaned
1 ½ tbsp olive oil
2 cloves garlic, minced
1 ½ tbsp capers
1 ¼ tbsp balsamic glaze
1 bunch parsley, chopped roughly
1 bunch baby fennel, chopped
200g semi-dried tomatoes, chopped
1 red onion, sliced
A handful of arugula
Salt and pepper to taste
70g chopped grilled Halloumi

1 long red chili, minced   350 ml water

DIRECTIONS

Pour the water in a pot and bring to boil over medium heat on a stovetop. Cut the octopus into bite sizes and add it to the boiling water for 45 seconds; drain the water. Add the garlic, olive oil, and octopus in a bowl. Coat the octopus with garlic and olive oil. Leave to marinate for 20 minutes.

Preheat the air fryer to 195 C. Place the octopus in the fryer basket and grill for 5 minutes. In a salad mixing bowl, add the capers, halloumi, chili, tomatoes, olives, parsley, red onion, fennel, octopus, arugula, and balsamic glaze. Season with salt and pepper and mix. Serve with a side of toasts.

100. Greek-Style Salmon with Dill Sauce

Total Time: 25min | **Serves**: 4 | **Per serving**: Calories : 240; Carbs: 4g; Fat: 6g; Protein: 16g

INGREDIENTS

4 (6-oz) salmon pieces   2 tsp olive oil   240g sour cream
Salt and pepper to taste   3 tbsp fresh dill + extra for garnishing   250g Greek yogurt

DIRECTIONS

For the dill sauce, in a bowl, mix well the sour cream, yogurt, dill, and salt. Preheat the air fryer to 140 C.

Drizzle the olive oil over the salmon, and rub with salt and pepper. Arrange the salmon pieces in the fryer basket and cook them for 15 minutes. Remove salmon to a platter and top with the sauce. Serve with steamed asparagus.

101. Hot Crab Cakes

Total Time: 20 min | **Serves**: 8 | **Per serving**: Calories: 184; Carbs: 9.2g; Fat: 12.1g; Protein: 15.4g

INGREDIENTS

1 lb crabmeat, shredded   20g parsley, chopped   Salt and black pepper
2 eggs, beaten   1 tbsp mayonnaise   Cooking spray
60g breadcrumbs   1 tsp sweet chili sauce
50g finely chopped green onion   ½ tsp paprika

DIRECTIONS

In a bowl, add meat, eggs, crumbs, green onion, parsley, mayo, chili sauce, paprika, salt, and black pepper and mix well with hands. Shape into 8 cakes and grease them lightly with oil. Arrange the cakes into a fryer, without overcrowding. Cook for 8 minutes at 200 C, turning once halfway through cooking.

102. Crispy Prawn in Bacon Wraps

Total Time: 30 min | **Serves**: 4 | **Per serving**: Calories: 153; Carbs: 0.2g; Fat: 9.1g; Protein: 11.6g

INGREDIENTS

8 bacon slices   8 jumbo prawns, peeled and deveined   Lemon Wedges for garnishing

DIRECTIONS

Wrap each prawn from head to tail with each bacon slice overlapping to keep the bacon in place. Secure the end of the bacon with a toothpick. It's ok not to cover the ends of the cheese with bacon. Refrigerate for 15 minutes.

Preheat the air fryer to 200 C. Arrange the bacon-wrapped prawns in the fryer's basket, close and cook for 7 minutes or until the bacon is browned and crispy. Transfer prawns to a paper towel to cool for 2 minutes. Remove the toothpicks and serve the bacon-wrapped prawns with lemon wedges and a side of steamed green vegetables.

103. Frozen Sesame Fish Fillets

Total Time: 20 min | **Serves**: 5 | **Per serving**: Calories: 257.6; Carbs: 16.4g; Fat: 14g; Protein: 19.1g

INGREDIENTS

5 frozen fish fillets
5 biscuits, crumbled
3 tbsp flour
1 egg, beaten
A pinch of salt
A pinch of black pepper
¼ tsp rosemary
3 tbsp olive oil divided
A handful of sesame seeds

DIRECTIONS

Preheat the air fryer to 195 C. Combine the flour, pepper and salt, in a shallow bowl. In another shallow bowl, combine the sesame seeds, crumbled biscuits, oil, and rosemary. Dip the fish fillets into the flour mixture first, then into the beaten egg, and finally, coat them with the sesame mixture.

Arrange them in the air fryer on a sheet of aluminum foil; cook the fish for 8 minutes. Flip the fillets over and cook for an additional 4 minutes. Serve and enjoy.

104. Full Baked Trout en Papillote with Herbs

Total Time: 30 min | **Serves**: 2 | **Per serving**: Calories: 243; Carbs: 2.9g; Fat: 8.1g; Protein: 15.6g

INGREDIENTS

¾ lb whole trout, scaled and cleaned
¼ bulb fennel, sliced
½ brown onion, sliced
3 tbsp chopped parsley
3 tbsp chopped dill
2 tbsp olive oil
1 lemon, sliced
Salt and pepper to taste

DIRECTIONS

In a bowl, add the onion, parsley, dill, fennel, and garlic. Mix and drizzle the olive oil over. Preheat the air fryer to 175 C. Open the cavity of the fish and fill with the fennel mixture.

Wrap the fish completely in parchment paper and then in foil. Place the fish in the fryer basket and cook for 10 minutes. Remove the paper and foil, and top with lemon slices. Serve with a side of cooked mushrooms.

105. Air Fried Dilly Trout

Total Time: 30 min | **Serves**: 3 | **Per serving**: Calories: 386; Carbs: 27g; Fat: 31g; Protein: 38g

INGREDIENTS

3 pieces trout, 5-6 oz each
3 tbsp olive oil
1 pinch salt

DILL SAUCE:

120g greek yogurt
120g sour cream
2 tbsp finely chopped dill
1 pinch salt

DIRECTIONS

Preheat the air fryer to 150 C. Drizzle the trout with oil and season with a pinch of salt. Place the seasoned trout into the air fryer's cooking basket. Cook for 20 minutes and top with the dill sauce before serving. For the dill sauce, in a large bowl, mix the yogurt, the sour cream, the chopped dill and salt.

106. Air Fried Calamari

Total Time: 130 min | **Serves**: 3 | **Per serving**: Calories: 317; Carbs: 43.4g; Fat: 28g; Protein: 21.3g

INGREDIENTS

½ lb calamari rings
120g cornmeal or cornstarch
2 large eggs, beaten
2 mashed garlic cloves
120g breadcrumbs
lemon juice

DIRECTIONS

Coat the calamari rings with the cornmeal. The first mixture is prepared by mixing the eggs and the garlic. Dip the calamari in the eggs' mixture. Then dip them in the breadcrumbs. Put the rings in the fridge for 2 hours.

Then, line them in the air fryer and add oil generously. Fry for 10 to 13 minutes at 195 C, shaking once halfway through. Serve with garlic mayonnaise and top with lemon juice.

107. Breaded Scallops

Total Time: 5 min | **Serves**: 6 | **Per serving**: Calories: 280; Carbs: 3.2g; Fat: 32g; Protein: 2.8g

INGREDIENTS

12 fresh scallops
3 tbsp flour
4 salt and black pepper
1 egg, lightly beaten
120g breadcrumbs
Cooking spray

DIRECTIONS

Coat the scallops with flour. Dip into the egg, then into the breadcrumbs. Spray them with olive oil and arrange them in the air fryer. Cook for 6 minutes at 180 C, turning once halfway through cooking.

108. Hot Salmon & Broccoli

Total Time: 25 min | **Serves**: 2 | **Per serving**: Calories: 368; Carbs: 5.8g; Fat: 26.8g; Protein: 4g

INGREDIENTS

2 salmon fillets
1 tsp olive oil
Juice of 1 lime
1 tsp chili flakes
Salt and black pepper
1 head of broccoli, cut into florets
1 tsp olive oil
1 tbsp soy sauce

DIRECTIONS

In a bowl, add oil, lime juice, flakes, salt, and black pepper; rub the mixture onto fillets. Lay the florets into your air fryer and drizzle with oil. Arrange the fillets around or on top and cook at 175 C for 10 minutes. Drizzle the florets with soy sauce to serve!

109. Fish Tacos

Total Time: 15 min | **Serves**: 4 | **Per serving**: Calories: 369; Carbs: 52g; Fat: 8.8g; Protein: 14.2g

INGREDIENTS

4 corn tortillas
1 halibut fillet
2 tbsp olive oil1
60g flour, divided
1 can of beer
1 tsp salt
4 tbsp peach salsa
4 tsp chopped coriander
1 tsp baking powder

DIRECTIONS

Preheat the air fryer to 195 C, and combine 1 cup of flour, baking, powder and salt. Pour in some of the beer, enough to form a batter-like consistency. Save the rest of the beer to gulp with the taco.

Slice the fillet into 4 strips and toss them in half cup of flour. Dip them into the beer batter and arrange on a lined baking sheet. Cook in the air fryer for 8 minutes. Spread the peach salsa on the tortillas. Top each tortilla with one fish strip and chopped coriander.

110. Flatten Salmon Balls

Total Time: 13 min | **Serves**: 2 | **Per serving**: Calories: 312; Carbs: 21g; Fat: 28.4g; Protein: 21g

INGREDIENTS

4 oz tinned salmon
4 tbsp celery, chopped
4 tbsp spring onion, sliced
4 tbsp wheat germ
4 tbsp olive oil
1 large egg
1 tbsp dill, fresh and chopped
½ tsp garlic powder

DIRECTIONS

Preheat the air fryer to 195 C. In a large bowl, mix the tinned salmon, egg, celery, onion, dill and garlic. Shape the mixture into 2-inch size balls and roll them in wheat germ. Heat the oil in a skillet and add the salmon balls; carefully flatten them. Then place them in the air fryer and fry for 8 minutes. Serve with yogurt or garlic mayo.

111. Peppery and Lemony Haddock

Total Time: 15 min | **Serves**: 4 | **Per serving**: Calories: 310; Carbs: 26.9g; Fat: 6.3g; Protein: 34.8g

INGREDIENTS

4 haddock fillets
120g breadcrumbs
2 tbsp lemon juice
½ tsp black pepper
40g dry air fryer to flakes
1 egg, beaten
30g Parmesan cheese
3 tbsp flour
¼ tsp salt

DIRECTIONS

Combine the flour, black pepper and salt, in a small bowl. In another bowl, combine the lemon, breadcrumbs, Parmesan cheese, and potato flakes. Dip the fillets in the flour first, then in the beaten egg, and coat them with the lemony crumbs. Arrange on a lined sheet and place in the air fryer. Cook for 8 to 10 minutes at 185 C.

112. Fish Finger Sandwich

Total Time: 20 min | **Serves**: 4 | **Per serving**: Calories: 360; Carbs: 39.2g; Fat: 10.4g; Protein: 29.3g

INGREDIENTS

4 cod fillets
2 tbsp flour
10 capers
4 bread rolls
2 oz breadcrumbs
4 tbsp pesto sauce
4 lettuce leaves
Salt and pepper, to taste

DIRECTIONS

Preheat the air fryer to 185 C. Season the fillets with salt and pepper, and coat them with the flour; dip in the breadcrumbs. You should get a really thin layer of breadcrumbs, that's why we don't use eggs for this recipe.

Arrange the fillets onto a baking mat and cook in the fryer for 10 to 15 minutes. Cut the bread rolls in half. Place a lettuce leaf on top of the bottom halves; put the fillets over. Spread a tbsp of pesto sauce on top of each fillet, and top with the remaining halves.

113. Delicious Coconut Shrimp

Total Time: 30 min | Serves: 2 | Per serving: Calories: 436; Carbs: 69.9g; Fat: 16.4g; Protein: 7.6g

INGREDIENTS

8 large shrimp
60g breadcrumbs
8 oz coconut milk
50g shredded coconut
¼ tsp salt
¼ tsp pepper
160g orange jam
1 tsp mustard
1 tbsp honey
½ tsp cayenne pepper
¼ tsp hot sauce

DIRECTIONS

Combine the breadcrumbs, cayenne pepper, shredded coconut, salt, and pepper in a bowl. Dip the shrimp in the coconut milk, first, and then in the coconut crumbs. Arrange on a lined sheet, and cook in the fryer for 20 minutes at 175 C. Whisk the jam, honey, hot sauce, and mustard. Serve shrimp drizzled with the sauce.

114. Crab Cakes

Total Time: 55 min | Serves: 4 | Per serving: Calories: 159; Carbs: 5.1g; Fat: 10.4g; Protein: 11.3g

INGREDIENTS

100g cooked crab meat
40g chopped red onion
1 tbsp chopped basil
40g chopped celery
50g chopped red pepper
3 tbsp mayonnaise
zest of half a lemon
30g breadcrumbs
2 tbsp chopped parsley
Old bay seasoning, as desired
Cooking spray

DIRECTIONS

Preheat the air fryer to 195 C. Place all ingredients in a large bowl, and mix well. Make 4 large crab cakes from the mixture and place them on a lined sheet. Refrigerate for 30 minutes, to set. Spay the air basket with cooking spray and arrange the crab cakes inside it. Cook for 7 minutes on each side, until crispy.

115. Cajun-Rubbed Jumbo Shrimp

Total Time: 10 min | Serves: 2 to 3 | Per serving: Calories : 80; Carbs: 1g; Fat: 1g; Protein: 15g

INGREDIENTS

1 lb jumbo shrimp
Salt to taste
¼ tsp old bay seasoning
⅓ tsp smoked paprika
¼ tsp cayenne pepper
1 tbsp olive oil

DIRECTIONS

Preheat the air fryer to 195 C. In a bowl, add the shrimp, paprika, oil, salt, old bay seasoning, and cayenne pepper; mix well. Place the shrimp in the fryer, close and cook for 5 minutes. Serve with mayo and rice.

116. Soy Sauce Glazed Cod

Total Time: 15 min | Serve: 1 | Per serving: Calories: 148; Carbs: 2.9g; Fat: 5.8g; Protein: 21g

INGREDIENTS

1 cod fillet
1 tsp olive oil
A pinch of sea salt
A pinch of pepper
1 tbsp soy sauce
Dash of sesame oil
¼ tsp ginger powder
¼ tsp honey

DIRECTIONS

Preheat the air fryer to 185 C. Combine the olive oil, salt and pepper, and brush that mixture over the cod.

Place the cod onto an aluminum sheet and into the air fryer; cook for 6 minutes. Combine the soy sauce, ginger, honey, and sesame oil. Brush the glaze over the cod. Flip the fillet over and cook for 3 more minutes.

117. Salmon Cakes

Total Time: 1 hr 15 min | **Serves**: 4 | **Per serving**: Calories: 248; Carbs: 28.6g; Fat: 6.4g; Protein: 17.7g

INGREDIENTS

- 10 oz cooked salmon
- 14 oz boiled and mashed potatoes
- 2 oz flour
- A handful of capers
- A handful of chopped parsley
- 1 tsp olive oil
- zest of 1 lemon

DIRECTIONS

Place the mashed potatoes in a large bowl and flake the salmon over. Stir in capers, parsley, and lemon zest. Shape small cakes out of the mixture. Dust them with flour and place in the fridge to set, for 1 hour. Preheat the air fryer to 175 C. Brush the olive oil over the basket's bottom and add the cakes. Cook for 7 minutes.

118. Pistachio Crusted Salmon

Total Time: 15 min | **Serve**: 1 | **Per serving**: Calories: 357; Carbs: 8.2g; Fat: 23.8g; Protein: 28.8g

INGREDIENTS

- 1 salmon fillet
- 1 tsp mustard
- 3 tbsp pistachios
- A pinch of sea salt
- A pinch of garlic powder
- A pinch of black pepper
- 1 tsp lemon juice
- 1 tsp grated Parmesan cheese
- 1 tsp olive oil

DIRECTIONS

Preheat the air fryer to 175 C, and whisk mustard and lemon juice together. Season the salmon with salt, pepper, and garlic powder. Brush the olive oil on all sides. Brush the mustard mixture onto salmon.

Chop the pistachios finely and combine them with the Parmesan cheese; sprinkle on top of the salmon. Place the salmon in the air fryer basket with the skin side down. Cook for 12 minutes, or to your liking.

119. Favorite Shrimp Risotto

Total Time: 25 min | **Serves**: 4 | **Per serving**: Calories: 226; Carbs: 19g; Fat: 9g; Protein: 16g

INGREDIENTS

- 4 whole eggs, beaten
- Pinch salt
- 100g rice, cooked
- Cooking spray
- 30g baby spinach
- 60g Monterey Jack cheese, grated
- 50g shrimp, chopped and cooked

DIRECTIONS

Preheat your air fryer to 160 C, and in a small bowl, add eggs and season with salt and basil; stir until frothy. Spray baking pan with non-stick cooking spray. Add rice, spinach and shrimp to the pan.

Pour egg mixture over and garnish with cheese. Place the pan in the air fryer's basket and cook for 14-18 minutes until the frittata is puffed and golden brown. Serve immediately.

120. Tuna Patties

Total Time: 50 min | **Serves**: 2 | **Per serving**: Calories: 235; Carbs: 20.5g; Fat: 6.6g; Protein: 24.6g

INGREDIENTS

- 5 oz of canned tuna
- 1 tsp lime juice
- 1 tsp paprika
- 30g flour
- 120 ml milk
- 1 small onion, diced
- 2 eggs
- 1 tsp chili powder, optional
- ½ tsp salt

DIRECTIONS

Place all ingredients in a bowl and mix well to combine. Make two large patties, or a few smaller ones, out of the mixture. Place them on a lined sheet and refrigerate for 30 minutes. Cook the patties for 7 minutes on each side at 175 C.

121. County Baked Crab Cakes

Total Time: 20 min | **Serves**: 4 | **Per serving**: Calories: 126; Carbs: 1.6g; Fat: 5g; Protein: 16g

INGREDIENTS

- ½ pound jumbo crab
- Lemon juice to taste
- 2 tbsp parsley, chopped
- Old bay seasoning as needed
- 1 tbsp basil, chopped
- 3 tbsp real mayo
- ¼ tsp dijon mustard
- zest of ½ lemon
- 30g panko breadcrumbs

DIRECTIONS

Preheat your Fryer to 200 C, and in a bowl, mix mayo, lemon zest, old bay seasoning, mustard, and oil. Blend crab meat in food processor and season with salt. Transfer to the mixing bowl and combine well.

Form cakes using the mixture and dredge the mixture into breadcrumbs. Place the cakes in your air fryer's basket and cook for 15 minutes. Serve garnished with parsley and lemon juice.

122. Chinese Garlic Shrimp

Total Time: 15 min | **Serves**: 5 | **Per serving**: Calories: 285; Carbs: 18g; Fat: 5g; Protein: 40g

INGREDIENTS

- 1 ½ pound shrimp
- Juice of 1 lemon
- 1 tsp sugar
- 3 tbsp peanut oil
- 2 tbsp cornstarch
- 2 scallions, chopped
- ¼ tsp Chinese powder
- Chopped chili to taste
- 1 tsp salt
- 4 garlic cloves
- 1 tsp pepper

DIRECTIONS

Preheat the air fryer to 185 C, and in a Ziploc bag, mix lemon juice, sugar, pepper, oil, cornstarch, powder, Chinese powder and salt. Add in the shrimp and massage to coat evenly. Let sit for 10 minutes.

Add garlic cloves, scallions and chili to a pan, and fry for a few minutes over medium heat. Place the marinated shrimp, garlic, chili and scallions in your air fryer's basket and cook for 10 minutes, until nice and crispy.

123. Beautiful Calamari Rings

Total Time: 20 min | **Serves**: 5 | **Per serving**: Calories: 227; Carbs: 14g; Fat: 14g; Protein: 11g

INGREDIENTS

12 oz frozen squid
1 large egg, beaten
120g all-purpose flour
1 tsp ground coriander seeds
1 tsp cayenne pepper
½ tsp pepper
½ tsp salt
Lemon wedges, to garnish
olive oil for spray

DIRECTIONS

In a bowl, mix flour, ground pepper, paprika, cayenne pepper and salt. Dredge calamari in eggs, followed by the floured mixture. Preheat your air fryer to 195 C and cook them for 15 minutes, until golden brown. Do it in batches if needed to avoid overcrowding. Garnish with lemon wedges and enjoy!

124. Asian Shrimp Medley

Total Time: 20 min | **Serves**: 4 | **Per serving**: Calories: 167; Carbs: 10g; Fat: 6.8g; Protein: 15g

INGREDIENTS

1 pound shrimp
2 whole onions, chopped
3 tbsp butter
1 ½ tbsp sugar
2 tbsp soy sauce
2 cloves garlic, chopped
2 tsp lime juice
1 tsp ginger, chopped

DIRECTIONS

Preheat your air fryer to 175 C, and in a bowl, mix lime juice, soy sauce, ginger, garlic, sugar and butter.

Add the mixture to a frying pan and warm over medium heat. Add in the chopped onions, and cook for 1 minute until translucent. Pour the mixture over shrimp, toss well and set aside for 30 minutes. Then, place the mixture in the air fryer's basket and cook for 8 minutes.

125. Greek Style Fried Mussels

Total Time: 25 min | **Serves**: 4 | **Per serving**: Calories: 123; Carbs: 18g; Fat: 2g; Protein: 10g

INGREDIENTS

4 pounds mussels
2 tbsp olive oil
240 ml white wine
2 tsp salt
2 bay leaves
1 tbsp pepper
200g flour
1 tbsp fenugreek
2 tbsp vinegar
5 garlic cloves
4 bread slices
50g mixed nuts

DIRECTIONS

Preheat the air fryer to 175 C. Add oil, garlic, vinegar, salt, nuts, fenugreek, pepper and bread to a food processor, and process until you obtain a creamy texture. Add bay leaves, wine, and mussels to a pan.

Bring to a boil over medium heat, lower heat to low and simmer the mixture until the mussels have opened up. Take the mussels out and drain; remove from shells. Add flour to the creamy mixture prepared before.

Cover the mussels with the sauce and cook them in your air fryer for 10 minutes. Serve with fenugreek to enjoy.

126. Panko Fish Nuggets

Total Time: 20 min | **Serves**: 4 | **Per serving**: Calories: 280; Carbs: 27g; Fat: 3g; Protein: 35g

INGREDIENTS

28 oz fish fillets
Lemon juice to taste
Salt and pepper to taste
1 tsp drilled dill
4 tbsp mayonnaise
1 whole egg, beaten
1 tbsp garlic powder
3 ½ oz breadcrumbs
1 tbsp paprika

DIRECTIONS

Preheat your air fryer to 200 C, and season fish fillets with salt and pepper. In a bowl, mix beaten egg, lemon juice, and mayonnaise. In a separate bowl, mix breadcrumbs, paprika, dill, and garlic powder.

Dredge fillets in egg mixture and then the garlic-paprika mix; repeat until all fillets are prepared. Place the fillets in your air fryer's cooking basket and cook for 15 minutes. Serve and enjoy!

127. Lemony Salmon

Total Time: 20 min | **Serves**: 2 | **Per serving**: Calories: 345; Carbs: 2g; Fat: 32.1g; Protein: 4.8g

INGREDIENTS

2 salmon fillets
Cooking spray
Salt, to taste
Zest of a lemon

DIRECTIONS

Spray the fillets with olive oil and rub them with salt and lemon zest. Line baking paper in your air fryer's basket to avoid sticking. Cook the fillets for 10 minutes at 180 C, turning once halfway through. Serve with steamed asparagus and a drizzle of lemon juice.

128. Wild Alaskan Salmon with Parsley Sauce

Total Time: 30 min | **Serves**: 4 | **Per serving**: Calories: 251; Carbs: 3g; Fat: 19g; Protein: 17g

INGREDIENTS

For Salmon
4 Alaskan wild salmon fillets, 6 oz each
2 tsp olive oil
A pinch of salt

For Dill Sauce
120g heavy cream
60 ml milk
A pinch of salt
2 tbsp chopped parsley

DIRECTIONS

Preheat your air fryer to 160 C, and in a mixing bowl, add salmon and drizzle 1 tsp of oil. Season with salt and pepper. Place the salmon in your air fryer's cooking basket and cook for 20-25 minutes, until tender and crispy.

In a bowl, mix milk, chopped parsley, salt, and whipped cream. Serve the salmon with the sauce.

129. A Worthy Sockeye Fish

Total Time: 25 min | **Serves**: 2 | **Per serving**: Calories: 224; Carbs: 6g Fat: 11g; Protein: 25g

INGREDIENTS

2-3 fingerling potatoes, thinly sliced
½ bulb fennel, thinly sliced
4 tbsp melted butter
Salt and pepper to taste
1-2 tsp fresh dill
2 sockeye salmon fillets (6 oz each)
8 cherry tomatoes, halved
60 ml fish stock

DIRECTIONS

Preheat your air fryer to 200 C, and boil salted water in a small saucepan over medium heat. Add the potatoes and blanch for 2 minutes; drain the potatoes. Cut 2 large-sized rectangles of parchment paper of 13x15 inch size.

In a large bowl, mix potatoes, melted butter, fennel, fresh ground pepper, and salt. Divide the mixture between parchment paper pieces and sprinkle dill on top. Place fillet on top of veggie piles; season with salt and pepper. Add cherry tomato on top of each veggie pile and drizzle butter; pour fish stock on top. Fold the squares and seal them. Preheat your air fryer to 200 C, and cook the packets for 10 minutes. Garnish with a bit of dill and enjoy!

130. Air-Fried Seafood

Total Time: 15 min | **Serves**: 4 | **Per serving**: Calories: 133; Carbs: 8.2g; Fat: 3.1g; Protein: 17.4g

INGREDIENTS

- 1 lb fresh scallops, mussels, fish fillets, prawns, shrimp
- 2 eggs, lightly beaten
- Salt and black pepper
- 120g breadcrumbs mixed with zest of 1 lemon

DIRECTIONS

Clean the seafood as needed. Dip each piece into the egg; and season with salt and pepper. Coat in the crumbs and spray with oil. Arrange into your air fryer and cook for 6 minutes at 200 C, turning once halfway through.

131. Lovely & Slightly "Blackened" Catfish

Total Time: 20 min | **Serves**: 2 | **Per serving**: Calories: 283; Carbs: 1.3g; Fat: 16g; Protein: 27g

INGREDIENTS

- 2 catfish fillets
- 2 tsp blackening seasoning
- Juice of 1 lime
- 2 tbsp butter, melted
- 1 garlic clove, mashed
- 2 tbsp coriander

DIRECTIONS

Preheat your air fryer to 180 C, and in a bowl, blend in garlic, lime juice, cilantro and butter. Divide the sauce into two parts, pour 1 part of the sauce over your fillets; cover the fillets with seasoning. Place the fillets in your air fryer's basket and cook for 15 minutes. Serve the cooked fish with remaining sauce.

132. Crumbly Fishcakes

Total Time: 15 min | **Serves**: 2 | **Per serving**: Calories: 210; Carbs: 25g; Fat: 7g; Protein: 10g

INGREDIENTS

- 8 oz salmon, cooked
- 1 ½ oz potatoes, mashed
- A handful of capers
- A handful of parsley, chopped
- zest of 1 lemon
- 1 ¾ oz plain flour

DIRECTIONS

Carefully flake the salmon. In a bowl, mix flaked salmon, zest, capers, dill, and mashed potatoes. Form small cakes using the mixture and dust the cakes with flour; refrigerate for 60 minutes. Preheat your air fryer to 350 and cook the cakes for 7 minutes. Serve chilled.

133. Cod Fennel Platter

Total Time: 15 min | **Serves**: 4 | **Per serving**: Calories: 269; Carbs: 5g; Fat: 1g; Protein: 32g

INGREDIENTS

- 2 black cod fillets
- Salt and pepper to taste
- 150g grapes, halved
- 1 small fennel bulb, sliced
- 50g pecans
- 2 tsp white balsamic vinegar
- 2 tbsp extra virgin olive oil

DIRECTIONS

Preheat your air fryer to 200 C, and season the fillets with salt and pepper; drizzle oil on top. Place the fillet in the air fryer basket and cook for 10 minutes; set the fish aside to cool. In a bowl, add grapes, pecans, and fennels. Drizzle oil over the grape mixture, and season with salt and pepper. Add the mixture to the basket and cook for 3 minutes. Add balsamic vinegar and oil to the mixture, season with salt and pepper. Pour over the fish, and serve.

134. Sautéed Shrimp

Total Time: 10 min | **Serves**: 4 | **Per serving**: Calories: 215; Carbs: 17g; Fat: 11g; Protein: 28g

INGREDIENTS

5-6 oz tiger shrimp, 12 to 16 pieces
1 tbsp olive oil
½ a tbsp old bay seasoning
¼ a tbsp cayenne pepper
¼ a tbsp smoked paprika
A pinch of sea salt

DIRECTIONS

Preheat the air fryer to 190 C, and mix all ingredients in a large bowl. Coat the shrimp with a little bit of oil and spices. Place the shrimp in the air fryer's basket and fry for 6-7 minutes. Serve with rice or salad.

135. The Great Cat Fish

Total Time: 25 min | **Serves**: 4 | **Per serving**: Calories: 199; Carbs: 14g; Fat: 12g; Protein: 16g

INGREDIENTS

4 catfish fillets, rinsed and dried
80g seasoned fish fry
1 tbsp olive oil
1 tbsp parsley, chopped

DIRECTIONS

Preheat your air fryer to 200 C, and add seasoned fish fry, and fillets in a large ziploc bag; massage well to coat. Place the fillets in your air fryer's cooking basket and cook for 10 minutes. Flip the fish and cook for 2-3 more minutes. Top with parsley and serve.

136. Quick and Easy Air Fried Salmon

Total Time: 13 min | **Serve**: 1 | **Per serving**: Calories: 172; Carbs: 1.7g; Fat: 7.2g; Protein: 23.7g

INGREDIENTS

1 salmon fillet
1 tbsp soy sauce
¼ tsp garlic powder
Salt and pepper

DIRECTIONS

Preheat the air fryer to 175 C, and combine soy sauce with garlic powder, salt and pepper. Brush the mixture over salmon. Place the salmon onto a sheet of parchment paper and into the air fryer; cook for 10 minutes, until crispy.

137. A Bowl of Shrimp

Total Time: 15 min | **Serves**: 6 | **Per serving**: Calories: 251; Carbs: 3g; Fat: 19g; Protein: 17g

INGREDIENTS

1 ¼ pound tiger shrimp
¼ tsp cayenne pepper
½ tsp old bay seasoning
¼ tsp smoked paprika
A pinch of salt
1 tbsp olive oil

DIRECTIONS

Preheat your air fryer to 195 C, and in a bowl, mix all listed ingredients. Place the mixture in your air fryer's cooking basket and cook for 5 minutes. Serve with warm rice and a drizzle of lemon juice.

138. Most-Authentic air fryer Fish & Cheese

Total Time: 15 min | **Serves:** 6 | **Per serving:** Calories: 284; Carbs: 5g; Fat: 11g; Protein: 38g

INGREDIENTS

1 Bunch of basil
2 garlic cloves, minced
1 tbsp olive oil
1 tbsp Parmesan cheese, grated
pepper and salt to taste
2 tbsp Pinenuts
6 white fish fillet
2 tbsp olive oil

DIRECTIONS

Season the fillets with salt and pepper. Preheat the air fryer to 175 C, and cook the fillets inside for 8 minutes. In a bowl, add basil, oil, pine nuts, garlic and Parmesan cheese; blend with your hand. Serve with the fish and enjoy!

139. The Great Air Fried Cod Fish

Total Time: 20 min | **Serves:** 4 | **Per serving:** Calories: 190; Carbs: 3g; Fat: 2g; Protein: 41g

INGREDIENTS

7 ¼ oz cod fish fillets
4 tbsp chopped coriander
Salt to taste
A handful of green onions, chopped
120 ml water
5 slices of ginger
5 tbsp light soy sauce
3 tbsp oil
1 tsp dark soy sauce
5 cubes rock sugar

DIRECTIONS

Preheat your air fryer to 180 C, and cover codfish with salt and coriander; drizzle with oil. Place the fish fillet in your air fryer's cooking basket and cook for 15 minutes. Place the remaining ingredients in a frying pan over medium heat; cook for 5 minutes. Serve the fish with the sauce, and enjoy.

140. Parmesan Tilapia

Total Time: 15 min | **Serves:** 4 | **Per serving:** Calories: 228; Carbs: 1.3g; Fat: 11.1g; Protein: 31.9g

INGREDIENTS

30g grated Parmesan cheese
1 tbsp olive oil
2 tsp paprika
1 tbsp chopped parsley
¼ tsp garlic powder
4 tilapia fillets

DIRECTIONS

Preheat the air fryer to 175 C, and mix parsley, Parmesan cheese, garlic, salt, and paprika in a shallow bowl. Brush the olive oil over the fillets, and then coat them with the Parmesan mixture. Place the tilapia onto a lined baking sheet, and then into the air fryer. Cook for 4 to 5 minutes on all sides.

141. Rosemary Garlic Prawns

Total Time: 1 h 15 min | **Serves:** 2 | **Per serving:** Calories: 152; Carbs: 1.5g; Fat: 2.9g; Protein: 8.3g

INGREDIENTS

8 large prawns
3 garlic cloves, minced
1 rosemary sprig, chopped
½ tbsp melted butter
Salt and pepper, to taste

DIRECTIONS

Combine garlic, butter, rosemary, salt and pepper, in a bowl. Add the prawns to the bowl and mix to coat them well. Cover the bowl and refrigerate for an hour. Preheat the air fryer to 175 C, and cook for 6 minutes. Increase the temperature to 195 C, and cook for one more minute.

142. Cajun Salmon with Lemon

Total Time: 10 min | **Serve**: 1 | **Per serving**: Calories: 170; Carbs: 9g; Fat: 7.2g; Protein: 22.6g

INGREDIENTS

1 salmon fillet
¼ tsp brown sugar
Juice of ½ lemon
1 tbsp cajun seasoning
2 lemon wedges
1 tbsp fresh parsley, for garnishing

DIRECTIONS

Preheat the air fryer to 175 C, and combine sugar and lemon; coat the salmon with this mixture. Coat with the Cajun seasoning as well. Place a parchment paper into the air fryer and cook the fish for 7 minutes. Serve with lemon wedges and chopped parsley.

143. Cod Cornflakes Nuggets

Total Time: 25 min | **Serves**: 4 | **Per serving**: Calories: 267; Carbs: 15.9g; Fat: 5.8g; Protein: 35.1g

INGREDIENTS

1 ¼ lb cod fillets, cut into chunks
60g flour
1 egg
1 tbsp water
100g cornflakes
1 tbsp olive oil
Salt and pepper, to taste

DIRECTIONS

Place the oil and cornflakes in a food processor and process until crumbed. Season the fish chunks with salt and pepper. In a bowl, beat the egg along with water. Dredge the chunks in flour first, then dip in the egg, and coat with cornflakes. Arrange on a lined sheet, and cook in the air fryer at 175 C for 15 minutes, until crispy.

144. Authentic Alaskan Crab Legs

Total Time: 15 min | **Serves**: 3 | **Per serving**: Calories: 203; Carbs: 0g; Fat: 2g; Protein: 26g

INGREDIENTS

3 pounds crab legs
450g butter
120 ml salted water

DIRECTIONS

Preheat the air fryer to 190 C, and dip the crab legs in salted water; let stay for a few minutes. Place the crab legs in the basket and cook for 10 minutes. Melt the butter in a bowl in the microwave. Pour over crab legs to serve.

145. Herbed Garlic Lobster

Total Time: 15 min | **Serves**: 3 | **Per serving**: Calories: 450; Carbs: 48g; Fat: 24g; Protein: 9g

INGREDIENTS

4 oz lobster tails
1 tsp garlic, minced
1 tbsp butter
Salt and pepper to taste
½ tbsp lemon juice

DIRECTIONS

Add all the ingredients to a food processor, except shrimp, and blend well. Wash lobster and halve using a meat knife; clean the skin of the lobster and cover the lobster with the marinade. Preheat your air fryer to 190 C.

Place the lobster in your air fryer's cooking basket and cook for 10 minutes. Serve with fresh herbs and enjoy!

146. Air Fried Fresh Broiled Tilapia

Total Time: 15 min | **Serves**: 4 | **Per serving**: Calories: 177; Carbs: 1.2g; Fat: 10g; Protein: 25g

INGREDIENTS

1 pound tilapia fillets
1 tbsp old bay seasoning
2 tbsp canola oil
2 tbsp lemon pepper
Salt to taste
2-3 butter buds

DIRECTIONS

Preheat your Fryer to 200 C, and drizzle oil over tilapia fillet. In a bowl, mix salt, lemon pepper, butter buds, and seasoning; spread on the fish. Place the fillets in the air fryer and cook for 10 minutes, until tender and crispy.

147. Original Trout Frittata

Total Time: 12 min | **Serves**: 6 | **Per serving**: Calories: 186; Carbs: 4g; Fat: 10g; Protein: 19g

INGREDIENTS

2 tbsp olive oil
1 onion, sauce and sliced
1 egg, beaten
6 tbsp crème fraiche
½ tbsp horseradish sauce
2 trout fillet, hot and smoked
A handful of fresh dill

DIRECTIONS

Heat oil in a frying pan over medium heat. Add onion and stir-fry until tender; season the onions well. Preheat your air fryer to 160 C, and in a bowl, mix egg, crème Fraiche, and horseradish. Add cooked onion and trout, and mix well. Place the mixture in your fryer's cooking basket and cook for 20 minutes. Serve and enjoy!

SNACKS AND SIDE DISHES

148. Rosemary Crispy Potatoes

Total Time: 35 min | **Serves**: 4 | **Per serving**: Calories: 195; Carbs: 30.7 g; Fat: 6.5 g; Protein: 3.7 g

INGREDIENTS

1.5 pounds potatoes, halved
2 tbsp olive oil
3 garlic cloves, grated
1 tbsp minced fresh rosemary
1 tsp salt
¼ tsp freshly ground black pepper

DIRECTIONS

In a bowl, mix potatoes, olive oil, garlic, rosemary, salt, and pepper, until they are well-coated. Arrange the potatoes in the air fryer and cook on 180 C for 25 minutes, shaking twice during the cooking. Cook until crispy on the outside and tender on the inside.

149. Air-Fried Spiced Wings

Total Time: 45 min | **Serves**: 8 | **Per serving**: Calories: 145; Carbs: 0.7 g; Fat: 4.1 g; Protein: 25.7 g

INGREDIENTS

½ tsp celery salt
½ tsp bay leaf powder
½ tsp ground black pepper
½ tsp paprika
¼ tsp dry mustard
¼ tsp cayenne pepper
¼ tsp allspice
2 pounds chicken wings

DIRECTIONS

Grease the air fryer basket and preheat to 175 C. In a bowl, mix celery salt, bay leaf powder, black pepper, paprika, dry mustard, cayenne pepper, and allspice. Coat the wings thoroughly in this mixture.

Arrange the wings in an even layer in the basket of the air fryer. Cook the chicken until it's no longer pink around the bone, for 30 minutes. Then, increase the temperature to 190 C and cook for 6 minutes more, until crispy on the outside.

150. Teriyaki Chicken Wings

Total Time: 55 min | **Serves**: 4 | **Per serving**: Calories: 331; Carbs: 40.7 g; Fat: 4.5 g; Protein: 31.7 g

INGREDIENTS

1 pound chicken wings
200ml soy sauce
100g brown sugar
100ml apple cider vinegar
2 tbsp fresh ginger, minced
2 tbsp fresh garlic, minced
1 tsp finely ground black pepper
2 tbsp cornstarch
2 tbsp cold water
1 tsp sesaOme seeds

DIRECTIONS

In a bowl, add chicken wings, and pour in half cup soy sauce. Refrigerate for 20 minutes; drain and pat dry. Arrange the wings in the air fryer and cook for 30 minutes at 190 C, turning once halfway through. Make sure you check them towards the end to avoid overcooking.

In a skillet and over medium heat, stir sugar, half cup soy sauce, vinegar, ginger, garlic, and black pepper. Cook until sauce has reduced slightly, about 4 to 6 minutes.

Dissolve 2 tbsp of cornstarch in cold water, in a bowl, and stir in the slurry into the sauce, until it thickens, for 2 minutes. Pour the sauce over wings and sprinkle with sesame seeds.

151. Smoked Fish Balls

Total Time: 45 min | **Serves**: 6 | **Per serving**: Calories: 339; Carbs: 36g; Fat: 19g; Protein: 19g

INGREDIENTS

150g smoked fish, flaked
350g cooked rice
2 eggs, lightly beaten
80g grated Grana Padano cheese
15g finely chopped thyme
Salt and pepper to taste
50g panko crumbs
Cooking spray

DIRECTIONS

In a bowl, add fish, rice, eggs, Grana Padano cheese, thyme, salt and pepper into a bowl; stir to combine. Shape the mixture into 12 even-sized balls. Roll the balls in the crumbs then spray with oil.

Arrange the balls into the fryer and cook for 16 minutes at 200 C, until crispy.

152. Spring Rolls

Total Time: 30 min | **Serves**: 8 | **Per serving**: Calories: 182; Carbs: 2g; Fat: 37g; Protein: 4g

INGREDIENTS

180g cooked and cooled vermicelli noodles
1 red bell pepper, seeds removed, chopped
8 spring roll wrappers
2 garlic cloves, finely chopped
1 tbsp minced fresh ginger
2 tbsp soy sauce
1 tsp sesame oil
100g finely chopped mushrooms
130g finely chopped carrot
50g finely chopped scallions
Cooking spray

DIRECTIONS

In a saucepan, add garlic, ginger, soy sauce, pepper, mushroom, carrot and scallions, and stir-fry over high heat for a few minutes, until soft. Add in vermicelli noodles; remove from the heat.

Place the spring roll wrappers onto a working board. Spoon dollops of veggie and noodle mixture at the center of each spring roll wrapper. Roll the spring rolls and tuck the corners and edges in to create neat and secure rolls.

Spray with oil and transfer them to the air fryer. Cook for 12 minutes at 175 C, turning once halfway through. Cook until golden and crispy. Serve with soy or sweet chili sauce.

153. Prawn & Cabbage in Egg Rolls

Total Time: 50 min | **Serves**: 4 | **Per serving**: Calories: 381; Carbs: 42.7 g; Fat: 16.5 g; Protein: 14.7 g

INGREDIENTS

2 tbsp vegetable oil
1-inch piece fresh ginger, grated
1 tbsp minced garlic
1 carrot, cut into strips
50ml chicken broth
2 tbsp reduced-sodium soy sauce
1 tbsp sugar
1 cup shredded Napa cabbage
1 tbsp sesame oil
8 cooked prawns, minced
1 egg
8 egg roll wrappers
Cooking spray

DIRECTIONS

In a skillet over high heat, heat vegetable oil, and cook ginger and garlic for 40 seconds, until fragrant. Stir in carrot and cook for another 2 minutes. Pour in chicken broth, soy sauce, and sugar and bring to a boil.

Add cabbage and let simmer until softened, for 4 minutes. Remove skillet from the heat and stir in sesame oil. Let cool for 15 minutes. Strain cabbage mixture, and fold in minced prawns. Whisk an egg in a small bowl. Fill each egg roll wrapper with prawn mixture, arranging the mixture just below the center of the wrapper.

Fold the bottom part over the filling and tuck under. Fold in both sides and tightly roll-up. Use the whisked egg to seal the wrapper. Repeat until all egg rolls are ready. Place the rolls into a greased air fryer basket, spray them with oil and cook for 12 minutes at 185 C, turning once halfway through.

154. Vanilla & Chocolate Cookies

Total Time: 15 min | **Serves**: 5 | **Per serving**: Calories: 281; Carbs: 42.7 g; Fat: 3.5 g; Protein: 11.7 g

INGREDIENTS

100g flour
¼ tsp baking soda
¾ tsp salt
40g brown sugar
30g unsalted butter, softened
2 tbsp white sugar
1 egg yolk
½ tbsp vanilla extract
½ cup (64g chocolate chips

DIRECTIONS

Preheat air fryer to 175 C. Line the basket or rack with foil. Whisk flour, baking soda, and salt together in a small bowl. Combine brown sugar, butter, and white sugar in a separate bowl.

Add egg yolk and vanilla extract and whisk until well-combined. Stir flour mixture into butter mixture until dough is just combined; gently fold in chocolate chips. Scoop dough by the spoonfuls and roll into balls; place onto the foil-lined air fryer basket, 2 inches apart.

Cook dough in the air fryer until cookies start getting crispy, 5 to 6 minutes. Transfer foil and cookies to wire racks or a plate, and let cool completely. Repeat with remaining dough.

155. Cauliflower with Buffalo Sauce

Total Time: 25 min | **Serves**: 4 | **Per serving**: Calories: 198; Carbs: 5.7 g; Fat: 3.5 g; Protein: 10.7 g

INGREDIENTS

3 tbsp butter, melted
3 tbsp buffalo hot sauce
1 egg white
120g panko breadcrumbs
½ tsp salt
¼ tsp freshly ground black pepper
½ head cauliflower, cut into florets
Cooking spray

DIRECTIONS

In a bowl, stir in butter, hot sauce, and egg white. Mix breadcrumbs with salt and pepper, in a separate bowl. Toss the florets in the hot sauce mixture until well-coated.

Toss the coated cauliflower in crumbs until coated, then transfer the coated florets to the air fryer. Spray with cooking spray. Cook for 18 minutes at 175 C, in batches if needed, until golden brown and cooked through.

156. Crispy Chicken Nuggets

Total Time: 25 min | **Serves**: 4 | **Per serving**: Calories: 253; Carbs: 4.2 g; Fat: 14.2 g; Protein: 25.6 g

INGREDIENTS

1 lb chicken breasts, boneless, skinless, cubed
Salt and black pepper to taste
2 tbsp olive oil
5 tbsp plain breadcrumbs
2 tbsp panko breadcrumbs
2 tbsp grated Parmesan cheese
Cooking spray

DIRECTIONS

Preheat the air fryer to 190 C. Season the chicken with pepper, kosher salt, and seasoned salt; set aside. In a bowl, pour olive oil. In a separate bowl, add crumb, and Parmesan cheese.

Place the chicken pieces in the oil to coat, then dip into breadcrumb mixture, and transfer to the air fryer. Work in batches if needed. Lightly spray chicken with cooking spray.

Cook the chicken for 10 minutes, flipping once halfway through. Cook until golden brown on the outside and no more pink on the inside.

157. Crispy Squash

Total Time: 25 min | **Serves**: 4 | **Per serving**: Calories: 41; Carbs: 2.1 g; Fat: 3.2 g; Protein: 0.6 g

INGREDIENTS

400g butternut squash, peeled and cubed
1 tbsp olive oil
Salt and black pepper to taste
¼ tsp dried thyme
1 tbsp finely chopped fresh parsley

DIRECTIONS

In a bowl, add squash, oil, salt, pepper, and thyme, and toss until squash is well-coated. Place squash in the air fryer and cook for 14 minutes at 180 C. When ready, sprinkle with freshly chopped parsley and serve chilled.

158. Air-Fried Chicken Tenders

Total Time: 30 min | **Serves**: 4 | **Per serving**: Calories: 424; Carbs: 21.5 g; Fat: 17.8 g; Protein: 41.3 g

INGREDIENTS

1 ½ lb chicken breasts, boneless, cut into strips
1 egg, lightly beaten
100g seasoned breadcrumbs
Salt and ground black pepper
½ tsp dried oregano
Cooking spray

DIRECTIONS

Preheat the air fryer to 195 C. Season the chicken with oregano, salt, and black pepper. In a small bowl, whisk in some salt and pepper to the beaten egg. In a separate bowl, add the crumbs. Dip chicken tenders in the egg wash, then in the crumbs.

Roll the strips in the breadcrumbs and press firmly so the breadcrumbs stick well. Spray the chicken tenders with cooking spray and arrange them in the air fryer. Cook for 14 minutes, until no longer pink in the center, and nice and crispy on the outside.

159. Delicious Chicken Taquitos

Total Time: 25 min | **Serves**: 4 | **Per serving**: Calories: 478; Carbs: 52.6 g; Fat: 18.8 g; Protein: 23.9 g

INGREDIENTS

150g cooked chicken, shredded
220g shredded mozzarella cheese
70g salsa
70g Greek yogurt
Salt and black pepper to taste
8 flour tortillas
Cooking spray

DIRECTIONS

In a bowl, mix chicken, cheese, salsa, and sour cream, and season with salt and pepper. Spray one side of the tortilla with cooking spray. Lay 2 tbsp of the chicken mixture at the center of the non-oiled side of each tortilla. Roll tightly around the mixture. Arrange taquitos into your air fryer basket, without overcrowding. Cook in batches if needed. Place the seam side down, or it will unravel during cooking crisps. Cook for 12 to 14 minutes, or until crispy at 190 C.

160. Crispy Kale Chips

Total Time: 25 min | **Serves**: 4 | **Per serving**: Calories: 71; Carbs: 2.2 g; Fat: 7.2 g; Protein: 0.6 g

INGREDIENTS

400g chopped kale, stems removed
2 tbsp olive oil
1 tsp garlic powder
½ tsp salt
¼ tsp onion powder
¼ tsp black pepper

DIRECTIONS

In a bowl, mix kale and oil together, until well-coated. Add in garlic, salt, onion, and pepper and toss until well-coated. Arrange half the kale leaves to air fryer, in a single layer. Cook for 8 minutes at 175 C, shaking once halfway through. Remove chips to a sheet to cool; do not touch.

161. Herby Meatballs

Total Time: 30 min | **Serves**: 4 | **Per serving**: Calories: 424; Carbs: 32g; Fat: 21g; Protein: 44g

INGREDIENTS

1 lb ground beef
1 onion, finely chopped
3 garlic cloves, finely chopped
2 eggs
120g breadcrumbs
30g fresh mixed herbs
Salt and pepper to taste
Olive oil

DIRECTIONS

In a bowl, add beef, onion, garlic, eggs, crumbs, herbs, salt and pepper and mix with hands to combine. Shape into balls and arrange them in the air fryer's basket. Drizzle with oil and cook for 16 minutes at 190 C, turning once halfway through.

162. Air-Fried Cheesy Broccoli with Garlic

Total Time: 25 min | **Serves**: 2 | **Per serving**: Calories: 207; Carbs: 6.2 g; Fat: 17.1 g; Protein: 10.3 g

INGREDIENTS

2 tbsp butter, melted
1 egg white
1 garlic clove, grated
¼ tsp salt
A pinch of black pepper
½ lb broccoli florets
30g grated Parmesan cheese

DIRECTIONS

In a bowl, whisk together the butter, egg, garlic, salt, and black pepper. Toss in broccoli to coat well. Top with Parmesan cheese and; toss to coat. Arrange broccoli in a single layer in the air fryer, without overcrowding. Cook in batches for 10 minutes at 180 C. Remove to a serving plate and sprinkle with Parmesan cheese.

163. Thyme & Garlic Sweet Potato Wedges

Total Time: 30 min | **Serves**: 2 | **Per serving**: Calories: 126; Carbs: 15.5 g; Fat: 6.7 g; Protein: 1.3 g

INGREDIENTS

1 sweet potato, cut into wedges
1 tbsp olive oil
¼ tsp salt
½ tsp chili powder
½ tsp garlic powder
½ tsp smoked paprika
½ tsp dried thyme
A pinch of cayenne pepper

DIRECTIONS

In a bowl, mix olive oil, salt, chili powder, garlic powder, smoked paprika, thyme, and cayenne. Toss in the potato wedges, until well-coated. Arrange the wedges evenly in the air fryer, and cook for 25 minutes at 190 C, flipping once halfway through.

164. Air-Fried Pumpkin Seeds with Cardamom

Total Time: 50 min | **Serves**: 4 | **Per serving**: Calories: 204; Carbs: 6.5 g; Fat: 17.3 g; Protein: 8.8 g

INGREDIENTS

40g pumpkin seeds, rinsed
1 tbsp butter, melted
1 tbsp brown sugar
1 tsp orange zest
½ tsp cardamom
½ tsp salt

DIRECTIONS

Cook the seeds for 4 minutes at 160 C, in your air fryer, to avoid moisture. In a bowl, whisk melted butter, sugar, zest, cardamom and salt. Add the seeds to the bowl and toss to coat well. Transfer the seeds to the air fryer and cook for 35 minutes at 150 C, shaking the basket every 10-12 minutes. Cook until lightly browned.

165. Chicken Wings with Alfredo Sauce

Total Time: 60 min | **Serves**: 4 | **Per serving**: Calories: 233; Carbs: 2.5 g; Fat: 7.3 g; Protein: 37.5 g

INGREDIENTS

1 ½ lb chicken wings
Salt to taste
120g Alfredo sauce

DIRECTIONS

Preheat the air fryer to 370°F. Season the wings with salt. Arrange them in the air fryer, without touching.

Cook in batches if needed, for 20 minutes, until no longer pink in the center. Increase the temperature to 195 C and cook for 5 minutes more. Remove to a big bowl and coat well with the sauce, to serve.

166. BBQ Chicken Pizza

Total Time: 15 min | **Serves**: 1 | **Per serving**: Calories: 635; Carbs: 52.7 g; Fat: 25.2 g; Protein: 45.6 g

INGREDIENTS

30g shredded Monterrey Jack cheese
1 piece naan bread
Cooking spray
60g barbeque sauce
60g shredded mozzarella cheese
2 tbsp red onion, thinly sliced
½ chicken herby sausage
Chopped coriander for garnish

DIRECTIONS

Spray naan's bread bottom with cooking spray and arrange it in the air fryer. Brush well with barbeque sauce, sprinkle mozzarella cheese, Monterrey Jack cheese, and red onion on top. Top with the sausage over and spray the crust with cooking spray. Cook for 8 minutes in a preheated air fryer at 200 C.

167. Homemade Croquettes

Total Time: 45 min | Serves: 4 | Per serving: Calories: 367; Carbs: 46g; Fat: 21g; Protein: 18g

INGREDIENTS

500g cooked rice
1 brown onion, chopped
2 garlic cloves, chopped
2 eggs, lightly beaten
50g grated Parmesan cheese
Salt and pepper to taste
50g breadcrumbs
1 tsp dried mixed herbs
Cooking spray

DIRECTIONS

Combine rice, onion, garlic, eggs, Parmesan, salt and pepper. Shape into 10 croquettes. Spread the crumbs onto a plate and coat each croquette in the crumbs. Spray each croquette with oil.

Arrange the croquettes in the air fryer and cook for 16 minutes at 190 C, turning once halfway through cooking. They should be golden and crispy. Serve with plum sauce.

168. Crispy Pepperoni Pizza

Total Time: 25 min | Serves: 2 | Per serving: Calories: 448; Carbs: 41.7 g; Fat: 20.9 g; Protein: 21.6 g

INGREDIENTS

8 ounces fresh pizza dough
Cooking spray
80g tomato sauce
80g mozzarella cheese, shredded
8 pepperonis, sliced
Flour, to dust

DIRECTIONS

On a floured surface, place dough and dust with flour. Stretch with hands into an air-fryer fitting shape. Spray the air fryer basket with cooking spray and arrange the pizza inside.

Brush generously with sauce, leaving some space at the border. scatter with mozzarella and top with pepperonis. Cook for 15 minutes, or until crispy, at 175 C.

169. Air-Frier Baked Potatoes

Total Time: 45 min | Serves: 4 | Per serving: Calories: 348; Carbs: 62.1 g; Fat: 7.2 g; Protein: 7.6 g

INGREDIENTS

4 yukon gold potatoes, clean and dried
2 tbsp olive oil
Salt and ground black pepper to taste

DIRECTIONS

Rub each potato with half tbsp of olive oil. Season generously with salt and pepper, and arrange them in the air fryer. Cook for 40 minutes at 200 C.

Let cool slightly, then make a slit on top. Use a fork to fluff the insides of the potatoes. Fill the potato with cheese or garlic mayo.

170. Beef Meatballs

Total Time: 25 min | Serves: 3 | Per serving: Calories 283; Carbs 24g; Fat 13g; Protein 21g

INGREDIENTS

½ lb ground beef
1 small finger ginger, crushed
1 tbsp hot sauce

3 tbsp vinegar
1 ½ tsp lemon juice

120g tomato ketchup, reduced sugar
2 tbsp sugar

¼ tsp dry mustard
Salt and pepper to taste, if needed

DIRECTIONS

In a bowl, add beef, ginger, hot sauce, vinegar, lemon juice, tomato ketchup, sugar, mustard, pepper, and salt, and mix well using a spoon. Shape 2-inch sized balls, with hands. Add the balls to the fryer without overcrowding.

Cook at 185 C for 15 minutes, shaking once halfway through. Cook in batches if needed. Serve with tomato or cheese dip.

171. BBQ Chicken

Total Time: 35 min | **Serves**: 3 | **Per serving**: Calories: 354; Carbs: 7 g; Fat: 46.4 g; Protein: 8.9 g

INGREDIENTS

1 whole small chicken, cut into pieces
1 tsp salt
1 tsp smoked paprika
1 tsp garlic powder
200 ml BBQ sauce

DIRECTIONS

Mix salt, paprika, and garlic powder and coat chicken pieces. Place them skin-side down in the air fryer. Cook for around 18 minutes at 200 C, until slightly golden. Remove to a plate and brush with barbecue sauce.

Wipe fryer out from the chicken fat. Return the chicken to the air fryer, skin-side up, and cook for 5 minutes at 175 C. Serve with more barbecue sauce.

172. Homemade Crispy Croutons

Total Time: 20 min | **Serves**: 4 | **Per serving**: Calories: 102; Carbs: 9.7 g; Fat: 6.4 g; Protein: 1.8 g

INGREDIENTS

240g bread, cubed
2 tbsp butter, melted
Garlic salt and black pepper to taste

DIRECTIONS

In a bowl, toss the bread with butter, garlic salt, and pepper until well-coated. Place the cubes in the air fryer and cook for 12 minutes at 190 C, or until golden brown and crispy.

173. Air-Fried Chicken Breasts

Total Time: 30 min | **Serves**: 4 | **Per serving**: Calories: 331; Carbs: 1.7 g; Fat: 7.2 g; Protein: 51.6 g

INGREDIENTS

4 boneless, skinless chicken breasts
Cooking spray
Salt and black pepper to taste
1 tsp garlic powder

DIRECTIONS

Spray the breasts and the air fryer tray, with cooking spray. Rub chicken with salt, garlic powder, and black pepper. Arrange the breasts in the basket, without overcrowding. Cook in batches if needed. Cook for 20 minutes at 360°F, until nice and crispy.

174. Air-Fried Crispy Chicken Thighs

Total Time: 30 min | **Serves**: 4 | **Per serving**: Calories: 252; Carbs: 0.6 g; Fat: 18.7 g; Protein: 18.5 g

INGREDIENTS

1 pound chicken thighs
½ tsp salt
¼ tsp black pepper
¼ tsp garlic powder

DIRECTIONS

Season the thighs with salt, pepper, and garlic powder. Arrange thighs, skin side down, in the air fryer and cook until golden brown, for 20 minutes at 175 C.

175. Whole Roasted Chicken

Total Time: 60 min | **Serves**: 4 | **Per serving**: Calories: 303; Carbs: 2.2 g; Fat: 10 g; Protein: 48.5 g

INGREDIENTS

1 chicken (around 3.5 lb), rinsed, pat-dried
1 tbsp olive oil
1 tsp salt
¼ tsp black pepper
1 lemon, cut into quarters
5 garlic cloves

DIRECTIONS

Rub chicken with olive oil and season with salt and pepper. Stuff with lemon and garlic cloves into the cavity.

Arrange chicken, breast-side down, into the air fryer. Tuck the legs and wings tips under. Cook for 45 minutes at 175 C. Let rest for 5-6 minutes, then carve and enjoy.

176. Air-Fried Chickpeas with Herbs

Total Time: 20 min | **Serves**: 4 | **Per serving**: Calories: 236; Carbs: 28.6 g; Fat: 10.3 g; Protein: 8.9 g

INGREDIENTS

2 (14.5-ounce) can chickpeas, rinsed, dried
2 tbsp olive oil
1 tsp dried rosemary
½ tsp dried thyme
¼ tsp dried sage
¼ tsp salt

DIRECTIONS

In a bowl, mix together chickpeas, oil, rosemary, thyme, sage, and salt. Transfer them to the air fryer and spread in an even layer. Cook 14 minutes at 190 C, shaking once, halfway through cooking.

177. Classic French Fries

Total Time: 25 min | **Serves**: 2 | **Per serving**: Calories: 331; Carbs: 65.6 g; Fat: 4.8 g; Protein: 7.9 g

INGREDIENTS

Cooking spray
2 russet potatoes, cut into strips
2 tbsp olive oil
Salt and black pepper to taste

DIRECTIONS

Spray the air fryer basket or rack with cooking spray. In a bowl, toss the strips with olive oil until well-coated, and season with salt and pepper. Arrange in the air fryer and cook for 18 minutes at 200 C, turning once halfway through. Check for crispiness and serve immediately, with garlic aioli, ketchup or crumbled cheese.

178. Air-Fried Brussels Sprouts

Total Time: 15 min | **Serves:** 2 | **Per serving:** Calories: 109; Carbs: 7.1 g; Fat: 10.4 g; Protein: 3.9 g

INGREDIENTS

½ pound Brussels sprouts, trimmed and halved
1 tbsp butter, melted
Salt and black pepper to taste
¼ tsp cayenne pepper

DIRECTIONS

In a bowl, mix Brussels sprouts, butter, cayenne pepper, salt, and pepper. Place Brussels sprouts in air fryer basket. Cook for 10 minutes at 190 C. Serve with sautéed onion rings.

179. Garlicky Chips with Herbs

Total Time: 60 min | **Serves:** 2 | **Per serving:** Calories: 424; Carbs: 68g; Fat: 13g; Protein: 8g

INGREDIENTS

2 potatoes, sliced
2 tbsp olive oil
3 garlic cloves, crushed
1 tsp each of fresh rosemary, thyme, oregano, chopped
Salt and black pepper

DIRECTIONS

In a bowl, add oil, garlic, herbs, salt and pepper, and toss with hands until well-coated. Arrange the slices in the air fryer's basket and cook for 14 minutes at 180 C, shaking it every 4-5 minutes. Enjoy with onion dip.

180. Cheesy Stuffed Mushrooms

Total Time: 30 min | **Serves:** 10 | **Per serving:** Calories: 73; Carbs: 7g; Fat: 3g; Protein: 4g

INGREDIENTS

10 Swiss brown mushrooms
Olive oil to brush the mushrooms
200g cooked brown rice
90g grated Grana Padano cheese
1 tsp dried mixed herbs
Salt and black pepper

DIRECTIONS

Brush every mushroom with oil and set aside. In a bowl, mix rice, cheese, herbs, salt and pepper. Stuff the mushrooms with the mixture. Arrange the mushrooms in the air fryer and cook for 14 minutes at 180 C. Make sure the mushrooms cooked until golden and the cheese has melted. Serve with fresh herbs.

181. Pita Pizzas

Total Time: 25 min | **Serves:** 5 | **Per serving:** Calories: 356; Carbs: 18g; Fat: 23g; Protein: 19g

INGREDIENTS

5 pita bread
5 tbsp marinara sauce
10 rounds of chorizo
10 button mushrooms, sliced
10 fresh basil leaves
200g grated cheddar cheese
1 tsp chili flakes
Cooking spray

DIRECTIONS

Spray the pitas with oil and scatter the sauce over. Top with chorizo, mushrooms, basil, cheddar and chili flakes. Cook for 14 minutes at 180 C, checking it at least once halfway through not to overcook them.

182. Spicy Fries

Total Time: 25 min | **Serves**: 4 | **Per serving**: Calories: 242; Carbs: 48g; Fat: 3g; Protein: 6g

INGREDIENTS

- 3 potatoes, sliced, rinsed
- 2 tsp olive oil
- 2 tsp cayenne pepper
- 1 tsp paprika
- Salt and black pepper

DIRECTIONS

Place the fries into a bowl and sprinkle with oil, cayenne, paprika, salt, and black pepper. Toss and place them in the fryer. Cook for 14 minutes at 180 C, until golden and crispy. Give it a toss after 7-8 minutes.

183. Mediterranean Bruschetta

Total Time: 25 min | **Serves**: 10 | **Per serving**: Calories: 206; Carbs: 17g; Fat: 12g; Protein: 8g

INGREDIENTS

- 10 slices of french baguette
- Olive oil
- 3 garlic cloves, minced
- 90g grated cheddar cheese
- 1 tsp dried oregano
- Salt and pepper to taste

DIRECTIONS

Brush the bread with oil and sprinkle with garlic. Scatter the cheese on top, then oregano, salt and pepper. Arrange the slices in the fryer and cook for 14 minutes at 180 C, turning once halfway through cooking.

184. Fried Agnolotti

Total Time: 25 min | **Serves**: 6 | **Per serving**: Calories: 367; Carbs: 56g; Fat: 9g; Protein: 14g

INGREDIENTS

- 2 packages of fresh agnolotti
- 120g flour
- Salt and black pepper
- 4 eggs, beaten
- 200g breadcrumbs
- Cooking spray

DIRECTIONS

Mix flour with salt and black pepper. Dip the pasta into the flour, then into the egg, and finally in the breadcrumbs. Spray with oil and arrange in the air fryer in an even layer. Set to 200 C and cook for 14 minutes, turning once halfway through cooking. Cook until nice and golden. Serve with goat cheese.

185. Plums and Pancetta Bombs

Total Time: 25 min | **Serves**: 10 | **Per serving**: Calories: 223; Carbs: 18g; Fat: 12g; Protein: 12g

INGREDIENTS

- 16 oz soft goat cheese
- 2 tbsp fresh rosemary, finely chopped
- 160g almonds, chopped into small pieces
- Salt and black pepper
- 15 dried plums, chopped
- 15 pancetta slices

DIRECTIONS

Line the air fryer basket with baking paper. In a bowl, add cheese, rosemary, almonds, salt, pepper and plums; stir well. Roll into balls and wrap with a pancetta slice. Arrange the bombs in the fryer and cook for 10 minutes at 200 C.

Check at the 5-minute mark, to avoid overcooking. When ready, let cool before removing them from the air fryer. Serve with toothpicks!

186. Salmon Tarts

Total Time: 20 min | **Serves**: 15 | **Per serving**: Calories: 415; Carbs: 43g; Fat: 23g; Protein: 10g

INGREDIENTS

15 mini tart cases
4 eggs, lightly beaten
120g heavy cream
Salt and black pepper
3 oz smoked salmon
6 oz cream cheese, divided into 15 pieces
6 fresh dill

DIRECTIONS

Mix together eggs and cream in a pourable measuring container. Arrange the tarts into the air fryer. Pour in mixture into the tarts, about halfway up the side and top with a piece of salmon and a piece of cheese. Cook for 10 minutes at 170 C, regularly check to avoid overcooking. Sprinkle dill and serve chilled.

187. Parmesan Crusted Pickles

Total Time: 35 min | **Serves**: 4 | **Per serving**: Calories 335; Carbs 34g; Fat 14g; Protein 17g

INGREDIENTS

450g dill pickles, sliced, drained
2 eggs
90g grated Parmesan cheese
160g breadcrumbs, smooth
Black pepper to taste
Cooking spray

DIRECTIONS

Season the breadcrumbs with black pepper in a bowl and mix well; set aside. In another bowl, crack the eggs and beat with 2 tsp of water. Set aside. Add the cheese to a separate bowl; set aside. Preheat the air fryer to 200 C.

Pull out the fryer basket and spray it lightly with cooking spray. Dredge the pickle slices in the egg mixture, then in breadcrumbs and then in cheese. Place them in the fryer without overlapping.

Slide the fryer basket back in and cook for 4 minutes. Turn them and cook for further for 5 minutes, until crispy. Serve with a cheese dip.

188. Breaded Mushrooms

Total Time: 55 min | **Serves**: 4 | **Per serving**: Calories 487; Carbs 49g; Fat 22g; Protein 31g

INGREDIENTS

1 pound small Button mushrooms, cleaned
200g breadcrumbs
2 eggs, beaten
Salt and pepper to taste
180g Parmesan cheese, grated

DIRECTIONS

Preheat the air fryer to 180 C. Pour the breadcrumbs in a bowl, add salt and pepper and mix well. Pour the cheese in a separate bowl and set aside. Dip each mushroom in the eggs, then in the crumbs, and then in the cheese.

Slide-out the fryer basket and add 6 to 10 mushrooms. Cook them for 20 minutes, in batches, if needed. Serve with cheese dip.

189. Cheesy Sticks with Sweet Thai Sauce

Total Time: 2 hrs 20 min | **Serves**: 4 | **Per serving**: Calories 158; Carbs 14g; Fat 7g; Protein 9g

INGREDIENTS

12 mozzarella string cheese
200g breadcrumbs
3 eggs
280g sweet thai sauce
4 tbsp skimmed milk

DIRECTIONS

Pour the crumbs in a medium bowl. Crack the eggs into another bowl and beat with the milk. One after the other, dip each cheese sticks in the egg mixture, in the crumbs, then egg mixture again and then in the crumbs again.

Place the coated cheese sticks on a cookie sheet and freeze for 1 to 2 hours. Preheat the air fryer to 190 C. Arrange the sticks in the fryer without overcrowding. Cook for 5 minutes, flipping them halfway through cooking to brown evenly. Cook in batches. Serve with a sweet thai sauce.

190. Bacon-Wrapped Avocados

Total Time: 40 min | **Serves**: 6 | **Per serving**: Calories 193; Carbs 10g; Fat 16g; Protein 4g

INGREDIENTS

12 thick strips bacon
3 large avocados, sliced
⅓ tsp salt
⅓ tsp chili powder
⅓ tsp cumin powder

DIRECTIONS

Stretch the bacon strips to elongate and use a knife to cut in half to make 24 pieces. Wrap each bacon piece around a slice of avocado from one end to the other end. Tuck the end of bacon into the wrap. Arrange on a flat surface and season with salt, chili and cumin on both sides.

Arrange 4 to 8 wrapped pieces in the fryer and cook at 175 C for 8 minutes, or until the bacon is browned and crunchy, flipping halfway through to cook evenly. Remove onto a wire rack and repeat the process for the remaining avocado pieces.

191. Hot Chicken Wingettes

Total Time: 45 min | **Serves**: 3 | **Per serving**: Calories 563; Carbs 2g; Fat 28g; Protein 35g

INGREDIENTS

15 chicken wingettes
Salt and pepper to taste
100g hot sauce
80g butter
½ tbsp vinegar

DIRECTIONS

Preheat the air fryer to 180 C. Season the wingettes with pepper and salt. Add them to the air fryer and cook for 35 minutes. Toss every 5 minutes. Once ready, remove them into a bowl. Over low heat, melt the butter in a saucepan. Add the vinegar and hot sauce. Stir and cook for a minute.

Turn the heat off. Pour the sauce over the chicken. Toss to coat well. Transfer the chicken to a serving platter. Serve with a side of celery strips and blue cheese dressing.

192. Bacon & Chicken Wrapped Jalapenos

Total Time: 40 min | **Serves**: 4 | **Per serving**: Calories 244; Carbs 13g; Fat 12.8g; Protein 9.3g

INGREDIENTS

8 jalapeño peppers, halved lengthwise and seeded
4 chicken breasts, butterflied and halved
6 oz cream cheese
6 oz Cheddar cheese
16 slices bacon
100g breadcrumbs
Salt and pepper to taste
2 eggs
Cooking spray

DIRECTIONS

Season the chicken with pepper and salt on both sides. In a bowl, add cream cheese, cheddar, a pinch of pepper and salt. Mix well. Take each jalapeno and spoon in the cheese mixture to the brim. On a working board, flatten each piece of chicken and lay 2 bacon slices each on them. Place a stuffed jalapeno on each laid out chicken and bacon set, and wrap the jalapenos in them.

Preheat the air fryer to 175 C. Add the eggs to a bowl and pour the breadcrumbs in another bowl. Also, set a flat plate aside. Take each wrapped jalapeno and dip it into the eggs and then in the breadcrumbs. Place them on the flat plate. Lightly grease the fryer basket with cooking spray. Arrange 4-5 breaded jalapenos in the basket, and cook for 7 minutes.

Prepare a paper towel-lined plate; set aside. Once the timer beeps, open the fryer, turn the jalapenos, and cook further for 4 minutes. Once ready, remove them onto the paper towel-lined plate. Repeat the cooking process for the remaining jalapenos. Serve with a sweet dip for an enhanced taste.

193. Mouth-Watering Salami Sticks

Total Time: 2 hrs 10 min | **Serves**: 3 | **Per serving**: Calories 428; Carbs 12g; Fat 16g; Protein 42g

INGREDIENTS

1 lb ground beef
3 tbsp sugar
A pinch garlic powder
A pinch chili powder
Salt to taste
1 tsp liquid smoke

DIRECTIONS

Place the meat, sugar, garlic powder, chili powder, salt and liquid smoke in a bowl. Mix with a spoon. Mold out 4 sticks with your hands, place them on a plate, and refrigerate for 2 hours. Cook at 175 C. for 10 minutes, flipping once halfway through.

194. Carrot Crisps

Total Time: 20 min | **Serves**: 2 | **Per serving**: Calories 35; Carbs 8g; Fat 3g; Protein 1g

INGREDIENTS

3 large carrots, washed and peeled
Salt to taste
Cooking spray

DIRECTIONS

Using a mandolin slicer, slice the carrots very thinly heightwise. Put the carrot strips in a bowl and season with salt to taste. Grease the fryer basket lightly with cooking spray, and add the carrot strips. Cook at 175 C for 10 minutes, stirring once halfway through.

195. Calamari with Olives

Total Time: 25 min | **Serves**: 3 | **Per serving**: Calories 128; Carbs 0g; Fat 3g; Protein 22g

INGREDIENTS

½ lb calamari rings
½ piece coriander, chopped
2 strips chili pepper, chopped
1 tbsp olive oil
130g pimiento-stuffed green olives, sliced

Salt and black pepper to taste

DIRECTIONS

In a bowl, add rings, chili pepper, salt, black pepper, oil, and coriander. Mix and let marinate for 10 minutes. Pour the calamari into an oven-safe bowl, that fits into the fryer basket.

Slide the fryer basket out, place the bowl in it, and slide the basket back in. Cook for 15 minutes stirring every 5 minutes using a spoon, at 200 C. After 15 minutes, and add in the olives.

Stir, close and continue to cook for 3 minutes. Once ready, transfer to a serving platter. Serve warm with a side of bread slices and mayonnaise.

196. Sweet Mixed Nuts

Total Time: 25 min | Serves: 5 | Per serving: Calories 147; Carbs 10g; Fat 12g; Protein 3g

INGREDIENTS

70g pecans
50g walnuts
70g almonds
A pinch cayenne pepper
2 tbsp sugar
2 tbsp egg whites
2 tsp cinnamon
Cooking spray

DIRECTIONS

Add the pepper, sugar, and cinnamon to a bowl and mix them well; set aside. In another bowl, mix in the pecans, walnuts, almonds, and egg whites. Add the spice mixture to the nuts and give it a good mix. Lightly grease the fryer basket with cooking spray.

Pour in the nuts, and cook them for 10 minutes. Stir the nuts using a wooden vessel, and cook for further for 10 minutes. Pour the nuts in the bowl. Let cool before crunching on them.

197. Cheesy Onion Rings

Total Time: 20 min | Serves: 3 | Per serving: Calories 205; Carbs 14g; Fat 11g; Protein 12g

INGREDIENTS

1 onion, peeled and sliced into 1-inch rings
70g Parmesan cheese, shredded
2 medium eggs, beaten
1 tsp garlic powder
A pinch of salt
120g flour
1 tsp paprika powder

DIRECTIONS

Add the eggs to a bowl; set aside In another bowl, add cheese, garlic powder, salt, flour, and paprika. Mix with a spoon. Dip each onion ring in egg, then in the cheese mixture, in the egg again and finally in the cheese mixture.

Add the rings to the basket and cook them for 8 minutes at 175 C. Remove onto a serving platter and serve with a cheese or tomato dip.

198. Cheesy Sausage Balls

Total Time: 50 min | Serves: 8 | Per serving: Calories 456; Carbs 23g; Fat 36g; Protein 36g

INGREDIENTS

1 ½ lb ground sausages
200g Cheddar cheese, shredded
200g flour
¾ tsp baking soda
4 eggs
180g sour cream
1 tsp dried oregano
1 tsp smoked paprika
2 tsp garlic powder

120 ml liquid coconut oil

DIRECTIONS

In a pan over medium heat, add the sausages and brown for 3-4 minutes. Drain the excess fat and set aside. In a bowl, sift in baking soda, and flour. Set aside. In another bowl, add eggs, sour cream, oregano, paprika, coconut oil, and garlic powder. Whisk to combine well. Combine the egg and flour mixtures using a spatula.

Add the cheese and sausages. Fold in and let it sit for 5 minutes to thicken. Rub your hands with coconut oil and mold out bite-size balls out of the batter. Place them on a tray, and refrigerate for 15 minutes. Then, add them in the air fryer, without overcrowding. Cook for 10 minutes per round, at 200 C, in batches if needed.

199. Crusted Coconut Shrimp

Total Time: 30 min | **Serves**: 5 | **Per serving**: Calories 149; Carbs 7g; Fat 2g; Protein 18g

INGREDIENTS

1 lb jumbo shrimp, peeled and deveined
70g shredded coconut
1 tbsp maple syrup
60g breadcrumbs
40g cornstarch
120 ml milk

DIRECTIONS

Pour the cornstarch in a zipper bag, add shrimp, zip the bag up and shake vigorously to coat with the cornstarch. Mix the syrup and milk in a bowl and set aside. In a separate bowl, mix the breadcrumbs and shredded coconut. Open the zipper bag and remove each shrimp while shaking off excess starch.

Dip each shrimp in the milk mixture and then in the crumbs mixture while pressing loosely to trap enough crumbs and coconut. Place the coated shrimp in the fryer without overcrowding. Cook 12 minutes at 175 C, flipping once halfway through. Cook until golden brown. Serve with a coconut-based dip.

200. Quick Cheese Sticks

Total Time: 5 min | **Serves**: 12 | **Per serving**: Calories 256; Carbs 8g; Fat 21g; Protein 16g

INGREDIENTS

6 oz bread cheese
2 tbsp butter
50g panko crumbs

DIRECTIONS

Put the butter in a bowl and melt in the microwave, for 2 minutes; set aside. With a knife, cut the cheese into equal sized sticks. Brush each stick with butter and dip into panko crumbs. Arrange the cheese sticks in a single layer on the fryer basket. Cook at 195 C for 10 minutes. Flip them halfway through, to brown evenly; serve warm.

201. Spicy Cheese Lings

Total Time: 25 min | **Serves**: 3 | **Per serving**: Calories 225; Carbs 35g; Fat 5.6g; Protein 8g

INGREDIENTS

4 tbsp grated cheese + extra for rolling
120g flour + extra for kneading
¼ tsp chili powder
½ tsp baking powder
3 tsp butter
A pinch of salt
Water

DIRECTIONS

In a bowl, mix in the cheese, flour, baking powder, chili powder, butter, and salt. The mixture should be crusty.

Add some drops of water and mix well to get a dough. Remove the dough on a flat surface.

Rub some extra flour in your palms and on the surface, and knead the dough for a while. Using a rolling pin, roll the dough out into a thin sheet. With a pastry cutter, cut the dough into your desired lings' shape. Add the cheese lings in the basket, and cook for 6 minutes at 175 C, flipping once halfway through.

202. Radish Chips

Total Time: 30 min | **Serves**: 4 | **Per serving**: Calories 25; Carbs 0.2g; Fat 2g; Protein 0.1g

INGREDIENTS

10 radishes, leaves removed and cleaned
Salt to season
Water
Cooking spray

DIRECTIONS

Using a mandolin, slice the radishes thinly. Place them in a pot and cover them with water. Heat the pot on a stovetop, and bring to boil, until the radishes are translucent, for 4 minutes. After 4 minutes, drain the radishes through a sieve; set aside. Grease the fryer basket with cooking spray.

Add in the radish slices and cook for 8 minutes, flipping once halfway through. Cook until golden brown, at 200 C. Prepare a paper towel-lined plate. Once the radishes are ready, transfer them to the paper towel-lined plate. Season with salt, and serve with ketchup or garlic mayo.

203. Zucchini Parmesan Chips

Total Time: 20 min | **Serves**: 3 | **Per serving**: Calories 268; Carbs 13g; Fat 16g; Protein 17g

INGREDIENTS

3 medium courgatte
120g breadcrumbs
2 eggs, beaten
90g grated Parmesan cheese
Salt and pepper to taste
1 tsp smoked paprika
Cooking spray

DIRECTIONS

With a mandolin cutter, slice the zucchinis thinly. Use paper towels to press out excess liquid. In a bowl, add crumbs, salt, pepper, cheese, and paprika. Mix well and set aside. Set a wire rack or tray aside. Dip each zucchini slice in egg and then in the cheese mix while pressing to coat them well.

Place them on the wire rack. Spray the coated slices with oil. Put the slices in the fryer basket in a single layer without overlapping. Cook at 175 C for 8 minutes for each batch. Serve sprinkled with salt and with a spicy dip.

204. Paprika Chicken Nuggets

Total Time: 1 hr 20 min | **Serves**: 4 | **Per serving**: Calories 548; Carbs 51g; Fat 23g; Protein 49g

INGREDIENTS

2 chicken breasts, bones removed
2 tbsp paprika
450 ml milk
2 eggs
4 tsp onion powder
1 ½ tsp garlic powder
Salt and pepper to taste
120g flour
200g breadcrumbs
Cooking spray

DIRECTIONS

Cut the chicken into 1-inch chunks. In a bowl, mix in paprika, onion, garlic, salt, pepper, flour, and breadcrumbs.

In another bowl, crack the eggs, add the milk and beat them together. Prepare a tray. Dip each chicken chunk in the egg mixture, place them on the tray, and refrigerate for 1 hour.

Preheat the air fryer to 185 C. Roll each chunk in the crumb mixture. Place the crusted chicken in the fryer's basket. Spray with cooking spray. Cook for 8 minutes at 180 C, flipping once halfway through. Serve with a tomato dip or ketchup. Yum!

205. Cool Chicken Croquettes

Total Time: 20 min | **Serves**: 4 | **Per serving**: Calories: 230; Carbs: 10g; Fat: 12g; Protein: 9g

INGREDIENTS

- 4 chicken breasts
- 1 whole egg
- Salt and pepper to taste
- 80g oats, crumbled
- ½ tsp garlic powder
- 1 tbsp parsley
- 1 tbsp thyme

DIRECTIONS

Preheat your air fryer to 180 C. Pulse chicken breast in a processor food until well blended. Add seasoning to the chicken alongside garlic, parsley, thyme and mix well. In a bowl, add beaten egg and beat until the yolk is mixed.

In a separate bowl, add crumbled oats. Form croquettes using the chicken mixture and dip in beaten egg, and finally in oats until coated. Place the nuggets in your fryer's cooking basket. Cook for 10 minutes, making sure to keep shaking the basket after every 5 minutes.

206. Herbed Croutons With Brie Cheese

Total Time: 20 min | Serve: 1 | **Per serving**: Calories: 20; Carbs: 1.5g; Fat: 1.3g; Protein: 0.5g

INGREDIENTS

- 2 tbsp olive oil
- 1 tbsp french herbs
- 7 oz brie cheese, chopped
- 2 slices bread, halved

DIRECTIONS

Preheat your air fryer to 170 C. Using a bowl, mix oil with herbs. Dip the bread slices in the oil mixture to coat. Place the coated slices on a flat surface. Lay the brie cheese on the slices. Place the slices into your air fryer's basket and cook for 7 minutes. Once the bread is ready, cut into cubes.

207. Cheesy Bacon Fries

Total Time: 25 min | **Serves**: 4 | **Per serving**: Calories: 447; Carbs: 44g; Fat: 28g; Protein: 5g

INGREDIENTS

- 2 large russet potatoes, sauce and cut strips
- 5 slices bacon, chopped
- 2 tbsp vegetable oil
- 200g Cheddar cheese, shredded
- 3 oz melted cream cheese
- Salt and pepper to taste
- 2 scallions, chopped

DIRECTIONS

Boil salted water in a large-sized pot. Add potatoes to the salted water and allow to boil for 4 minutes until blanched. Strain the potatoes in a colander and rinse thoroughly with cold water to remove starch from the surface. Dry them with a kitchen towel. Preheat your air fryer to 200 C.

Add chopped bacon to your air fryer's cooking basket and cook for 4 minutes until crispy, making sure to give the basket a shake after 2 minutes; set aside. Add dried potatoes to the cooking basket and drizzle oil on top to coat. Cook for 25 minutes, shaking the basket every 5 minutes. Season with salt and pepper after 12 minutes.

Once cooked, transfer the fries to an 8-inch pan. In a bowl, mix 2 cups of cheddar cheese with cream cheese. Pour over the potatoes and add in crumbled bacon. Place the pan into the air fryer's cooking basket and cook for 5 more minutes at 170 C. Sprinkle chopped scallions on top and serve with your desired dressing.

208. Chili Cheese Balls

Total Time: 50 min | **Serves**: 6 | **Per serving**: Calories 395; Carbs 45g; Fat 13g; Protein 23g

INGREDIENTS

300g crumbled Cottage cheese
180g grated Parmesan cheese
2 red potatoes, peeled and chopped
1 medium onion, finely chopped
1 ½ tsp red chili flakes
1 green chili, finely chopped
Salt to taste
4 tbsp chopped coriander leaves
120g flour
100g breadcrumbs
Water

DIRECTIONS

Place the potatoes in a pot, add water and bring them to boil over medium heat for 25 to 30 minutes until soft. Turn off the heat, drain the potatoes through a sieve, and place in a bowl. With a potato masher, mash the potatoes and leave to cool.

Add the cottage cheese, Parmesan cheese, onion, red chili flakes, green chili, salt, coriander, and flour to the potato mash. Use a wooden spoon to mix the ingredients well, then, use your hands to mold out bite-size balls. Pour the crumbs in a bowl and roll each cheese ball lightly in it.

Place them on a tray. Put 8 to 10 cheese balls in the fryer basket, and cook for 15 minutes at 175 C. Repeat the cooking process for the remaining cheese balls. Serve with tomato-basil dip.

209. Juicy Pickled Chips

Total Time: 20 min | **Serves**: 3 | **Per serving**: Calories: 140; Carbs: 17g; Fat: 7g; Protein: 2g

INGREDIENTS

36 sweet pickle chips
240g buttermilk
3 tbsp smoked paprika
240g flour
30g cornmeal
Salt and black pepper to taste

DIRECTIONS

Preheat your air fryer to 200 C. Using a bowl mix flour, paprika, pepper, salt, cornmeal and powder. Place pickles in buttermilk and set aside for 5 minutes. Dip the pickles in the spice mixture and place them in the air fryer's cooking basket. Cook for 10 minutes.

210. Hearty Apple Chips

Total Time: 25 min | **Serves**: 2 | **Per serving**: Calories: 140; Carbs: 20g; Fat: 7g; Protein: 0g

INGREDIENTS

1 tsp sugar
1 tsp salt
1 whole apple, sauce and sliced
½ tsp cinnamon
Confectioners' sugar for serving

DIRECTIONS

Preheat your air fryer to 200 C. In a bowl, mix cinnamon, salt and sugar; add the apple slices. Place the prepared apple spices in your fryer's cooking basket and bake for 8 minutes. Dust with confectioners' sugar and serve.

211. Appetizing Cod Fingers

Total Time: 25 min | **Serves**: 3 | **Per serving**: Calories: 245; Carbs: 24g; Fat: 10g; Protein: 14g

INGREDIENTS

240g flour
Salt and pepper to taste
1 tsp seafood seasoning
2 whole eggs, beaten
180g cornmeal
1 pound cod fillets, cut into fingers
2 tbsp milk
2 eggs, beaten
100g breadcrumbs

DIRECTIONS

Preheat your air fryer to 200 C. In a bowl, mix beaten eggs with milk. In a separate bowl, mix flour, cornmeal, and seafood seasoning. In another mixing bowl, mix spices with the eggs. In a third bowl, pour the breadcrumbs.

Dip cod fingers in the seasoned flour mixture, followed by a dip in the egg mixture and finally, coat with breadcrumbs. Place the prepared fingers in your air fryer's cooking basket and cook for 10 minutes.

212. Quick Rutabaga Chips

Total Time: 20 min | **Serves**: 12 | **Per serving**: Calories: 80; Carbs: 10g; Fat: 5g; Protein: 3g

INGREDIENTS

1 swede, sliced
1 tsp olive oil
1 tsp soy sauce
Salt to taste

DIRECTIONS

Preheat your air fryer to 200 C. In a bowl, mix oil, soy sauce and salt to form a marinade. Add rutabaga pieces and allow to stand for 5 minutes. Cook in your air fryer for 5 minutes, tossing once halfway through cooking.

213. Macaroni Quiche

Total Time: 30 min | **Serves**: 4 | **Per serving**: Calories: 279; Carbs: 21g; Fat: 2g; Protein: 47g

INGREDIENTS

8 tbsp leftover macaroni with cheese
Extra cheese for serving
Pastry as much needed for forming 4 shells
Salt and pepper to taste
1 tsp garlic puree
2 tbsp Greek yogurt
2 whole eggs
350 ml milk

DIRECTIONS

Preheat the fryer to 180 C. Roll the pastry to form 4 shells. Place them in the air fryer's basket. In a bowl, mix leftover macaroni with cheese, yogurt, eggs and milk and garlic puree. Pour this mixture over the pastry shells. Top with the cheese evenly. Place the basket into the air fryer, and cook for 20 minutes.

214. Pumpkin Wedges

Total Time: 30 min | **Serves**: 3 | **Per serving**: Calories: 123; Carbs: 26g; Fat: 2g; Protein: 2g

INGREDIENTS

½ pumpkin, washed and cut into wedges
1 tbsp paprika
1 whole lime, squeezed
250g paleo dressing
1 tbsp balsamic vinegar
Salt and pepper to taste
1 tsp turmeric

DIRECTIONS

Preheat your air fryer to 180 C. Add the pumpkin wedges in your air fryer's cooking basket, and cook for 20 minutes. In a mixing bowl, mix lime juice, vinegar, turmeric, salt, pepper and paprika to form a marinade. Pour the marinade over pumpkin, and cook for 5 more minutes.

215. Awesome Cheese Sticks

Total Time: 15 min | **Serves**: 6 | **Per serving**: Calories: 150; Carbs: 17g; Fat: 5g; Protein: 10g

INGREDIENTS

Marinara sauce
12 sticks mozzarella cheese
30g flour
200g breadcrumbs
2 whole eggs
30g Parmesan cheese, grated

DIRECTIONS

Preheat your air fryer to 175 C. Pour breadcrumbs in a bowl. Beat the eggs in a separate bowl. In a third bowl, mix Parmesan cheese and flour. Dip each cheese stick the flour mixture, then in eggs and finally in breadcrumbs. Place the sticks on a cookie sheet and freeze for 1 to 2 hours.

Put the sticks in your air fryer's basket and cook for 7 minutes, turning them once. Place on a serving plate, and serve with marinara sauce.

216. Elegant Carrot Cookies

Total Time: 30 min | **Serves**: 8 | **Per serving**: Calories: 300; Carbs: 38g; Fat: 15g; Protein: 3g

INGREDIENTS

6 carrots, sauce and sliced
Salt and pepper to taste
1 tbsp parsley
1¼ oz oats
1 whole egg, beaten
1 tbsp thyme

DIRECTIONS

Preheat your air fryer to 180 C. In a saucepan, add carrots and cover with hot water. Heat over medium heat for 10 minutes, until tender. Remove the oiled carrots to a plate. Season with salt, pepper and parsley and mash using a fork. Add the beaten egg, oats, and thyme as you continue mashing to mix well.

Form the batter into cookie shapes. Place in your air fryer's cooking basket and cook for 15 minutes until edges are browned.

217. Rice Pilaf with Cremini Mushrooms

Total Time: 40 min | **Serves**: 6 | **Per serving**: Calories: 221; Carbs: 36g; Fat: 3g; Protein: 3g

INGREDIENTS

3 tbsp olive oil
800 ml heated vegetable stock
400g long-grain rice
1 onion, chopped
2 garlic cloves, minced
180g cremini mushrooms, chopped
Salt and ground black pepper to taste
1 tbsp fresh chopped parsley

DIRECTIONS

Preheat your air fryer to 200 C. Place a frying pan over medium heat. Add oil, onion, garlic, and rice; cook for 5 minutes. Pour the vegetable stock and mushrooms and whisk well. Season with salt and pepper to taste. Transfer to your air fryer's basket and cook for 20 minutes. Serve sprinkled with fresh chopped parsley.

218. Simple Cheesy Melty Mushrooms

Total Time: 20 min | **Serves**: 2 | **Per serving**: Calories: 275; Carbs: 27g; Fat: 16g; Protein: 5g

INGREDIENTS

- 2-3 tbsp olive oil
- Salt and pepper to taste
- 10 button mushrooms
- 450g mozzarella cheese, chopped
- 240g cheddar cheese, chopped
- 3 tbsp mixture of Italian herbs
- 1 tbsp dried dill

DIRECTIONS

Wash the mushrooms thoroughly under cold water and clean. Preheat your air fryer to 170 C. In a bowl, mix oil, salt, pepper, herbs, and dill to form a marinade. Add button mushrooms to the marinade and toss to coat well.

In a separate bowl, mix both kinds of cheese. Stuff each mushroom with the cheese mixture. Place the mushrooms in your air fryer's cooking basket and cook for 10 minutes.

219. Super Cabbage Canapes

Total Time: 15 min | **Serves**: 2 | **Per serving**: Calories: 320; Carbs: 85g; Fat: 20g; Protein: 10g

INGREDIENTS

- 1 whole cabbage, cut into rounds
- 1 cube Amul cheese
- ½ carrot, cubed
- ¼ onion, cubed
- ¼ capsicum, cubed
- Fresh basil to garnish

DIRECTIONS

Preheat your air fryer to 180 C. Using a bowl, mix onion, carrot, capsicum and cheese. Toss to coat everything evenly. Add cabbage rounds to the air fryer's cooking basket. Top with the veggie mixture and cook for 5 minutes. Serve with a garnish of fresh basil.

220. Crispy Bacon with Butterbean Dip

Total Time: 10 min | **Serves**: 2 | **Per serving**: Calories: 74; Carbs: 7g; Fat: 5g; Protein: 2g

INGREDIENTS

- 1 (14 oz) can butter beans
- 1 tbsp chives
- 3 ½ oz feta
- Pepper to taste
- 1 tsp olive oil
- 3 ½ oz bacon, sliced

DIRECTIONS

Preheat your air fryer to 170 C. Blend beans, oil and pepper using a blender. Arrange bacon slices on your air fryer's cooking basket. Sprinkle chives on top and cook for 10 minutes. Add feta cheese to the butter bean blend and stir. Serve bacon with the dip.

221. Tender Eggplant Fries

Total Time: 20 min **Serves**: 2 | **Per serving**: Calories: 80; Carbs: 10g; Fat: 5g; Protein: 3g

INGREDIENTS

1 aubergine, sliced
1 tsp olive oil
1 tsp soy sauce
Salt to taste

DIRECTIONS
Preheat your air fryer to 200 C. Make a marinade of 1 tsp oil, soy sauce and salt. Mix well. Add in the eggplant slices and let stand for 5 minutes. Place the prepared eggplant slices in your air fryer's cooking basket and cook for 5 minutes. Serve with a drizzle of maple syrup.

222. Roasted Cashew Delight

Total Time: 20 min | Serve: 12 | **Per serving**: Calories: 168; Carbs: 9g; Fat: 12g; Protein: 5g

INGREDIENTS
280g cashews
3 tbsp liquid smoke
2 tsp salt
2 tbsp molasses

DIRECTIONS
Preheat your air fryer to 180 C. In a bowl, add salt, liquid, molasses, and cashews; toss to coat well. Place the coated cashews in your air fryer's cooking basket and cook for 10 minutes, shaking the basket every 5 minutes.

223. Rosemary Potato Chips

Total Time: 50 min | **Serves**: 3 | **Per serving**: Calories: 220; Carbs: 26g; Fat: 11g; Protein: 3g

INGREDIENTS
3 whole potatoes, cut into thin slices
60g olive oil
1 tbsp garlic
120g cream
2 tbsp rosemary

DIRECTIONS
Preheat your air fryer to 195 C. In a bowl, add oil, garlic and salt to form a marinade. In a separate bowl, add potato slices and top with cold water. Allow sitting for 30 minutes. Drain the slices and transfer them to marinade.

Allow sitting for 30 minutes. Lay the potato slices onto your air fryer's cooking basket and cook for 20 minutes. After 10 minutes, give the chips a turn, sprinkle with rosemary and serve.

224. Almond French Beans

Total Time: 25 min | **Serves**: 5 | **Per serving**: Calories: 160; Carbs: 7g; Fat: 13g; Protein: 6g

INGREDIENTS
1 ½ pounds French beans, drained
1 tbsp salt
1 tbsp pepper
½ pound shallots, chopped
3 tbsp olive oil
50g almonds, toasted

DIRECTIONS
Preheat your air fryer to 200 C. Put a pan over medium heat, mix beans in hot water and boil until tender, about 5-6 minutes. Mix the boiled beans with oil, shallots, salt, and pepper. Add the mixture to your air fryer's cooking basket and cook for 20 minutes. Serve with almonds and enjoy!

225. Spicy Cajun Shrimp

Total Time: 15 min | **Serves**: 3 | **Per serving**: Calories: 80; Carbs: 0g; Fat: 1g; Protein: 0g

INGREDIENTS

½ pound shrimp, sauce and deveined
½ tsp cajun seasoning
Salt as needed
1 tbsp olive oil
¼ tsp pepper
¼ tsp paprika

DIRECTIONS

Preheat your air fryer to 195 C. Using a bowl, make the marinade by mixing paprika, salt, pepper, oil and seasoning. Cut shrimp and cover with marinade. Place the prepared shrimp in your air fryer's cooking basket and cook for 10 minutes, flipping halfway through.

226. Roasted Brussels Sprouts

Total Time: 25 min | **Serves**: 4 | **Per serving**: Calories: 43; Carbs: 5g; Fat: 2g; Protein: 2g

INGREDIENTS

1 block brussels sprouts
½ tsp garlic, chopped
2 tbsp olive oil
Salt and black pepper to taste

DIRECTIONS

Wash the Brussels thoroughly under cold water and trim off the outer leaves, keeping only the head of the sprouts. In a bowl, mix oil and garlic. Season with salt and pepper. Add prepared sprouts to this mixture and preheat the air fryer to 200 C. Place the coated sprouts in and Bake for 15 minutes, strring once, until golden brown.

227. Hearty Grilled Ham and Cheese

Total Time: 15 min | **Serves**: 2 | **Per serving**: Calories: 230; Carbs: 21g; Fat: 13g; Protein: 3g

INGREDIENTS

4 slices bread
60g butter
2 slices ham
2 slices cheese

DIRECTIONS

Preheat your air fryer to 180 C. Place 2 bread slices on a flat surface. Spread butter on the exposed surfaces. Lay cheese and ham on two of the slices. Cover with the other 2 slices to form sandwiches. Place the sandwiches in the cooking basket and cook for 5 minutes.

228. Simple Cheese Sandwich

Total Time: 20 min | **Serve**: 1 | **Per serving**: Calories: 469; Carbs: 41g; Fat: 30g; Protein: 13g

INGREDIENTS

2 tbsp Parmesan cheese, shredded
2 scallions
2 tbsp butter
2 slices bread
60g Cheddar cheese

DIRECTIONS

Preheat your air fryer to 180 C. Lay the bread slices on a flat surface. On one slice, spread the exposed side with butter, followed by cheddar and scallions. On the other slice, spread butter and then sprinkle cheese.

Bring the buttered sides together to form sand. Place the sandwich in your air fryer's cooking basket and cook for 10 minutes. Serve with berry sauce.

229. Indian-Style Masala Cashew

Total Time: 25 min | **Serves**: 2 | **Per serving**: Calories: 140; Carbs: 11g; Fat: 8g; Protein: 4g

INGREDIENTS

8 oz Greek yogurt
2 tbsp mango powder
8 ¾ oz cashew nuts
Salt and black pepper to taste
1 tsp coriander powder
½ tsp masala powder

DIRECTIONS

Preheat your Fryer to 120 C. In a bowl, mix all powders. Season with salt and pepper. Add cashews and toss to coat well. Place the cashews in your air fryer's basket and cook for 15 minutes. Serve with a garnish of basil.

230. Cheesy Cheddar Biscuits

Total Time: 35 min | **Serves**: 8 | **Per serving**: Calories: 110; Carbs: 12g; Fat: 5g; Protein: 2g

INGREDIENTS

120g + 1 tbsp butter
2 tbsp sugar
380g flour
320g buttermilk
40g Cheddar, grated

DIRECTIONS

Preheat your air fryer to 190 C. Lay a parchment paper on a baking plate. In a bowl, mix sugar, flour, ½ cup butter, cheese and buttermilk to form a batter. Make 8 balls from the batter and roll in flour.

Place the balls in your air fryer's cooking basket and flatten into biscuit shapes. Sprinkle cheese and the remaining butter on top. Cook for 30 minutes, tossing every 10 minutes. Serve warm.

231. Hearty Curly Fries

Total Time: 20 min | **Serves**: 2 | **Per serving**: Calories: 438; Carbs: 65g; Fat: 15g; Protein: 11g

INGREDIENTS

2 whole potatoes, sauce
1 tbsp extra-virgin olive oil
1 tsp pepper
1 tsp salt
1 tsp paprika

DIRECTIONS

Preheat your Fryer to 175 C. Wash the potatoes thoroughly under cold water and pass them through a spiralizer to get curly shaped potatoes. Place the potatoes in a bowl and coat with oil. Transfer them to your air fryer's cooking basket and cook for 15 minutes. Sprinkle a bit of salt and paprika, to serve.

232. A Platter of French Fries

Total Time: 35 min | **Serves**: 6 | **Per serving**: Calories: 473; Carbs: 6g; Fat: 23g; Protein: 5g

INGREDIENTS

6 medium russet potatoes, sauce
2 tbsp olive oil
Salt as needed

DIRECTIONS

Cut potatoes into ¼ by 3-inch pieces and place in a bowl with cold water; let soak for 30 minutes. Strain and allow to dry. Preheat your air fryer to 180 C. Drizzle oil on the dried potatoes and toss to coat. Place the potatoes in your air fryer's cooking basket and cook for 30 minutes. Season with salt and pepper, to serve.

233. Bacon & Asparagus Spears

Serves: 4 | **Total Time**: 25 min | **Serves**: 4 | **Per serving**: Carbs: 3g; **Per serving**: Calories: 20; Fat: 26g; Protein: 5g

INGREDIENTS

20 spears asparagus
4 bacon slices

1 tbsp olive oil
1 tbsp sesame oil

1 tbsp brown sugar
1 garlic clove, crushed

DIRECTIONS

Preheat your air fryer to 190 C. In a bowl, mix the oils, sugar and crushed garlic. Separate the asparagus into 4 bunches (5 spears in 1 bunch) and wrap each bunch with a bacon slice. Coat the bunches with the sugar and oil mix. Place the bunches in your air fryer's cooking basket and cook for 8 minutes. Serve immediately.

234. The Mini Cheese Scones

Serve: 10 | **Total Time**: 25 min | **Serve**: 10 | **Per serving**: Calories: 396; Carbs: 41g; Fat: 19g; Protein: 11g

INGREDIENTS

6 ¼ oz flour
Salt and pepper to taste
¾ oz butter

1 tsp chives
1 whole egg
1 tbsp milk

330g Cheddar cheese, shredded

DIRECTIONS

Preheat your air fryer to 170 C. In a bowl, mix butter, flour, cheddar cheese, chives, milk and egg to get a sticky dough. Dust a flat surface with flour. Roll the dough into small balls. Place the balls in your air fryer's cooking basket and cook for 20 minutes. Serve and enjoy!

235. Tortilla Chips

Total Time: 55 min | **Serves**: 6 | **Per serving**: Calories 265; Carbs 17g; Fat 14g; Protein 13g

INGREDIENTS

120g flour
Salt and pepper to taste

1 tbsp golden flaxseed meal
230g shredded Cheddar cheese

Cooking spray

DIRECTIONS

Melt cheddar cheese in the microwave for 1 minute. Once melted, add the flour, salt, flaxseed meal, and pepper. Mix well with a fork. On a board, place the dough, and knead it with hands while warm until the ingredients are well combined. Divide the dough into 2 and with a rolling pin, roll them out flat into 2 rectangles.

Use a pastry cutter, to cut out triangle-shaped pieces and line them in 1 layer on a baking dish. Grease the fryer basket lightly with cooking spray. Arrange some triangle chips in 1 layer in the fryer basket without touching or overlapping; spray them with cooking spray. Close the air fryer and cook for 8 minutes. Serve with a cheese dip.

236. Salmon Croquettes

Total Time: 40 min | **Serves**: 4 | **Per serving**: Calories 415; Carbs 31g; Fat 18g; Protein 28.5g

INGREDIENTS

1 (15 oz) tinned salmon, deboned and flaked
50g grated onion
150g grated carrots
3 large eggs
1 ½ tbsp chopped chives
4 tbsp mayonnaise
4 tbsp breadcrumbs
2 ½ tsp Italian seasoning
Salt and pepper to taste
2 ½ tsp lemon juice
Cooking spray

DIRECTIONS

In a bowl, add salmon, onion, carrots, eggs, chives, mayo, crumbs, Italian seasoning, pepper, salt, and lemon juice and mix well. With hands, form 2-inch thick oblong balls from the mixture, resembling croquette shape. Put them on a flat tray and refrigerate for 45 minutes. Grease the air fryer's basket with cooking spray.

Remove the croquettes from the fridge and arrange in a single layer, in the fryer, without overcrowding. Spray with cooking spray. Cook for 10 minutes, flipping once, until crispy at 200 C. Serve with a dill-based dip.

PORK, BEEF AND LAMB

237. Sweet Pork Tenderloins

Total Time: 60 min | **Serves:** 4 | **Per serving:** Calories: 250; Carbs: 3.2g; Fat: 30.5g; Protein: 2.9g

INGREDIENTS

4 pork tenderloins
1 apple, wedged
1 cinnamon quill
1 tbsp olive oil
1 tbsp soy sauce
Salt and black pepper

DIRECTIONS

In a bowl, add pork, apple, cinnamon, olive oil, soy sauce, salt, and black pepper into; stir to coat well. Let sit at room temperature for 25-35 minutes. Put the pork and apples into the air fryer, and a little bit of marinade. Cook at 190 C for 14 minutes, turning once halfway through. Serve hot!

238. Pork and Apple Burger Patties

Total Time: 25 min | **Serves:** 2 | **Per serving:** Calories: 404; Carbs: 3.2g; Fat: 25.1g; Protein: 3g

INGREDIENTS

12 oz ground pork
1 apple, peeled and grated
100g breadcrumbs
2 eggs, beaten
½ tsp ground cumin
½ tsp ground cinnamon
Salt and pepper to taste

DIRECTIONS

In a bowl, add pork, apple, breadcrumbs, cumin, eggs, cinnamon, salt, and black pepper; mix with hands. Shape into 4 even-sized burger patties. Grease the fryer with oil, arrange the patties inside the basket and cook for 14 minutes at 170 C, turning once halfway through.

239. Crispy Pork Chops

Total Time: 25 min | **Serves:** 4 | **Per serving:** Calories: 430; Carbs: 1.2g; Fat: 29.1g; Protein: 4g

INGREDIENTS

4 pork chops, center-cut
2 tbsp flour
2 tbsp sour cream
Salt and black pepper
50g breadcrumbs
Cooking spray

DIRECTIONS

Coat the chops with flour. Drizzle the cream over and rub gently to coat well. Spread the breadcrumbs onto a bowl, and coat each pork chop with crumbs. Spray the chops with oil and arrange them in the basket of your air fryer. Cook for 14 minutes at 190 C, turning once halfway through. Serve with salad, slaw or potatoes.

240. Apple and Onion Topped Pork Chops

Total Time: 25 min | **Serves:** 3 | **Per serving:** Calories: 434; Carbs: 30g; Fat: 33g; Protein: 27g

INGREDIENTS

Topping:

1 small onion, sliced
2 tbsp olive oil
1 tbsp apple cider vinegar

Meat:
¼ tsp smoked paprika
1 tbsp olive oil

2 tsp thyme
¼ tsp brown sugar
180g sliced apples

3 pork chops
1 tbsp apple cider vinegar

2 tsp rosemary

Salt and pepper, to taste

DIRECTIONS

Preheat the air fryer to 175 C. Place all topping ingredients in a baking dish and then in the air fryer. Cook for 4 minutes. Place the pork chops in a bowl. Add oil, vinegar, paprika, and season with salt and pepper.

Stir to coat them well. Remove the topping from the dish. Add the pork chops in the dish and cook in the air fryer for 10 minutes. Top with the topping, return to the air fryer and cook for 5 more minutes. Serve immediately.

241. The Simples and Yummiest Rib Eye Steak

Total Time: 20 min | **Serves:** 6 | **Per serving:** Calories: 219; Carbs: 10g; Fat: 8g; Protein: 34g

INGREDIENTS

2 lb rib eye steak
1 tbsp. steak rub
1 tbsp. olive oil

DIRECTIONS

Preheat the fryer to 200 C. Combine the steak rub and olive oil. Rub the steak with the seasoning. Place in the air fryer and cook for 10 minutes. Flip the steak over and cook for 7 more minutes. Serve hot with roasted potatoes.

242. Pork Belly the Philippine Style

Total Time: 4 hrs 50 min | **Serves:** 6 | **Per serving:** Calories: 743; Carbs: 1.2g; Fat: 72g; Protein: 14g

INGREDIENTS

2 lb pork belly, cut in half, blanched
2 bay leaves
2 tbsp soy sauce

5 garlic cloves, coarsely chopped
1 tbsp peppercorns
1 tbsp peanut oil

1 tsp salt

DIRECTIONS

Let the blanched pork air fry for 2 hours; pat the excess water, if any. Take a mortar and pestle, and place bay leaves, garlic, salt, peppercorns, and peanut oil in it. Smash until a paste-like consistency has formed. Whisk the paste with the soy sauce. Pierce the skin of the pork belly with a fork or a skewer.

Rub the mixture onto the meat. Wrap the pork with a plastic foil and refrigerate for 2 hours. Preheat the fryer to 175 C. Place the pork inside and cook for 30 minutes. Set to 185 C and cook for 10 more minutes. Serve chilled.

243. Honey Barbecue Pork Ribs

Total Time: 4 h 35 min | **Serves:** 2 | **Per serving:** Calories: 735; Carbs: 15 g; Fat: 41 g; Protein: 65 g

INGREDIENTS

1 lb pork ribs
½ tsp five-spice powder
1 tsp salt
3 garlic cloves, chopped
1 tsp black pepper

1 tsp sesame oil
1 tbsp honey, plus some more for brushing
4 tbsp barbecue sauce
1 tsp soy sauce

DIRECTIONS

Chop the ribs into smaller pieces and place them in a large bowl. In a smaller bowl, whisk together all other ingredients. Add them to the bowl with the pork, and mix until the pork is fully coated.

Cover the bowl, place it in the fridge, and marinate for 4 hours. Preheat the air fryer to 175 C. Place the ribs in the basket and cook for 15 minutes. Brush the ribs with some honey and cook for another 15 minutes.

244. The Crispiest Roast Pork

Total Time: 3 hrs 10 min | **Serves**: 4 | **Per serving**: Calories: 840; Carbs: 22g; Fat: 69g; Protein: 55g

INGREDIENTS

1 ½ lb pork belly, blanched
1 tsp five spice seasoning
½ tsp white pepper
¾ tsp garlic powder
1 tsp salt

DIRECTIONS

After blanching the pork belly leave it at room temperature for 2 hours to air dry. Pat with paper towels if there is excess water. Preheat the air fryer to 170 C. Take a skewer and pierce the skin as many times as you can, so you can ensure crispiness. Combine the seasonings in a small bowl, and rub it onto the pork.

Place the pork into the air fryer and cook for 30 minutes. Increase the temperature to 175 C and cook for 30 more minutes. Let cool slightly before serving.

245. Char Siew Pork Ribs

Total Time: 55 min | **Serves**: 6 | **Per serving**: Calories: 753; Carbs: 15g; Fat: 37g; Protein: 33g

INGREDIENTS

2 lb pork ribs
2 tbsp char siew sauce
2 tbsp minced ginger
2 tbsp hoisin sauce
2 tbsp sesame oil
1 tbsp honey
4 garlic cloves, minced
1 tbsp soy sauce

DIRECTIONS

Whisk together all marinade ingredients in a small bowl; coat the ribs well with the mixture. Place in a container with a lid, and refrigerate for 4 hours. Preheat the air fryer to 170 C.

Place the ribs in the basket but do not throw away the liquid from the container; cook for 40 minutes. Stir in the liquid and cook 10 more minutes.

246. Zesty Breaded Chops

Total Time: 25 min | **Serves**: 3 | **Per serving**: Calories 421; Carbs 3.2g; Fat 39g; Protein 21g

INGREDIENTS

3 lean pork chops
Salt and pepper to season
2 eggs, cracked into a bowl
1 tbsp water
100g breadcrumbs
½ tsp garlic powder
3 tsp paprika
1 ½ tsp oregano
½ tsp cayenne pepper
¼ tsp dry mustard
1 lemon, zested
Cooking spray

DIRECTIONS

Put the pork chops on a chopping board and use a knife to trim off any excess fat. Add the water to the eggs and whisk; set aside. In another bowl, add the breadcrumbs, salt, pepper, garlic powder, paprika, oregano, cayenne pepper, lemon zest, and dry mustard. Use a fork to mix evenly.

Preheat the air fryer to 190 C and grease the basket with cooking spray. In the egg mixture, dip each pork chop and then in the breadcrumb mixture. Place the breaded chops in the fryer. Don't spray with cooking spray. The fat in the chops will be enough oil to cook them. Close the air fryer and cook for 12 minutes.

Flip to other side and cook for another 5 minutes. Once ready, place the chops on a chopping board to rest for 3 minutes before slicing and serving. Serve with a side of vegetable fries.

247. Bacon-Wrapped & Stuffed Pork Loins

Total Time: 40 min | Serves: 4 | Per serving: Calories : 604; Carbs: 3g; Fat: 51.8g; Protein: 30g

INGREDIENTS

16 bacon slices
16 oz pork tenderloin
30g spinach
3 oz cream cheese
1 small onion, sliced
1 tbsp olive oil
1 clove garlic, minced
½ tsp dried thyme
½ tsp dried rosemary

DIRECTIONS

Place the tenderloin on a chopping board, cover it with a plastic wrap and pound it using a kitchen hammer to a 2-inches flat and square piece. Trim the uneven sides with a knife to have a perfect square. Set aside on a flat plate. On the same chopping board, place and weave the bacon slices into a square of the size of the pork.

Place the pork on the bacon weave and set aside. Put a skillet over medium heat on a stovetop, add olive oil, onions, and garlic; sauté until transparent. Add the spinach, ½ tsp rosemary, ½ tsp thyme, a bit of salt, and pepper. Stir with a spoon and allow the spinach to wilt. Stir in the cream cheese, until the mixture is even. Turn off.

Preheat the air fryer to 180 C. Spoon and spread the spinach mixture onto the pork loin. Roll up the bacon and pork over the spinach stuffing. Secure the ends with as many toothpicks as necessary. Season with more salt and pepper. Place it in the fryer basket and cook for 15 minutes. Flip to other side and cook for another 5 minutes. Once ready, remove to a clean chopping board. Let sit for 4 minutes before slicing. Serve with steamed veggies.

248. Sausage Sticks Rolled in Bacon

Total Time: 1 hr 44 min | Serves: 4 | Per serving: Calories : 126; Carbs: 0.3g; Fat: 9.6g; Protein: 8.7g

INGREDIENTS

Sausage:
8 bacon strips
8 pork sausages

Relish:
8 large tomatoes
1 clove garlic, peeled
1 small onion, peeled
3 tbsp chopped parsley
A pinch of salt
A pinch of pepper
2 tbsp sugar
1 tsp smoked paprika
1 tbsp white wine vinegar

DIRECTIONS

Start with the relish; add the tomatoes, garlic, and onion in a food processor. Blitz them for 10 seconds until the mixture is pulpy. Pour the pulp into a saucepan, add the vinegar, salt, pepper, and place it over medium heat.

Bring to simmer for 10 minutes; add the paprika and sugar. Stir with a spoon and simmer for 10 minutes until pulpy and thick. Turn off the heat, transfer the relish to a bowl and chill it for an hour. In 30 minutes after putting the relish in the refrigerator, move on to the sausages. Wrap each sausage with a bacon strip neatly and stick in a bamboo skewer at the end of the sausage to secure the bacon ends.

Open the air fryer, place 3 to 4 wrapped sausages in the fryer basket and cook for 12 minutes at 175 C. Ensure that the bacon is golden and crispy before removing them. Repeat the cooking process for the remaining wrapped sausages. Remove the relish from the refrigerator. Serve the sausages and relish with turnip mash.

249. Roasted Pork Rack with Macadamia Nuts

Total Time: 50min | **Serves**: 2 to 3 | **Per serving**: Calories : 319; Carbs: 0g; Fat: 18g; Protein: 27g

INGREDIENTS

1 lb rack of pork
2 tbsp olive oil
1 clove garlic, minced
Salt and pepper to taste
120g chopped macadamia nuts
1 tbsp breadcrumbs
1 egg, beaten in a bowl
1 tbsp rosemary, chopped

DIRECTIONS

Add the olive oil and garlic to a bowl. Mix vigorously with a spoon to make garlic oil. Place the rack of pork on a chopping board and brush it with the garlic oil using a brush. Sprinkle with salt and pepper.

Preheat the air fryer to 125 C. In a bowl, add breadcrumbs, nuts, and rosemary. Mix with a spoon and set aside. Brush the meat with the egg on all sides and sprinkle the nut mixture generously over the pork. Press with hands to avoid the nut mixture from falling off. Put the coated pork in the fryer basket, close and roast for 30 minutes.

Increase the temperature to 195 C and cook further for 5 minutes. Once ready, remove the meat onto a chopping board. Allow a sitting time of 10 minutes before slicing. Serve with a side of parsnip fries and tomato dip.

250. Aromatic Pork Chops

Total Time: 2 hrs 20 min | **Serves**: 3 | **Per serving**: Calories : 163; Carbs: 0g; Fat: 6.8g; Protein: 24.1g

INGREDIENTS

3 slices pork chops
2 garlic cloves, minced
1 ½ tbsp sugar
4 stalks lemongrass, trimmed and chopped
2 shallots, chopped
2 tbsp olive oil
1 ¼ tsp soy sauce
1 ¼ tsp fish sauce
1 ½ tsp black pepper

DIRECTIONS

In a bowl, add the garlic, sugar, lemongrass, shallots, olive oil, soy sauce, fish sauce, and black pepper; mix well. Add the pork chops, coat them with the mixture and allow to marinate for around 2 hours to get nice and savory.

Preheat the air fryer to 200 C. Cooking in 2 to 3 batches, remove and shake each pork chop from the marinade and place it in the fryer basket. Cook it for 7 minutes. Turn the pork chops with kitchen tongs and cook further for 5 minutes. Remove the chops and serve with a side of sautéed asparagus.

251. Tangy Pork Roast

Preparation 4 hrs 30 min | **Serves**: 8 | **Per serving**: Calories : 447; Carbs: 2g; Fat: 42g; Protein: 8.2g

INGREDIENTS

1 ½ lb pork belly
1 ½ tsp garlic powder
1 ½ tsp coriander powder
⅓ tsp salt
1 ½ tsp black pepper
1 ½ dried thyme
1 ½ tsp dried oregano
1 ½ tsp cumin powder
700 ml water
1 lemon, halved

DIRECTIONS

Leave the pork to air fry for 3 hours. In a small bowl, add the garlic powder, coriander powder, ½ tsp of salt, black pepper, thyme, oregano, and cumin powder. After the pork is well dried, poke holes all around it using a fork. Smear the oregano rub thoroughly on all sides with your hands and squeeze the lemon juice all over it.

Leave to sit for 5 minutes. Put the pork in the center of the fryer basket and cook for 30 minutes. Turn the pork with the help of two spatulas, increase the temperature to 175 C and continue cooking for 25 minutes.

Once ready, remove it and place it in on a chopping board to sit for 4 minutes before slicing. Serve the pork slices with a side of sautéed asparagus and hot sauce.

252. Best Ever Pork Burgers

Total Time: 35 min | **Serves**: 2 | **Per serving**: Calories : 470; Carbs: 1g; Fat: 42g; Protein: 22g

INGREDIENTS

½ lb ground pork
1 medium onion, chopped
1 tbsp mixed herbs
2 tsp garlic powder
1 tsp dried basil
1 tbsp tomato puree
1 tsp mustard
Salt and pepper to taste
2 bread buns, halved

Assembling:
1 large onion, sliced in 2-inch rings
1 large tomato, sliced in 2-inch rings
2 small lettuce leaves, cleaned
4 slices Cheddar cheese

DIRECTIONS

In a bowl, add the minced pork, chopped onion, mixed herbs, garlic powder, dried basil, tomato puree, mustard, salt, and pepper. Use hands to mix evenly. Form two patties out of the mixture and place them on a flat plate.

Preheat the air fryer to 185 C. Place the pork patties in the fryer basket, and cook for 15 minutes. Slide-out the basket and turn the patties with a spatula. Reduce the temperature to 175 C and continue cooking for 5 minutes.

Once ready, remove them onto a plate and start assembling the burger. Place two halves of the bun on a clean flat surface. Add the lettuce in both, then a patty each, followed by an onion ring each, a tomato ring each, and then 2 slices of cheddar cheese each. Cover the buns with their other halves. Serve with ketchup and french fries.

253. Spicy Tricolor Pork Kebabs

Total Time: 1 hr 20 min | **Serves**: 3 to 4 | **Per serving**: Calories : 240; Carbs: 0g; Fat: 10.4g; Protein: 8g

INGREDIENTS

1 lb pork steak, cut in cubes
60 ml soy sauce
2 tsp smoked paprika
1 tsp powdered chili
1 tsp garlic salt
1 tsp red chili flakes
1 tbsp white wine vinegar
3 tbsp steak sauce

Skewing:
1 green pepper, cut in cubes
1 red pepper, cut in cubes
1 yellow squash, seeded and cubed
1 green squash, seeded and cubed
Salt and pepper to taste

DIRECTIONS

In a mixing bowl, add the pork cubes, soy sauce, smoked paprika, powdered chili, garlic salt, red chili flakes, white wine vinegar, and steak sauce. Mix them using a ladle. Refrigerate to marinate them for 1 hour. After one hour, remove the marinated pork from the fridge and preheat the air fryer to 185 C.

On each skewer, stick the pork cubes and vegetables in the order that you prefer. Have fun doing this. Once the pork cubes and vegetables are finished, arrange the skewers in the fryer basket and grill them for 8 minutes. You can do them in batches. Once ready, remove them onto the serving platter and serve with salad.

254. Pulled Pork Sliders with Bacon and Cheddar

Total Time: 50 min | **Serves**: 2 | **Per serving**: Calories : 237; Carbs: 3g; Fat: 8g; Protein: 14g

INGREDIENTS

½ pork steak
1 tsp steak seasoning
Salt and pepper to taste

5 thick bacon slices, chopped
120g grated Cheddar cheese
½ tbsp Worcestershire sauce

2 bread buns, halved

DIRECTIONS

Preheat the air fryer to 200 C. Place the pork steak on a plate and season with pepper, salt, and the steak seasoning. Pat it with your hands. Slide-out the fryer basket and place the pork in it. Grill for 15 minutes, turn using tongs, slide the fryer in and continue cooking for 6 minutes.

Once ready, remove the steak onto a chopping board and use two forks to shred the pork into small pieces. Place the chopped bacon in a small heatproof bowl and place the bowl in the fryer's basket. Close the air fryer and cook the bacon at 185 C for 10 minutes. Remove the bacon into a bigger heatproof bowl, add the pulled pork, Worcestershire sauce, and the cheddar cheese. Season with salt and pepper.

Place the bowl in the fryer basket and cook at 175 C for 4 minutes. Slide-out the fryer basket, stir the mixture with a spoon, slide the fryer basket back in and cook further for 1 minute. Spoon to scoop the meat into the halved buns and serve with a cheese or tomato dip.

255. Pork Chops with Mustardy-Sweet Marinade

Total Time: 15 min | **Serves**: 3 | **Per serving**: Calories : 165; Carbs: 1g; Fat: 5g; Protein: 15g

INGREDIENTS

3 pork chops, ½-inch thick
Salt and pepper to season

1 tbsp maple syrup
1 ½ tbsp minced garlic

3 tbsp mustard

DIRECTIONS

In a bowl, add maple syrup, garlic, mustard, salt, and pepper; mix well. Add the pork and toss it in the mustard sauce to coat well. Slide-out the fryer basket and place the chops in the basket; cook at 175 C for 6 minutes.

Open the air fryer and flip the pork with a spatula and cook further for 6 minutes. Once ready, remove them onto a serving platter and serve with a side of steamed asparagus.

256. Sweet and Hot Ribs

Total Time: 5 hrs 30 min | **Serves**: 2 to 3 | **Per serving**: Calories 296; Carbs 3.3g; Fat 22.6g; Protein 21.7g

INGREDIENTS

1 lb pork ribs
1 tsp soy sauce
Salt and pepper to season

1 tsp oregano
1 tbsp + 1 tbsp maple syrup
3 tbsp reduced sugar barbecue sauce

2 cloves garlic, minced
1 tbsp cayenne pepper
1 tsp sesame oil

DIRECTIONS

Put the chops on a chopping board and use a knife to cut them into smaller pieces of desired sizes. Put them in a mixing bowl, add the soy sauce, salt, pepper, oregano, one tablespoon of maple syrup, barbecue sauce, garlic, cayenne pepper, and sesame oil. Mix well and place the pork in the fridge to marinate in the spices for 5 hours.

Preheat the air fryer to 175 C. Open the air fryer and place the ribs in the fryer basket. Slide the fryer basket in and cook for 15 minutes. Open the air fryer, turn the ribs using tongs, apply the remaining maple syrup with a brush, close the air fryer, and continue cooking for 10 minutes.

257. Spicy-Sweet Beef and Veggie Stir Fry

Total Time: 25 min | **Serves**: 4 | **Per serving**: Calories: 404; Carbs: 3.2g; Fat: 32.1g; Protein: 4g

INGREDIENTS

2 beef steaks, sliced into thin strips
2 garlic cloves, chopped
2 tsp maple syrup
1 tsp oyster sauce
1 tsp cayenne pepper
½ tsp olive oil
Juice of 1 lime
Salt and black pepper
1 cauliflower, cut into florets
2 carrots, cut into chunks
130g green peas

DIRECTIONS

In a bowl, add beef, garlic, maple syrup, oyster sauce, cayenne, oil, lime juice, salt, and black pepper, and stir to combine. Place the beef along with the garlic and some of the juices into your air fryer and top with the veggies. Cook at 200 C for 8 minutes, turning once halfway through.

258. Meatloaf

Total Time: 30 min | **Serves**: 4 | **Per serving**: Calories: 404; Carbs: 3.2g; Fat: 32.1g; Protein: 4g

INGREDIENTS

1 lb ground beef
2 eggs, lightly beaten
50g breadcrumbs
2 garlic cloves, crushed
1 onion, finely chopped
2 tbsp tomato puree
1 tsp mixed dried herbs

DIRECTIONS

Line a loaf pan that fits in your fryer with baking paper. In a bowl, mix beef, eggs, breadcrumbs, garlic, onion, puree, and herbs. Gently press the mixture into the pan and slide in the air fryer. Cook for 25 minutes on 190 C. If undercooked, and slightly moist, cook for 5 more minutes. Wait 15 minutes before slicing it.

259. Spice-Coated Steaks

Total Time: 15 min | **Serves**: 2 | **Per serving**: Calories: 404; Carbs: 3.2g; Fat: 32.1g; Protein: 4g

INGREDIENTS

2 steaks, 1-inch thick
½ tsp black pepper
½ tsp cayenne pepper
1 tbsp olive oil
½ tsp ground paprika
Salt and pepper to taste

DIRECTIONS

Preheat the air fryer to 195 C. Mix olive oil, black pepper, cayenne, paprika, salt and pepper and rub onto steaks. Spread evenly. Put the steaks in the fryer, and cook for 6 minutes, turning them halfway through.

260. Healthier Burgers

Total Time: 20 min | **Serves**: 4 | **Per serving**: Calories: 366; Carbs: 6 g; Fat: 31 g; Protein: 18 g

INGREDIENTS

1 lb ground beef
½ tsp onion powder
½ tsp salt

½ tsp oregano
1 tbsp Worcestershire sauce
½ tsp garlic powder

½ tsp pepper
1 tsp parsley
1 tsp Maggi seasoning sauce

1 tsp olive oil

DIRECTIONS

Preheat the air fryer to 175 C. Combine all of the sauces and seasonings, except oil, in a small bowl. Place the beef in a bowl and stir in the seasonings. Mix until the mixture is well incorporated.

Divide the meat mixture into four equal pieces and form patties. Spread the olive oil in the air fryer. Arrange the 4 burgers inside and cook for 10 to 15 minutes, until thoroughly cooked.

261. Air Fried Beef Empanada

Total Time: 25 min | **Serves**: 4 | **Per serving**: Calories: 495; Carbs: 17g; Fat: 36g; Protein: 23g

INGREDIENTS

1 lb ground beef
½ onion, diced
1 garlic clove, minced
50g tomato salsa

4 empanada shells
1 egg yolk
2 tsp milk
½ tsp cumin

Salt and pepper, to taste
½ tbsp olive oil

DIRECTIONS

Grease the fryer with olive oil and set to 175 C. Combine the beef, onion, cumin, and garlic, in a bowl. Season with some salt and pepper. Place the beef in the air fryer and cook for 7 minutes, flipping once halfway through.

Stir in the tomato salsa and set aside. In a small bowl, combine the milk and yolk. Place the empanada shells on a dry and clean surface. Divide the beef mixture between the shells. Fold the shells and seal the ends with a fork. Brush with the egg wash. Bake them in the air fryer for 10 minutes. Serve with a cheese dip.

262. Beef Quesadillas

Total Time: 25 min | **Serves**: 4 | **Per serving**: Calories: 305; Carbs: 2.2g; Fat: 31.1g; Protein: 4g

INGREDIENTS

8 soft round taco shells
1 pound beefsteak, sliced
220g mozzarella cheese, grated

30g fresh coriander, chopped
1 jalapeno chili, chopped
160g corn kernels, canned

Salt and black pepper
Oil for greasing

DIRECTIONS

Place sliced beef on each taco, top with cheese, cilantro, chili, corn, salt and pepper. Fold gently in half and secure with toothpicks if necessary. Grease the rack with oil and arrange the tacos into the basket. Cook at 190 C for 14 minutes, turning once halfway through. Serve with mexican sauces and guacamole!

263. Liver Muffins with Eggs

Total Time: 25 min | **Serves**: 2 | **Per serving**: Calories: 345; Carbs: 45g; Fat: 26g; Protein: 43g

INGREDIENTS

1 lb beef liver, sliced
2 large eggs

1 tbsp butter
½ tbsp black truffle oil

1 tbsp cream
Salt and black pepper

DIRECTIONS

Preheat the air fryer to 160 C. Cut the liver into thin slices and refrigerate for 10 minutes. Separate the whites from the yolks and put each yolk in a cup. In another bowl, add the cream, truffle oil, salt and pepper and mix with a fork. Arrange half of the mixture in a small ramekin.

Pour the white of the egg and divide it equally between ramekins. Top with the egg yolks. Surround each yolk with a liver. Cook for 15 minutes and serve cool.

264. Meatballs in Tomato Sauce

Total Time: 20 min | **Serves**: 4 | **Per serving**: Calories: 386; Carbs: 26g; Fat: 21g; Protein: 35g

INGREDIENTS

½ lb ground beef
1 medium onion
1 egg
4 tbsp breadcrumbs
1 tbsp fresh parsley, chopped
½ tbsp thyme leaves, chopped
10 oz of tomato sauce
Salt and pepper

DIRECTIONS

Place all ingredients into a bowl and mix very well. Shape the mixture into 10 to 12 balls. Preheat the air fryer to 190 C. Place the meatballs in the air fryer basket, and cook them for 10 minutes.

Remove the meatballs to an oven plate. Add in the tomato sauce and bring them back to the air fryer. Lower the temperature to 150 C. Cook for 6 more minutes.

265. Thai Roasted Beef

Total Time: 4 hrs 20 min | **Serves**: 2 | **Per serving**: Calories: 687; Carbs: 21g; Fat: 39g; Protein: 64g

INGREDIENTS

1 lb ground beef
½ tsp salt
2 tbsp soy sauce
½ tsp pepper
Thumb-sized piece of ginger, chopped
3 chilies, deseeded and chopped
4 garlic cloves, chopped
1 tsp brown sugar
Juice of 1 lime
2 tbsp mirin
2 tbsp coriander, chopped
2 tbsp basil, chopped
2 tbsp oil
2 tbsp fish sauce

DIRECTIONS

Place all ingredients, except the beef, salt and pepper, in a blender; process until smooth. Season the beef with salt and pepper. Place all in a zipper bag; shake well to combine. Marinate in the fridge for 4 hours.

Preheat the air fryer to 175 C. Place the beef in the air fryer and cook for 12 minutes, or more if you like it really well done. Let sit for a couple of minutes before serving. Serve with cooked rice and fresh veggies.

266. Crunchy Beef Schnitzel

Total Time: 25 min | **Serves**: 4 | **Per serving**: Calories: 404; Carbs: 3.2g; Fat: 32.1g; Protein: 4g

INGREDIENTS

4 beef schnitzel cutlets
70g flour
2 eggs, beaten
Salt and black pepper
100g breadcrumbs
Cooking spray

DIRECTIONS

Coat the cutlets in flour and shake off any excess. Dip the coated cutlets into the beaten egg. Sprinkle with salt and black pepper. Then dip into the crumbs and to coat well. Spray them generously with oil and cook for 10 minutes at 180 C, turning once halfway through.

267. The Ultimate Beef Chili

Total Time: 50 min | **Serves**: 6 | **Per serving**: Calories: 485; Carbs: 38g; Fat: 28g; Protein: 39g

INGREDIENTS

- 1 lb ground beef
- ½ tbsp chili powder
- 1 tsp salt
- 1 can (8 oz) cannellini beans
- 1 tsp chopped coriander
- 1 tbsp olive oil
- ½ tsp parsley
- 50g chopped celery
- 1 onion, chopped
- 2 garlic cloves, minced
- 350 ml vegetable broth
- ¼ tsp pepper
- 1 can diced tomatoes
- 80g finely chopped bell pepper

DIRECTIONS

Preheat the air fryer to 175 C. Place the oil, garlic, onion, bell pepper, and celery, in an ovenproof bowl. Place the bowl in the air fryer and cook for 5 minutes. Add the beef and cook for 6 more minutes.

Stir in broth, tomatoes, chili, parsley, and coriander. Let cook for 20 minutes. Stir in beans, salt, and pepper. Cook for 10 more minutes. Sprinkle with cilantro, to serve.

268. Roast Beef

Total Time: 60 min | **Serves**: 8 | **Per serving**: Calories: 366; Carbs: 7g; Fat: 31g; Protein: 18g

INGREDIENTS

- 2 lb beef loin
- ½ tsp black pepper, salt
- 1 tsp thyme
- 1 tsp rosemary
- ½ tsp oregano
- ½ tsp garlic powder
- 1 tsp onion powder
- 1 tbsp olive oil

DIRECTIONS

Preheat the air fryer to 170 C. In a bowl, combine olive oil and seasonings. Rub the mixture onto beef. Place the beef in the air fryer and cook for 30 minutes. Turn the roast over and cook for 20 to 30 more minutes, until well-roasted. Serve with mushrooms sauce, cooked rice, and steamed veggies.

269. Peppercorn Meatloaf

Total Time: 35 min | **Serves**: 8 | **Per serving**: Calories: 613; Carbs: 18g; Fat: 27g; Protein: 41g

INGREDIENTS

- 4 lb ground beef
- 1 tbsp basil
- 1 tbsp oregano
- 1 tbsp parsley
- 1 onion, diced
- 1 tbsp Worcestershire sauce
- 3 tbsp ketchup
- ½ tsp salt
- 1 tsp ground peppercorns
- 10 whole peppercorns, for garnishing
- 100g breadcrumbs

DIRECTIONS

Preheat the air fryer to 175 C. Place the beef in a large bowl. Add all of the ingredients except the whole peppercorns and the breadcrumbs. Mix with your hand until well combined; stir in the breadcrumbs.

Place the meatloaf on a lined baking dish. Place in the air fryer and cook for 25 minutes. Garnish the meatloaf with the whole peppercorns and let cool slightly before serving.

270. Liver Soufflé

Total Time: 40 min | **Serves:** 4 | **Per serving:** Calories: 216; Carbs: 25g; Fat: 17g; Protein: 42g

INGREDIENTS

½ lb of liver
3 eggs
3 oz buns
250 ml warm milk
Salt and pepper

DIRECTIONS

Cut the liver in slices and put it in the fridge for 15 minutes. Divide the buns into pieces and soak them in milk for 10 minutes. Put the liver in a blender, and add the yolks, the bread mixture, and the spices. Grind the components and stuff in the ramekins. Line the ramekins in the air fryer's basket; cook for 20 minutes at 175 C.

271. Panko Beef Schnitzel

Total Time: 22 min | **Serve:** 1 | **Per serving:** Calories: 487; Carbs: 41g; Fat: 39.5g; Protein: 40g

INGREDIENTS

2 tbsp olive oil
1 thin beef cutlet
1 egg, beaten
2 oz breadcrumbs
1 tsp paprika
¼ tsp garlic powder
Salt and pepper, to taste

DIRECTIONS

Preheat the air fryer to 175 C. Combine olive oil, breadcrumbs, paprika, garlic powder, and salt, in a bowl. Dip the beef in with the egg first, and then coat it with the breadcrumb mixture completely. Line a baking dish with parchment paper and place the breaded meat on it. Cook for 12 minutes. Serve and enjoy.

272. Beef Bulgogi

Total Time: 3 hrs 15 min | **Serve:** 1 | **Per serving:** Calories: 599; Carbs: 10 g; Fat: 24 g; Protein: 33 g

INGREDIENTS

6 oz beef
50g sliced mushrooms
2 tbsp bulgogi marinade
1 tbsp diced onion

DIRECTIONS

Cut the beef into small pieces and place them in a bowl. Add the bulgogi and mix to coat the beef completely. Cover the bowl and place in the fridge for 3 hours to marinate. Preheat the air fryer to 175 C.

Transfer the beef to a baking dish; stir in the mushroom and onion. Cook for 10 minutes, until nice and tender. Serve with some roasted potatoes and a green salad.

273. Beef Veggie Mix with Hoisin Sauce

Total Time: 55 min | **Serves:** 4 | **Per serving:** Calories 210; Carbs 2g; Fat 10.2g; Protein 18.2g

INGREDIENTS

Hoisin Sauce:
2 tbsp soy sauce
1 tbsp peanut butter
½ tsp Sriracha hot sauce
1 tsp sugar
1 tsp rice vinegar
3 cloves garlic, minced

Beef Veggie Mix:
- 2 lb beef sirloin steak, cut in strips
- 2 yellow peppers, cut in strips
- 2 green peppers, cut in strips
- 2 green peppers, cut in strips
- 2 white onions, cut in strips
- 1 red onion, cut in strips
- 2 lb broccoli, cut in florets
- 2 tbsp soy sauce
- 2 tsp sesame oil
- 3 tsp minced garlic
- 2 tsp ground ginger
- 120 ml water
- 1 tbsp olive oil

DIRECTIONS

Make the hoisin sauce first:

In a pan, add the soy sauce, peanut butter, sugar, hot sauce, rice vinegar, and minced garlic. Bring to simmer over low heat until reduced, about 15 minutes. Stir occasionally using a vessel and let it cool.

For the beef veggie mix: Add to the chilled hoisin sauce, garlic, sesame oil, soy sauce, ginger, and water; mix well.

Add meat, mix with a spoon, and refrigerate for 20 minutes, to marinate. Add the florets, peppers, onions, and olive oil to a bowl; mix to coat well. Add the veggies in the fryer basket and cook for 5 minutes at 200 C. Open the air fryer, stir the veggies, and cook further for 5 minutes, if not soft.

Remove the veggies to a serving plate and set aside. Remove the meat from the fridge and drain the liquid into a bowl. Add the beef into the fryer, and cook at 190 C for 8 minutes. Slide-out the basket and shake. Cook for 7 more minutes. Remove to the veggie plate; season with salt and pepper and pour the cooking sauce over, to serve.

274. Simple Roast Beef with Herbs

Total Time: 50 min | **Serves:** 2 | **Per serving:** Calories 268; Carbs 1g; Fat 9.3g; Protein 26.4g

INGREDIENTS
- 2 tsp olive oil
- 1 lb beef roast
- ½ tsp dried rosemary
- ½ tsp dried thyme
- ½ tsp dried oregano
- Salt and black pepper to taste

DIRECTIONS

Preheat the air fryer to 200 C. Drizzle oil over the beef, and sprinkle with salt, pepper, and herbs. Rub onto the meat with hands. Cook for 45 minutes for medium-rare and 50 minutes for well-done.

Check halfway through, and flip to ensure they cook evenly. Wrap the beef in foil for 10 minutes after cooking to allow the juices to reabsorb into the meat. Slice the beef using a knife and serve with a side of steamed asparagus.

275. Beef & Tomato Meatballs

Total Time: 25 min | **Serves:** 6 | **Per serving:** Calories: 194; Carbs: 5g; Fat: 15g; Protein: 8g

INGREDIENTS
- 1 small onion, chopped
- ¾ pound grounded beef
- 1 tbsp fresh parsley, chopped
- ½ tbsp fresh thyme leaves, chopped
- 1 whole egg, beaten
- 3 tbsp breadcrumbs
- Salt and pepper to taste
- Tomato sauce for coating

DIRECTIONS

Preheat your air fryer to 195 C. In a mixing bowl, mix all the ingredients except tomato sauce. Roll the mixture into 10-12 balls. Place the balls in your air fryer's cooking basket, and cook for 8 minutes. Add tomato sauce to the balls to coat and cook for 5 minutes at 150 C. Gently stir and enjoy!

276. Mexican-Style Beef in Savoy Wraps

Total Time: 35 min | Serves: 3 | Per serving: Calories 227; Carbs 3.2g; Fat 14.1g; Protein 27.1g

INGREDIENTS

½ lb ground beef
8 savoy cabbage leaves
1 small onion, chopped
¼ packet Taco seasoning
1 tbsp coriander lime rotel
60g shredded Mexican cheese
2 tsp olive oil
Salt and pepper to taste
2 cloves garlic, minced
1 tsp chopped coriander
Cooking spray

DIRECTIONS

Preheat the air fryer to 200 C. Grease a skillet with cooking spray and place it over medium heat on a stovetop. Add the onions and garlic; sauté until fragrant. Add the beef, pepper, salt, and taco seasoning. Cook until the beef browns while breaking the meat with a vessel as it cooks. Add the cilantro rotel and stir well to combine.

Turn off the heat. Lay 4 of the savoy cabbage leaves on a flat surface and scoop the beef mixture in the center, and sprinkle with the Mexican cheese. Wrap diagonally and double wrap with the remaining 4 cabbage leaves.

Arrange the 4 rolls in the fryer basket and spray with cooking spray. Close the fryer and cook for 8 minutes. Flip the rolls, spray with cooking spray, and continue to cook for 4 minutes. Remove, garnish with cilantro and allow them to cool. Serve with cheese dip.

277. Spicy Meatloaf with Tomato-Basil Sauce

Total Time: 40 min | Serves: 5 | Per serving: Calories 260; Carbs 2g; Fat 13g; Protein 26g

INGREDIENTS

230g tomato basil sauce, divided in 2
1 ½ lb ground beef
70g diced onion
2 tbsp minced garlic
2 tbsp minced ginger
50g breadcrumbs
50g grated Parmesan cheese
Salt and pepper to season
2 tsp cayenne pepper
½ tsp dried basil
20g chopped parsley
2 egg whites
Cooking spray

DIRECTIONS

Preheat the air fryer to 180 C. In a bowl, add the beef, half of the tomato sauce, onion, garlic, ginger, breadcrumbs, cheese, salt, pepper, cayenne pepper, dried basil, parsley, and egg whites; mix well.

Grease an 8 or 10-inch pan with cooking spray and scoop the meat mixture into it. Shape the meat into the pan while pressing firmly. Brush the remaining tomato sauce onto meat. Place the pan in the fryer basket and close the air fryer; cook for 25 minutes.

After 15 minutes, open the fryer, and use a meat thermometer to ensure the meat has reached 160 C internally. If not, cook further for 5 minutes. Remove the pan, drain any excess liquid and fat. Let meatloaf cool for 20 minutes before slicing. Serve with a side of sautéed green beans.

278. Ginger-Garlic Beef Ribs with Hot Sauce

Total Time: 35 min | Serves: 2 | Per serving: Calories 210; Carbs 0g; Fat 15g; Protein 17g

INGREDIENTS

1 rack rib steak
Salt to season
1 tsp white pepper
1 tsp garlic powder
½ tsp red pepper flakes
1 tsp ginger powder
Hot sauce

DIRECTIONS

Preheat the air fryer to 180 C. Place the rib rack on a flat surface and pat dry using a paper towel. Season the ribs with salt, garlic, ginger, white pepper, and red pepper flakes.

Place the ribs in the fryer's basket and cook for 15 minutes. Turn the ribs with kitchen tongs and cook further for 15 minutes. Remove the ribs onto a chopping board and let sit for 3 minutes before slicing. Plate and drizzle hot sauce over and serve.

279. Crispy Sweet and Spicy Beef Tenderloin

Total Time: 30 min | Serves: 3 | Per serving: Calories 180; Carbs 6g; Fat 11g; Protein 11g

INGREDIENTS

Beef:
2 lb beef tenderloin, cut into strips
60g flour
Cooking spray

Sauce:
1 tbsp minced ginger
1 tbsp minced garlic
50g chopped green onions
2 tbsp olive oil
120 ml soy sauce
120 ml water
60 ml vinegar
50g sugar
1 tsp cornstarch
½ tsp red chili flakes
Salt and pepper to taste

DIRECTIONS

Pour the flour in a bowl, add the beef strips and dredge them in the flour. Spray the fryer basket with cooking spray and arrange the beef strips in it; spray with cooking spray. Cook the beef at 200 C for 4 minutes. Slide-out and shake the fryer basket to toss the beef strips. Cook further for 3 minutes; set aside.

To make the sauce, pour the cornstarch in a bowl and mix it with 3 to 4 teaspoons of water until well dissolve; set aside. Place a wok or saucepan over medium heat on a stovetop and add the olive oil, garlic, and ginger. Stir continually for 10 seconds. Add the soy sauce, vinegar, and remaining water.

Stir well and bring to boil for 2 minutes. Stir in the sugar, chili flakes, and cornstarch mixture. Add the beef strips, stir and cook for 3 minutes. Stir in the green onions and cook for 1 to 2 minutes. Season with pepper and salt as desired. Turn off the heat. Serve with a side of steamed rice.

280. Chipotle Steak with Avocado-Lime Salsa

Total Time: 35 min | Serves: 4 | Per serving: Calories 523; Carbs 6.5g; Fat 45g; Protein 32g

INGREDIENTS

1 ½ lb rib eye steak
2 tsp olive oil
1 tbsp chipotle chili pepper
Salt and black pepper to taste
1 avocado, diced
Juice from ½ lime

DIRECTIONS

Place the steak on a chopping board. Pour the olive oil over and sprinkle with the chipotle pepper, salt, and black pepper. Use your hands to rub the spices on the meat. Leave it to sit and marinate for 10 minutes.

Preheat the air fryer to 200 C. Pull out the fryer basket and place the meat inside. Slide it back into the air fryer and cook for 14 minutes. Turn the steak and continue cooking for 6 minutes. Remove the steak, cover with foil, and let it sit for 5 minutes before slicing.

Meanwhile, prepare the avocado salsa by mashing the avocado with potato mash. Add in the lime juice and mix until smooth. Taste, adjust the seasoning, slice and serve with salsa.

281. Dreamy Beef Roast

Total Time: 25 min | **Serves**: 3 | **Per serving**: Calories: 183; Carbs: 10g; Fat: 5g; Protein: 11g

INGREDIENTS

- 2 tbsp olive oil
- 4 pound top round roast beef
- 1 tsp salt
- ¼ tsp fresh ground black pepper
- 1 tsp dried thyme
- ½ tsp fresh rosemary, chopped
- 3 pounds red potatoes, halved
- Olive oil, black pepper and salt for garnish

DIRECTIONS

Preheat your air fryer to 180 C. In a small bowl, mix rosemary, salt, pepper and thyme; rub oil onto beef. Season with the spice mixture. Place the prepared meat in your air fryer's cooking basket and cook for 20 minutes.

Give the meat a turn and add potatoes, more pepper and oil. Cook for 20 minutes more. Take the steak out and set aside to cool for 10 minutes. Cook the potatoes in your air fryer for 10 more minutes at 200 C. Serve hot.

282. Crazy Beef Schnitzel

Total Time: 25 min | **Serves**: 2 | **Per serving**: Calories: 275; Carbs: 12g; Fat: 11g; Protein: 33g

INGREDIENTS

- 2 tbsp vegetable oil
- 2 oz breadcrumbs
- 1 whole egg, whisked
- 1 thin beef schnitzel, cut into strips
- 1 whole lemon

DIRECTIONS

Preheat your fryer to 356 F. In a bowl, add breadcrumbs and oil and stir well to get a loose mixture. Dip schnitzel in egg, then dip in breadcrumbs coat well. Place the prepared schnitzel your air fryer's cooking basket and cook for 12 minutes. Serve with a drizzle of lemon juice.

283. Burgundy Beef Dish

Total Time: 35 min | **Serves**: 5 | **Per serving**: Calories: 161; Carbs: 8g; Fat: 9g; Protein: 10g

INGREDIENTS

- 1 ½ pounds beef steak
- 1 package egg noodles, cooked
- 1 ounce dry onion soup mix
- 1 can (14.5 oz) cream mushroom soup
- 180g mushrooms, sliced
- 1 whole onion, chopped
- 100 ml beef broth
- 3 garlic cloves, minced

DIRECTIONS

Preheat your air fryer to 180 C. Drizzle onion soup mix all over the meat. In a mixing bowl, mix the sauce, garlic cloves, beef broth, chopped onion, sliced mushrooms and mushroom soup.

Top the meat with the prepared sauce mixture. Place the prepared meat in the air fryer's cooking basket and cook for 25 minutes. Serve with cooked egg noodles.

284. Easy Homemade Beef Satay

Total Time: 25 min | **Serves**: 4 | **Per serving**: Calories 174; Carbs 0g; Fat 11.82g; Protein 15.93g

INGREDIENTS

- 2 lb flank steaks, cut in long strips
- 2 tbsp fish sauce
- 2 tbsp soy sauce
- 2 tbsp sugar
- 2 tbsp ground garlic
- 2 tbsp ground ginger
- 2 tsp hot sauce
- 2 tbsp chopped coriander
- 60g roasted peanuts, chopped

DIRECTIONS

Preheat the air fryer to 200 C. In a zipper bag, add the beef, fish sauce, swerve sweetener, garlic, soy sauce, ginger, half of the cilantro, and hot sauce. Zip the bag and massage the ingredients with your hands to mix well.

Open the bag, remove the beef, shake off the excess marinade and place the beef strips in the fryer basket in a single layer; avoid overlapping. Close the air fryer and cook for 5 minutes. Turn the beef and cook further for 5 minutes. Dish the cooked meat in a serving platter, garnish with the peanuts and the remaining coriander.

285. Broccoli And Beef Dish

Total Time: 35 min | **Serves**: 4 | **Per serving**: Calories: 338; Carbs: 50g; Fat: 18g; Protein: 20g

INGREDIENTS

¾ pound circular beef steak, cut into strips
1 pound broccoli, cut into florets
160 ml oyster sauce
2 tbsp sesame oil
80 ml sherry
1 tsp soy sauce
1 tsp white sugar
1 tsp cornstarch
1 tbsp olive oil
1 garlic clove, minced

DIRECTIONS

In a bowl, mix cornstarch, sherry, oyster sauce, sesame oil, soy sauce, sugar and beef steaks. Set aside for 45 minutes. Add garlic, oil and ginger to the steaks. Place the steaks in your air fryer's cooking basket and cook for 12 minutes at 195 C.

286. Delicious Beef Rice

Total Time: 40 min | **Serves**: 2 | **Per serving**: Calories 445; Carbs 11.3g; Fat 21g; Protein 49g

INGREDIENTS

Beef:
1 lb beef steak
Salt and pepper to season

Fried Rice:
300g rice
1 ½ tbsp. soy sauce
2 tsp sesame oil
2 tsp minced ginger
2 tsp vinegar
1 clove garlic, minced
3 oz chopped broccoli
150g green beans

DIRECTIONS

Put the beef on a chopping board and use a knife to cut it in 2-inch strips. Add the beef to a bowl, sprinkle with pepper and salt, and mix it with a spoon. Let it sit for 10 minutes. Preheat the air fryer to 200 C. Add the beef to the fryer basket, and cook for 5 minutes. Turn the beef strips with kitchen tongs and cook further for 3 minutes.

Once ready, remove the beef to a safe-oven dish that fits in the fryer's basket. Add the rice, broccoli, green beans, garlic, ginger, sesame oil, vinegar and soy sauce. Mix evenly using a spoon.

Place the dish in the fryer basket, close, and cook at 185 C for 10 minutes. Open the air fryer, mix the rice well, and cook for 4 minutes; season with salt and pepper. Dish the rice into serving bowls and serve with hot sauce.

287. Yummy Worcestershire Beef Burgers

Total Time: 255 min | **Serves**: 4 | **Per serving**: Calories 421; Carbs 3.2g; Fat 39g; Protein 21g

INGREDIENTS

Beef:
- 1 ½ lb ground beef
- Salt and pepper to season

Burgers:
- 4 buns
- 4 trimmed lettuce leaves
- ¼ tsp liquid smoke
- 2 tsp onion powder
- 4 tbsp mayonnaise
- 1 large tomato, sliced
- 1 tsp garlic powder
- 1 ½ tbsp Worcestershire sauce
- 4 slices Cheddar cheese

DIRECTIONS

Preheat the air fryer to 185 C. In a bowl, combine the beef, salt, pepper, liquid smoke, onion powder, garlic powder and Worcestershire sauce using your hands. Form 3 to 4 patties out of the mixture. Place the patties in the fryer basket making sure to leave enough space between them.

Ideally, work with two patties at a time. Close the air fryer and cook for 10 minutes. Turn the beef with kitchen tongs, reduce the temperature to 175 C, and cook further for 5 minutes. Remove the patties onto a plate. Assemble burgers with the lettuce, mayonnaise, sliced cheese, and sliced tomato.

288. Beer Dredged Corned Beef

Total Time: 35 min | **Serves**: 3 | **Per serving**: Calories: 320; Carbs: 10g; Fat: 22g; Protein: 21g

INGREDIENTS

- 1 tbsp beef spice
- 1 whole onion, chopped
- 4 carrots, chopped
- 12 oz bottle beer
- 300g chicken broth
- 4 pounds corned beef

DIRECTIONS

Preheat your air fryer to 190 C. Cover beef with beer and set aside for 20 minutes. Place carrots, onion and beef in a pot and heat over high heat. Add in broth and bring to a boil. Drain boiled meat and veggies; set aside.

Top with beef spice. Place the meat and veggies in your air fryer's cooking basket and cook for 30 minutes.

289. Beef Stroganoff

Total Time: 20 min | **Serves**: 3 | **Per serving**: Calories: 361; Carbs: 16g; Fat: 16g; Protein: 35g

INGREDIENTS

- 1 pound thin steak
- 4 tbsp butter
- 1 whole onion, chopped
- 240g sour cream
- 8 oz mushrooms, sliced
- 800 ml beef broth
- 16 oz egg noodles, cooked

DIRECTIONS

Preheat your air fryer to 200 C. Using a microwave proof bowl, melt butter in a microwave oven. In a mixing bowl, mix the melted butter, sliced mushrooms, cream, onion, and beef broth.

Pour the mixture over steak and set aside for 10 minutes. Place the marinated beef in your fryer's cooking basket, and cook for 10 minutes. Serve with cooked egg noodles and enjoy!

290. American Beef Roll

Total Time: 30 min | **Serves**: 4 | **Per serving**: Calories: 380; Carbs: 40g; Fat: 18g; Protein: 11g

INGREDIENTS

- 2 pounds beef steak, sliced
- 1 tsp pepper
- 3 tbsp pesto

1 tsp salt
6 slices cheese

50g spinach, chopped
3 oz bell pepper, deseeded and sliced

DIRECTIONS

Preheat your air fryer to 200 C. Top the steak slices with pesto, cheese, spinach, bell pepper. Roll up the slices and secure using a toothpick. Season with salt and pepper accordingly. Place the prepared slices in your air fryer's cooking basket and cook for 15 minutes. Serve and enjoy!

291. Traditional Beef Meatballs

Total Time: 15 min | **Serves**: 5 | **Per serving**: Calories: 338; Carbs: 50g; Fat: 18g; Protein: 20g

INGREDIENTS

1 pound beef, ground
1 tbsp extra-virgin olive oil

1 large red onion, chopped
1 tsp garlic, minced

2 whole eggs, beaten
Salt and pepper to taste

DIRECTIONS

Preheat your air fryer to 175 C. Using a pan over high heat, heat the oil. Add the chopped onion and garlic, cook for 1 minute until tender; transfer to a bowl. Add ground beef and egg and mix well. Season with salt and pepper. Roll the mixture golf ball shapes. Place the balls in the air fryer cooking basket and cook for 4 minutes.

292. Original Rib Eye

Total Time: 20 min | **Serves**: 4 | **Per serving**: Calories: 305; Carbs: 2g; Fat: 24g; Protein: 21g

INGREDIENTS

2 pounds ribeye steak

1 tbsp olive oil

Salt and pepper to taste

DIRECTIONS

Preheat your fryer to 175 C. Rub both sides of the steak with oil; season with salt and pepper. Place the steak in your air fryer's cooking basket and cook for 8 minutes. Serve and enjoy!

293. Honey & Pork Dish

Total Time: 20 min | **Serves**: 3 | **Per serving**: Calories: 297; Carbs: 10g; Fat: 22g; Protein: 15g

INGREDIENTS

1 pound pork ribs
1 tsp salt
1 tsp pepper
1 tbsp sugar

1 tsp ginger juice
1 tsp five-spice powder
1 tbsp teriyaki sauce
1 tbsp light soy sauce

1 garlic clove, minced
2 tbsp honey
1 tbsp water
1 tbsp tomato sauce

DIRECTIONS

In a bowl, mix pepper, sugar, five-spice powder, salt, ginger juice, teriyaki sauce. Add pork ribs to the marinade and let marinate for 2 hours. Preheat your air fryer to 175 C.

Add pork ribs to your air fryer's cooking basket and cook for 8 minutes. In a separate mixing bowl, mix soy sauce, garlic, honey, water, tomato sauce. Over medium heat, add oil and garlic in a pan and fry for 30 seconds. Add fried pork ribs and pour the prepared sauce. Stir-fry for a few minutes, serve and enjoy!

294. Mexican Pork And Rice

Total Time: 40 min | **Serves**: 4 | **Per serving**: Calories: 370; Carbs: 35g; Fat: 10g; Protein: 31g

INGREDIENTS

2 pork chops
1 lime juice
Salt and pepper to taste
1 tsp garlic powder
300g white rice, cooked
2 tbsp olive oil
1 can (14.5 oz) tomato sauce
1 onion, chopped
3 garlic cloves, minced
½ tsp oregano
1 tsp chipotle chili

DIRECTIONS

Preheat your air fryer to 175 C. Season pork chops with salt, pepper and garlic powder. Next, in a bowl, mix onion, garlic, chipotle, oregano, and tomato sauce. Add the pork to the mixture. Let marinate for an hour.

Remove the meat from the mixture and allow the mixture to sit for 15 minutes. After, place them into the wire basket of your air fryer and cook for 25 minutes, make sure you check them halfway through and turn to ensure they get nicely cooked on both sides. Serve with cooked rice.

295. Awesome Onion and Sausage Balls

Total Time: 20 min | **Serves**: 4 | **Per serving**: Calories: 52; Carbs: 7g; Fat: 1g; Protein: 0g

INGREDIENTS

3 ½ oz sausages, sliced
Salt and pepper to taste
1 onion, chopped
3 tbsp breadcrumbs
½ tsp garlic puree
1 tsp sage

DIRECTIONS

Preheat your air fryer to 170 C. In a bowl, mix onions, sausage meat, sage, garlic puree, salt and pepper. Add breadcrumbs to a plate. Form balls using the mixture and roll them in breadcrumbs. Add onion balls in your air fryer's cooking basket and cook for 15 minutes. Serve and enjoy!s

296. Juicy Double Cut Pork Chops

Total Time: 45 min | **Serves**: 4 | **Per serving**: Calories: 519; Carbs: 9g; Fat: 26g; Protein: 56g

INGREDIENTS

2 tbsp tamarind paste
2 whole caramelized potatoes
1 tbsp garlic, minced
120ml green mole sauce
3 tbsp corn syrup
1 tbsp olive oil
2 tbsp molasses
4 tbsp southwest seasoning
2 tbsp ketchup
4 pork chops
2 tbsp water

DIRECTIONS

Preheat your air fryer to 175 C. In a bowl, mix all the ingredients except potatoes, pork chops and mole sauce.

Let the pork chops marinate in the mixture for 30 minutes. Place pork chops to your air fryer's cooking basket and cook for 25 minutes. Serve with caramelized potatoes and mole sauce.

297. Sweet Pork Balls

Total Time: 25 min | **Serves**: 4 to 6 | **Per serving**: Calories : 225; Carbs: 0g; Fat: 17g; Protein: 13g

INGREDIENTS

1 lb ground pork
1 large onion, chopped
½ tsp maple syrup
2 tsp mustard
10g chopped basil leaves
2 tbsp grated Cheddar cheese

DIRECTIONS

In a mixing bowl, add the ground pork, onion, maple syrup, mustard, basil leaves, salt, pepper, and cheddar cheese; mix well. Use your hands to form bite-size balls. Place in the fryer basket and cook at 200 C for 10 minutes.

Slide-out the fryer basket and shake it to toss the meatballs. Cook further for 5 minutes. Remove them onto a wire rack and serve with zoodles and marinara sauce.

298.   Ultimate Ham Quiche Cups

Total Time: 25 min | Serve: 6 | **Per serving**: Calories: 80; Carbs: 0g; Fat: 5g; Protein: 7g

INGREDIENTS

5 whole eggs, beaten
2 ¼ oz ham
250 ml milk
¼ tsp pepper
130g swiss cheese, grated
¼ tsp salt
2 green onions, chopped
½ tsp thyme

DIRECTIONS

Preheat your Fryer to 175 C. In a bowl, mix beaten eggs, thyme, onion, salt, Swiss cheese, pepper, and milk. Prepare baking forms and place ham slices in each baking form. Top with the egg mixture. Place the prepared muffin forms in your air fryer's cooking basket and cook for 15 minutes. Serve and enjoy!

299.   Herbed Pork

Total Time: 30 min | **Serves**: 4 | **Per serving**: Calories: 140; Carbs: 3g; Fat: 8g; Protein: 14g

INGREDIENTS

4 slices pork chops, sliced
2-3 tbsp olive oil
Salt and pepper to taste
1 whole egg, beaten
1 tbsp flour
Breadcrumbs as needed
A bunch of Italian herbs

DIRECTIONS

Preheat your air fryer to 200 C. Mix oil, salt, and pepper to form a marinade. Place the beaten egg on a plate. In a separate plate, add the breadcrumbs. Add pork to the marinade and allow to rest for 15 minutes.

Add one slice in egg and then to breadcrumbs; repeat with all slices. Place the prepared slices in your air fryer's cooking basket and cook for 20 minutes. Season with your desired herbs and serve.

300.   Sweet & Tender Pork Chops

Total Time: 40 min | **Serves**: 4 | **Per serving**: Calories: 118; Carbs: 0g; Fat: 7g; Protein: 13g

INGREDIENTS

8 pork chops
¼ tsp pepper
800g stuffing mix
½ tsp salt
2 tbsp olive oil
4 garlic cloves, minced
2 tbsp sage leaves

DIRECTIONS

Preheat your air fryer to 175 C. Cut a hole in pork chops and fill chops with stuffing mix. In a bowl, mix sage leaves, garlic cloves, oil, salt and pepper. Cover chops with marinade and let marinate for 10 minutes. Place the chops in your air fryer's cooking basket and cook for 25 minutes. Serve and enjoy!

301. Special Crackling Pork Belly

Total Time: 35 min | Serves: 8 | Per serving: Calories: 280; Carbs: 0g; Fat: 17g; Protein: 32g

INGREDIENTS

2 pounds pork belly
½ tsp pepper
1 tbsp olive oil
1 tbsp salt
3 tbsp honey

DIRECTIONS

Preheat your air fryer to 200 C. Season the pork belly with salt and black pepper. Grease the basket with oil. Bake the seasoned meat for 15 minutes. Flip, top with honey and cook for 10 minutes more. Serve with green salad.

302. The Butterbean Pork Ratatouille

Total Time: 25 min | Serves: 4 | Per serving: Calories: 114; Carbs: 10g; Fat: 6g; Protein: 7g

INGREDIENTS

4 pork sausages

For Ratatouille

1 pepper, chopped
2 courgatte, chopped
1 aubergine, chopped
1 medium red onion, chopped

1 tbsp olive oil
1-ounce butterbean, drained
15 oz tomatoes, chopped
2 sprigs fresh thyme

1 tbsp balsamic vinegar
2 garlic cloves, minced
1 red chili, chopped

DIRECTIONS

Preheat your air fryer to 185 C. Mix pepper, eggplant, oil, onion, zucchinis, and add to the cooking basket. Roast for 20 minutes. Set aside to cool. Reduce air fryer temperature to 356 F. In a saucepan, mix prepared vegetables and the remaining ratatouille ingredients, and bring to a boil over medium heat.

Let the mixture simmer for 10 minutes; season with salt and pepper. Add sausages to your air fryer's basket and cook for 10-15 minutes. Serve the sausages with ratatouille.

303. The Feisty Air Fried Pigs in Blanket

Total Time: 20 min | Serves: 4 | Per serving: Calories: 104; Carbs: 5g; Fat: 8g; Protein: 3g

INGREDIENTS

12 oz cocktail franks
8 oz can crescent rolls

DIRECTIONS

Use a paper towel to pat the cocktail franks to drain completely. Cut the dough in 1 by 1.5-inch rectangles using a knife. Gently roll the franks in the strips, making sure the ends are visible Place in freezer for 5 minutes.

Preheat the fryer to 170 C. Take the franks out of the freezer and place them in the air fryer's basket and cook for 6-8 minutes. Increase the temperature to 195 C. cook for another 3 minutes until a fine golden texture appears.

304. Fruity Pear and Ham

Total Time: 30 min | Serves: 2 | Per serving: Calories: 337; Carbs: 40g; Fat: 13g; Protein: 18g

INGREDIENTS

15 oz pears, halved
8 pound smoked ham
300g brown sugar
¾ tbsp allspice
1 tbsp apple cider vinegar
1 tsp black pepper
1 tsp vanilla extract

DIRECTIONS

Preheat your air fryer to 170 C. In a bowl, mix pears, brown sugar, cider vinegar, vanilla extract, pepper, and allspice. Place the mixture in a frying pan and fry for 2-3 minutes. Pour the mixture over ham. Add the ham to the air fryer cooking basket and cook for 15 minutes. Serve ham with hot sauce, to enjoy!

305. Garlic & Bacon Platter

Total Time: 40 min | **Serves**: 4 | **Per serving**: Calories: 418; Carbs: 65g; Fat: 13g; Protein: 12g

INGREDIENTS

4 potatoes, halved and sauce
6 garlic cloves, squashed
4 streaky cut rashers bacon
2 sprigs rosemary
1 tbsp olive oil

DIRECTIONS

Preheat your air fryer to 185 C. In a mixing bowl, mix garlic, bacon, potatoes and rosemary; toss in oil. Place the mixture in your air fryer's cooking basket and roast for 25-30 minutes. Serve and enjoy!

306. Ham & Cheese Sandwich

Total Time: 15 min | **Serves**: 4 | **Per serving**: Calories: 294; Carbs: 25g; Fat: 15g; Protein: 16g

INGREDIENTS

8 slices whole wheat bread
4 slices lean pork ham
4 slices cheese
8 slices tomato

DIRECTIONS

Preheat your air fryer to 180 C. Lay four slices of bread on a flat surface. Spread the slices with cheese, tomato, and ham. Cover with the remaining slices to form sandwiches. Add the sandwiches to the air fryer cooking basket and cook for 10 minutes.

307. Savoury Apple Pork Bites

Total Time: 40 min | **Serve**: 10 | **Per serving**: Calories: 301; Carbs: 5g; Fat: 19g; Protein: 20g

INGREDIENTS

16 oz sausage meat
1 whole egg, beaten
3 ½ oz onion, chopped
2 tbsp dried sage
2 tbsp almonds, chopped
½ tsp pepper
3 ½ oz apple, sauce and sliced
½ tsp salt

DIRECTIONS

Preheat your air fryer to 175 C. In a bowl, mix onion, almonds, sliced apples, egg, pepper and salt. Add the almond mixture and sausage in a Ziploc bag. mix to coat well and set aside for 15 minutes Use the mixture to form cutlets. Add cutlets to your fryer's basket and cook for 25 minutes. Serve with heavy cream and enjoy!

308. Crunchy Cashew Lamb Rack

Total Time: 30 min | **Serves**: 4 | **Per serving**: Calories: 262 Carbs: 1.5g; Fat: 11.8g; Protein: 35g

INGREDIENTS

3 oz chopped cashews
1 tbsp chopped rosemary
1 ½ lb rack of lamb
1 garlic clove, minced
1 tbsp breadcrumbs
1 egg, beaten
1 tbsp olive oil salt and pepper, to taste

DIRECTIONS

Preheat the air fryer to 110 C. Combine olive oil with the garlic, and brush this mixture onto lamb. Combine rosemary, cashews, and crumbs, in a bowl. Brush egg over the lambs, and coat it with the cashew mixture.

Place the lamb into the air fryer's basket, cook for 25 minutes. Increase the temperature to 180 C, and cook for 5 more minutes. Cover with a foil and let sit for a couple of minutes before serving.

309. Oregano & Thyme Lamb Chops

Total Time: 30 min | **Serves**: 4 | **Per serving**: Calories: 270; Carbs: 0.2g; Fat: 13g; Protein: 34.8g

INGREDIENTS

4 lamb chops
1 garlic clove, peeled
1 tbsp plus
2 tsp olive oil
½ tbsp oregano
½ tbsp thyme
½ tsp salt
¼ tsp black pepper

DIRECTIONS

Preheat the air fryer to 195 C. Coat the garlic clove with 1 tsp. of olive oil and place it in the air fryer for 10 minutes. Mix the herbs and seasonings with the remaining olive oil.

Using a towel or a mitten, squeeze the hot roasted garlic clove into the herb mixture and stir to combine. Coat the lamb chops with the mixture well, and place in the air fryer. Cook for 8 to 12 minutes.

310. Lamb Meatballs

Total Time: 40 min | **Serve**: 12 | **Per serving**: Calories: 304; Carbs: 1.3g; Fat: 16g; Protein: 21g

INGREDIENTS

1 ½ lb ground lamb
1 minced onion
2 tbsp chopped mint leaves
3 garlic cloves, minced
2 tsp paprika
2 tsp coriander seeds
½ tsp cayenne pepper
1 tsp salt
1 tbsp chopped parsley
2 tsp cumin
½ tsp ground ginger

DIRECTIONS

Soak 24 skewers in water, until ready to use. Preheat the air fryer to 170 C. Combine all ingredients in a large bowl. Mix well with your hands until the herbs and spices are evenly distributed and the mixture is well incorporated.

Shape the lamb mixture into 12 sausage shapes around 2 skewers. Cook for 12 to 15 minutes, or until it reaches the preferred doneness. Served with tzatziki sauce and enjoy.

311. Lamb Steaks with Fresh Mint and Potatoes

Total Time: 25 min | **Serves**: 2 | **Per serving**: Calories: 420; Carbs: 3.2g; Fat: 28g; Protein: 4g

INGREDIENTS

2 lamb steaks
2 tbsp olive oil
2 garlic cloves, crushed
Salt and pepper, to taste
A handful of fresh thyme, chopped
4 red potatoes, cubed

DIRECTIONS

Rub the steaks with oil, garlic, salt, and black pepper. Put thyme in the fryer, and place the steaks on top. Oil the potato chunks and sprinkle with salt and pepper. Arrange the potatoes next to the steaks, and cook on 180 C for 14 minutes, turning once halfway through cooking.

VEGETABLES AND VEGETARIAN

312. Vegetable Croquettes

Total Time: 1 hr 30 min | Serves: 3 | Per serving: Calories: 24; Carbs: 2.6g; Fat: 0.3g; Protein: 3.3g

INGREDIENTS

1 lb red potatoes
450 ml water
300 ml milk
Salt to taste
2 tsp + 3 tsp butter
2 tsp olive oil
2 red peppers, chopped
30g baby spinach, chopped
3 mushrooms, chopped
1/6 broccoli florets, chopped
20g sliced green onion
½ red onion, chopped
2 cloves garlic, minced
1 medium carrot, grated
60g flour
2 tbsp cornstarch
180g breadcrumbs
Cooking spray

DIRECTIONS

Place the potatoes in a pot, add the water, and bring it to boil over medium heat on a stovetop. Boil until tender and mashable. Drain the potatoes through a sieve and place them in a bowl.

Add the 2 teaspoons of butter, 1 cup of milk, and salt. Use a potato masher to mash well; set aside.

Place a skillet over medium heat on a stovetop and melt the remaining butter. Add the onion, garlic, red peppers, broccoli, and mushrooms; stir-fry for 2 minutes. Add green onion and spinach, and cook until the spinach wilts.

Season with salt and stir. Turn the heat off and pour the veggie mixture into the potato mash. Use the potato masher to mash the veggies into the potatoes; allow cooling. Using your hands, form oblong balls of the mixture and place them on a baking sheet in a single layer. Refrigerate for 30 minutes.

In 3 separate bowls, add breadcrumbs in one, flour in another, and cornstarch, remaining milk and salt in a third bowl. Mix cornstarch, salt and 1 tbsp of water. Remove the patties from the fridge. Preheat the fryer to 195 C.

Dredge each veggie mold in flour, then in the cornstarch mixture, and then in the breadcrumbs. Place the patties in batches in a single layer in the basket without overlapping. Spray with olive oil and cook for 2 minutes. Flip, spray them with cooking spray and cook for more 3 minutes. Remove to a wire rack and serve with tomato sauce.

313. Crispy Air-Fried Tofu

Total Time: 25 min | Serves: 4 | Per serving: Calories: 487; Carbs: 23g; Fat: 31g; Protein: 41.5g

INGREDIENTS

3 blocks of firm tofu, cut into ½-inch thick
2 tbsp olive oil
120g flour
50g crushed cornflakes
Salt and black pepper to taste

DIRECTIONS

Sprinkle oil over tofu and massage gently until well-coated. On a plate, mix flour, cornflakes, salt, and pepper.

Dip each strip into the mixture to coat, spray with oil and arrange the strips in your air fryer lined with baking paper. Cook for 14 minutes at 180 C, turning once halfway through.

314. Air-Fried Veggie Sushi

Total Time: 60 min | Serves: 4 | Per serving: Calories: 434; Carbs: 54.2g; Fat: 27.3g; Protein: 13.4g

INGREDIENTS

300g cooked sushi rice
4 nori sheets
1 carrot, sliced lengthways
1 red bell pepper, seeded, sliced

1 avocado, sliced
1 tbsp olive oil mixed with
1 tbsp rice wine vinegar
90g panko crumbs

2 tbsp sesame seeds
Soy sauce, wasabi and pickled ginger to serve

DIRECTIONS

Prepare a clean working board, a small bowl of lukewarm water and a sushi mat. Wet hands, and lay a nori sheet onto sushi mat and spread half cup sushi rice, leaving a half inch of nori clear, so you can seal the roll. Place carrot, pepper and avocado sideways to the rice. Roll sushi tightly and rub warm water along the clean nori strip to seal.

In a bowl, mix olive oil and rice vinegar. In another bowl, mix the crumbs with the sesame seeds. Roll each sushi log in the vinegar mixture and then straight to the sesame bowl to coat. Arrange the coated sushi into the air fryer and cook for 14 minutes at 180 C, turning once halfway through. When ready, check if the sushi is golden and crispy on the outside. Slice and serve with soy sauce, pickled ginger and wasabi.

315. Roasted Balsamic Veggies

Total Time: 30 min | **Serves**: 4 | **Per serving**: Calories: 272; Carbs: 43.2g; Fat: 10.1g; Protein: 4.4g

INGREDIENTS

2 lb chopped veggies: potatoes, parsnips, courgatte, pumpkin, carrot, leeks

3 tbsp olive oil
1 tbsp balsamic vinegar
1 tbsp maple syrup

Salt and black pepper

DIRECTIONS

In a bowl, add oil, balsamic vinegar, agave syrup, salt, and black pepper; mix well with a fork. Arrange the veggies into the fryer, drizzle with the dressing and massage with hands until well-coated. Cook for 25 minutes at 180 C, tossing halfway through.

316. Corn Cakes

Total Time: 25 min | **Serves**: 8 | **Per serving**: Calories: 120; Carbs: 19.2g; Fat: 5.1g; Protein: 2.9g

INGREDIENTS

330g corn kernels, fresh or canned, drained
2 eggs, lightly beaten

40g finely chopped green onions
20g roughly chopped parsley
60g self-raising flour

60g all-purpose flour
½ tsp baking powder
Salt and black pepper

DIRECTIONS

In a bowl, add corn, eggs, parsley and onion, and season with salt and pepper; mix well to combine. Sift flour and baking powder into the bowl and stir. Line the air fryer's basket with baking paper and spoon batter dollops, making sure they are separated by at least an inch. Work in batches if needed.

Cook for 10 minutes at 200 C, turning once halfway through. Serve with sour cream and chopped scallions.

317. Air Fried Halloumi with Veggies

Total Time: 15 min | **Serves**: 2 | **Per serving**: Calories: 411; Carbs: 32.5g; Fat: 25.5g; Protein: 21g

INGREDIENTS

6 oz block of firm halloumi cheese, cubed

2 courgatte, cut into even chunks
1 large carrot, cut into chunks

1 large aubergine, peeled, cut into chunks

2 tsp olive oil

1 tsp dried mixed herbs

Salt and black pepper

DIRECTIONS

In a bowl, add halloumi, zucchini, carrot, eggplant, olive oil, herbs, salt and pepper. Sprinkle with oil, salt and pepper. Arrange halloumi and veggies in the air fryer and cook for 14 minutes at 175 C. When ready, make sure the veggies are tender and the halloumi is golden. Sprinkle with olive oil and scatter with fresh arugula leaves.

318. Vegetables Tacos

Total Time: 30 min | Serves: 3 | Per serving: Calories: 440; Carbs: 52g; Fat: 11.5g; Protein: 33.5g

INGREDIENTS

3 soft taco shells
180g kidney beans, drained
180g black beans, drained
120g tomato puree

1 fresh jalapeño chili, chopped
40g fresh coriander, chopped
170g corn kernels
½ tsp ground cumin

½ tsp cayenne pepper
Salt and black pepper
240g grated mozzarella cheese
Guacamole to serve

DIRECTIONS

In a bowl, add beans, beans, tomato puree, chili, cilantro, corn, cumin, cayenne, salt and pepper; stir well. Spoon the mixture onto one half of the taco, sprinkle the cheese over the top and fold over. Spray the basket, and lay the tacos inside. Cook for 14 minutes at 180 C, until the cheese melts. Serve hot with guacamole.

319. Tempura Veggies with Sesame Soy Sauce

Total Time: 20 min | Serves: 4 | Per serving: Calories: 287; Carbs: 55g; Fat: 6.3g; Protein: 8g

INGREDIENTS

2 lb chopped veggies: carrot, parsnip, green beans, courgatte, onion rings, asparagus, cauliflower

Dipping sauce:
4 tbsp soy sauce
Juice of 1 lemon

200g plain flour
Salt and black pepper
1 ½ tbsp vegan cornstarch

½ tsp sesame oil
½ tsp sugar

180 ml cold water
Cooking spray

½ garlic clove, chopped
½ tsp sweet chili sauce

DIRECTIONS

Line the air fryer's basket with baking paper. In a bowl, mix flour, salt, pepper and cornstarch; whisk to combine.

Keep whisking as you add water into the dry ingredients so a smooth batter is formed. Dip each veggie piece into the batter and place into your air fryer. Cook for 12 minutes at 180 C, turning once halfway through; cook until crispy. For the dipping sauce, mix all ingredients in a bowl.

320. Air-Fried Cauliflower

Total Time: 20 min | Serves: 4 | Per serving: Calories: 76; Carbs: 3.3g; Fat: 7.1g; Protein: 1.4g

INGREDIENTS

1 head of cauliflower, cut into florets

2 tbsp extra-virgin olive oil

½ tsp salt and ground black pepper

DIRECTIONS

In a bowl, toss cauliflower, oil, salt, and black pepper, until the florets are well-coated. Arrange the florets in the air fryer and cook for 8 minutes at 180 C; work in batches if needed. Serve the crispy cauliflower in lettuce wraps with chicken, cheese or mushrooms.

321. Polenta Fries

Total Time: 80 min | **Serves**: 4 | **Per serving**: Calories: 122; Carbs: 16g; Fat: 4.1g; Protein: 5.4g

INGREDIENTS

450 ml water
450 ml milk
150g instant polenta
Salt and black pepper
Cooking spray
Fresh thyme, chopped

DIRECTIONS

Line a tray with paper. Pour water and milk into a saucepan and let it simmer. Keep whisking as you pour in the polenta. Continue to whisk until polenta thickens and bubbles; season to taste.

Add polenta into the lined tray and spread out. Refrigerate for 45 minutes. Slice the cold, set polenta into batons and spray with oil. Arrange polenta chips into the air fryer basket and cook for 16 minutes at 190 C, turning once halfway through. Make sure the fries are golden and crispy.

322. Air-Fried Falafel

Total Time: 25 min | **Serves**: 6 | **Per serving**: Calories: 145; Carbs: 24.2g; Fat: 2.1g; Protein: 8.4g

INGREDIENTS

340g cooked chickpeas
50g chickpea flour
30g fresh parsley, chopped
Juice of 1 lemon
4 garlic cloves, chopped
1 onion, chopped
2 tsp ground cumin
2 tsp ground coriander
1 tsp chili powder
Salt and black pepper
Cooking spray

DIRECTIONS

In a blender, add chickpeas, flour, parsley, lemon juice, garlic, onion, cumin, coriander, chili, turmeric, salt and pepper, and blend until well-combined but not too battery; there should be some lumps. Shape the mixture into 15 balls and press them with hands, making sure they are still around.

Spray them with oil and arrange them in a paper-lined air fryer basket; work in batches if needed. Cook at 180 C for 14 minutes, turning once halfway through. They should be crunchy and golden.

323. Teriyaki Cauliflower

Total Time: 20 min | **Serves**: 4 | **Per serving**: Calories: 147; Carbs: 18.2g; Fat: 7.1g; Protein: 3.4g

INGREDIENTS

1 cauliflower head, cut into florets
130g soy sauce
3 tbsp brown sugar
1 tsp sesame oil
100 ml water
½ chili powder
2 cloves garlic, chopped
1 tsp cornstarch

DIRECTIONS

In a measuring cup, whisk soy sauce, sugar, sesame oil, water, chili powder, garlic and cornstarch, until smooth. In a bowl, add cauliflower, and pour teriyaki sauce over the top, toss with hands until well-coated.

Take the cauliflower to the air fryer's basket and cook for 14 minutes at 175 C, turning once halfway through. When ready, check if the cauliflower is cooked but not too soft. Serve with rice and edamame beans!

324. Sweet Potato French Fries

Total Time: 30 min | **Serves**: 4 | **Per serving**: Calories: 176; Carbs: 20.3g; Fat: 10.1g; Protein: 1.6g

INGREDIENTS

- ½ tsp salt
- ½ tsp garlic powder
- ½ tsp chili powder
- ¼ tsp cumin
- 3 tbsp olive oil
- 3 sweet potatoes, cut into thick strips

DIRECTIONS

In a bowl, mix salt, garlic powder, chili powder, and cumin, and whisk in oil. Coat the strips well in this mixture and arrange them in the air fryer's basket, without overcrowding. Cook for 20 minutes at 190 C, or until crispy.

325. Spicy Mixed Veggie Bites

Total Time: 1 hr 30 min | **Serves**: 13 to 16 bites | **Per serving**: Calories: 160; Carbs: 3g; Fat: 8g; Protein: 3g

INGREDIENTS

- 1 medium cauliflower, cut in florets
- 6 medium carrots, diced
- 1 medium broccoli, cut in florets
- 1 onion, diced
- 70g garden peas
- 2 leeks, sliced thinly
- 1 small courgatte, chopped
- 50g flour
- 1 tbsp garlic paste
- 2 tbsp olive oil
- 1 tbsp curry paste
- 2 tsp mixed spice
- 1 tsp coriander
- 1 tsp cumin powder
- 400 ml milk
- 1 tsp ginger paste
- Salt and pepper to taste

DIRECTIONS

In a pot, steam all vegetables, except the leek and courgette, for 10 minutes; set aside. Place a wok over medium heat, and add the onion, ginger, garlic and olive oil. Stir-fry until onions turn transparent. Add in leek, zucchini and curry paste. Stir and cook for 5 minutes. Add all spices and milk; stir and simmer for 10 minutes.

Once the sauce has reduced, add the steamed veggies; mix evenly. Transfer to a bowl and refrigerate for 1 hour. Remove the veggie base from the fridge and mold into bite sizes. Arrange the veggie bites in the fryer basket and cook at 175 C for 10 minutes. Once ready, serve warm with yogurt sauce.

326. Brussels Sprouts with Garlic Aioli

Total Time: 25 min | **Serves**: 4 | **Per serving**: Calories: 42; Carbs: 0g; Fat: 2.6g; Protein: 4.9g

INGREDIENTS

- 1 lb brussels sprouts, trimmed and excess leaves removed
- Salt and pepper to taste
- 1 ½ tbsp olive oil
- 2 tsp lemon juice
- 1 tsp powdered chili
- 3 cloves garlic
- 180g mayonnaise, whole egg
- 450 ml water

DIRECTIONS

Place a skillet over medium heat on a stovetop, add the garlic cloves with the peels on it and roast until lightly brown and fragrant. Remove the skillet and place a pot with water over the same heat; bring to a boil.

Using a knife, cut the brussels sprouts in halves lengthwise. Add to the boiling water to blanch for just 3 minutes. Drain through a sieve and set aside. Preheat the air fryer to 175 C. Remove the garlic from the skillet to a plate; peel, crush and set aside. Add olive oil to the skillet and light the fire to medium heat on the stovetop.

Stir in the brussels sprouts, season with pepper and salt; sauté for 2 minutes and turn off the heat. Pour the brussels sprouts in the fryer's basket and cook for 5 minutes.

Meanwhile, make the garlic aioli. In a bowl, add mayonnaise, crushed garlic, lemon juice, powdered chili, pepper and salt; mix well. Remove the brussels sprouts onto a serving bowl and serve with the garlic aioli.

327. Cheesy Stuffed Peppers

Total Time: 40 min | **Serves**: 4 | **Per serving**: Calories: 115; Carbs: 0g; Fat: 16g; Protein: 13g

INGREDIENTS

4 green peppers
Salt and pepper to taste
120 ml olive oil
1 red onion, chopped
1 large tomato, chopped
120g crumbled Goat cheese
320g cauliflower, chopped
2 tbsp grated Parmesan cheese
2 tbsp chopped basil
1 tbsp lemon zest

DIRECTIONS

Preheat the air fryer to 175 C, and cut the peppers a quarter way from the head down and lengthwise. Remove the membrane and seeds. Season the peppers with pepper, salt, and drizzle olive oil over.

Place the pepper bottoms in the fryer's basket and cook them for 5 minutes to soften a little bit.

In a mixing bowl, add the tomatoes, goat cheese, lemon zest, basil, and cauliflower; season with salt and pepper, and mix well. Remove the bottoms from the air fryer to a flat surface and spoon the cheese mixture into them.

Sprinkle Parmesan cheese on top of each and gently place in the basket; cook for 15 minutes. Serve warm.

328. Cheesy Mushroom and Cauliflower Balls

Total Time: 50 min | **Serves**: 4 | **Per serving**: Calories: 115; Carbs: 4.1g; Fat: 8.6g; Protein: 5.6g

INGREDIENTS

½ lb mushrooms, diced
3 tbsp olive oil
1 small red onion, chopped
3 cloves garlic, minced
200g cauliflower, chopped
2 tbsp chicken stock
120g breadcrumbs
90g Grana Padano cheese
60 ml coconut oil
2 sprigs chopped fresh thyme
Salt and pepper to taste

DIRECTIONS

Place a skillet over medium heat on a stovetop. Add olive oil, once heated, sauté garlic and onion, until translucent.

Add the mushrooms, stir-fry for 4 minutes; add the cauliflower and stir-fry for 5 minutes. Pour in the stock, thyme, and simmer until the cauliflower has absorbed the stock. Add Grana Padano cheese, pepper, and salt.

Stir and turn off the heat. Allow the mixture cool and make bite-size balls of the mixture. Place them on a plate and refrigerate for 30 minutes to harden. Preheat the air fryer to 175 C.

In a bowl, add the breadcrumbs and coconut oil and mix well. Remove the mushroom balls from the refrigerator, stir the breadcrumb mixture again, and roll the balls in the breadcrumb mixture.

Place the balls in the air fryer's basket without overcrowding, and cook for 15 minutes, tossing every 5 minutes for an even cook. Repeat until all the mushroom balls are fried. Serve with sautéed zoodles and tomato sauce.

329. Curried Cauliflower Florets

Total Time: 34 min | **Serves**: 4 | **Per serving**: Calories: 123; Carbs: 2g; Fat: 11g; Protein: 5g

INGREDIENTS

1 large cauliflower head
Salt to taste
1 ½ tbsp curry powder

100 ml olive oil

50g fried pine nuts

DIRECTIONS

Preheat the air fryer to 195 C, and mix the pine nuts and 1 tsp of olive oil, in a medium bowl. Pour them in the air fryer's basket and cook for 2 minutes; remove to cool.

Place the cauliflower on a cutting board. Use a knife to cut them into 1-inch florets. Place them in a large mixing bowl. Add the curry powder, salt, and the remaining olive oil; mix well. Place the cauliflower florets in the fryer's basket in 2 batches, and cook each batch for 10 minutes. Remove the curried florets onto a serving platter, sprinkle with the pine nuts, and toss. Serve the florets with tomato sauce or as a side to a meat dish.

330. Roasted Rosemary Squash

Total Time: 30 min | **Serves**: 2 | **Per serving**: Calories: 123; Carbs: 25.7g; Fat: 0.2g; Protein: 1.3g

INGREDIENTS

1 butternut squash
1 tbsp dried rosemary
Cooking spray
Salt to season

DIRECTIONS

Place the butternut squash on a cutting board and peel it; cut it in half and remove the seeds. Cut the pulp into wedges and season with salt.

Preheat the air fryer to 175 C, spray the squash wedges with cooking spray and sprinkle with rosemary. Grease the fryer's basket with cooking spray and place the wedges inside it without overlapping. Slide the fryer basket back in and cook for 20 minutes, flipping once halfway through. Serve with maple syrup and goat cheese.

331. Eggplant Gratin with Mozzarella Crust

Total Time: 30 min | **Serves**: 2 to 3 | **Per serving**: Calories: 317; Carbs: 2g; Fat: 16.83g; Protein: 12g

INGREDIENTS

100g cubed aubergine
80g chopped red pepper
80g chopped green pepper
20g chopped onion
80g chopped tomatoes
1 clove garlic, minced
1 tbsp sliced pimiento-stuffed olives
1 tsp capers
¼ tsp dried basil
¼ tsp dried marjoram
Salt and pepper to taste
Cooking spray
60g grated mozzarella cheese
1 tbsp breadcrumbs

DIRECTIONS

Preheat the air fryer to 150 C, and in a bowl, add the eggplant, green pepper, red pepper, onion, tomatoes, olives, garlic, basil marjoram, capers, salt, and pepper. Lightly grease a baking dish with the olive oil cooking spray.

Ladle the eggplant mixture into the baking dish and level it using the vessel. Sprinkle the mozzarella cheese on top and cover with the breadcrumbs. Place the dish in the air fryer and cook for 20 minutes. Serve with rice.

332. Three Veg Bake

Total Time: 30 min | **Serves**: 3 | **Per serving**: Calories: 50; Carbs: 4g; Fat: 2g; Protein: 2g

INGREDIENTS

3 turnips, sliced
1 large red onion, cut into rings
1 large courgatte, sliced
Salt and pepper to taste
2 cloves garlic, crushed
1 bay leaf, cut in 6 pieces

1 tbsp olive oil

Cooking spray

DIRECTIONS

Place the turnips, onion, and zucchini in a bowl. Toss with olive oil and season with salt and pepper.

Preheat the air fryer to 170 C, and place the veggies into a baking pan that fits in the air fryer. Slip the bay leaves in the different parts of the slices and tuck the garlic cloves in between the slices.

Insert the pan in the air fryer's basket and cook for 15 minutes. Serve warm with as a side to a meat dish or salad.

333. Easy Roast Winter Vegetable Delight

Total Time: 30 min | **Serves**: 2 | **Per serving**: Calories: 50; Carbs: 5g; Fat: 3g; Protein: 2g

INGREDIENTS

1 parsnip, peeled and sliced into 2-inch thickness
170g chopped butternut squash
2 small red onions, cut in wedges
100g chopped celery
1 tbsp chopped fresh thyme
Salt and pepper to taste
2 tsp olive oil

DIRECTIONS

Preheat the air fryer to 200 C, and in a bowl, add turnip, squash, red onions, celery, thyme, pepper, salt, and olive oil; mix well. Pour the vegetables into the fryer's basket and cook for 16 minutes, tossing once halfway through.

334. Potato, Eggplant, and Zucchini Chips

Total Time: 45 min | **Serves**: 4 | **Per serving**: Calories: 120; Carbs: 6g; Fat: 3.5g; Protein: 3g

INGREDIENTS

1 large aubergine
5 potatoes
3 courgatte
60g cornstarch
120ml water
100ml olive oil
Salt to season

DIRECTIONS

Preheat the air fryer to 195 C, and cut the eggplant and zucchini in long 3-inch strips. Peel and cut the potatoes into 3-inch strips; set aside. In a bowl, stir in cornstarch, water, salt, pepper, oil, eggplants, zucchini, and potatoes.

Place one-third of the veggie strips in the fryer's basket and cook them for 12 minutes. Once ready, transfer them to a serving platter. Repeat the cooking process for the remaining veggie strips. Serve warm.

335. Stuffed Mushrooms with Bacon & Cheese

Total Time: 20 min | **Serves**: 2 | **Per serving**: Calories: 188; Carbs: 5g; Fat: 10.5g; Protein: 4.7g

INGREDIENTS

14 small button mushrooms
1 clove garlic, minced
Salt and pepper to taste
4 slices bacon, chopped
60g grated Cheddar cheese
1 tbsp olive oil
1 tbsp chopped parsley

DIRECTIONS

Preheat the air fryer to 195 C, and in a bowl, add the oil, bacon, cheddar cheese, parsley, salt, pepper, and garlic. Mix well with a spoon. Cut the stalks of the mushroom off and fill each cup with the bacon mixture.

Press the bacon mixture into the caps to avoid falling off. Place the stuffed mushrooms in the fryer's basket and cook at 195 C for 8 minutes. Once golden and crispy, plate them and serve with a green salad.

336. Tomato Sandwiches with Feta and Pesto

Total Time: 60 min | **Serves**: 2 | **Per serving**: Calories: 241; Carbs: 11g; Fat: 24g; Protein: 12g

INGREDIENTS

1 heirloom tomato
1 (4-oz) block feta cheese
1 small red onion, thinly sliced
1 clove garlic
Salt to taste
2 tsp + 60ml olive oil
1 ½ tbsp toasted pine nuts
20g chopped parsley
30g grated Parmesan cheese
10g chopped basil

DIRECTIONS

Add basil, pine nuts, garlic and salt to a food processor. Process while adding the ¼ cup of olive oil slowly. Once the oil is finished, pour the basil pesto into a bowl and refrigerate for 30 minutes. Preheat the air fryer to 195 C.

Slice the feta cheese and tomato into ½ inch circular slices. Use a kitchen towel to pat the tomatoes dry. Remove the pesto from the fridge and use a tablespoon to spread some pesto on each slice of tomato. Top with a slice of feta cheese. Add the onion and remaining olive oil in a bowl and toss. Spoon on top of feta cheese.

Place the tomato in the fryer's basket and cook for 12 minutes. Remove to a serving platter, sprinkle lightly with salt and top with the remaining pesto. Serve with a side of rice or lean meat.

337. Italian Style Tofu

Total Time: 30 min | **Serves**: 2 | **Per serving**: Calories: 287; Carbs: 8.4g; Fat: 18.4g; Protein: 10g

INGREDIENTS

6 oz extra firm tofu
pepper to season
1 tbsp vegetable broth
1 tbsp soy sauce
⅓ tsp dried oregano
⅓ tsp garlic powder
⅓ tsp dried basil
⅓ tsp onion powder

DIRECTIONS

Place the tofu on a cutting board, and cut it into 3 lengthwise slices with a knife. Line a side of the cutting board with paper towels, place the tofu on it and cover with paper towel. Use your hands to press the tofu gently until as much liquid has been extracted from it.

Remove the paper towels and use a knife to chop the tofu into 8 cubes; set aside. In another bowl, add the soy sauce, vegetable broth, oregano, basil, garlic powder, onion powder, and black pepper; mix well with a spoon.

Pour the spice mixture on the tofu, stir the tofu until well coated; set aside to marinate for 10 minutes. Preheat the air fryer to 195 C, and arrange the tofu in the fryer's basket, in a single layer; cook for 10 minutes, flipping it at the 6-minute mark. Remove to a plate and serve with green salad.

338. Two-Cheese Vegetable Frittata

Total Time: 35 min | **Serves**: 2 | **Per serving**: Calories: 203; Carbs: 9.3g; Fat: 15.2g; Protein: 6.4g

INGREDIENTS

30g baby spinach
50g sliced mushrooms
1 large courgatte, sliced with a 1-inch thickness
1 small red onion, sliced
20g chopped chives
¼ lb asparagus, trimmed and sliced thinly
2 tsp olive oil
4 eggs, cracked into a bowl
100 ml milk
Salt and pepper to taste

50g grated Cheddar cheese

50g crumbled Feta cheese

DIRECTIONS

Preheat the air fryer to 160 C and line a 6 x 6 inches baking dish with parchment paper; set aside. In the egg bowl, add milk, salt, and pepper; beat evenly. Place a skillet over medium heat on a stovetop, and heat olive oil.

Add the asparagus, zucchini, onion, mushrooms, and baby spinach; stir-fry for 5 minutes. Pour the veggies into the baking dish and top with the egg mixture. Sprinkle feta and cheddar cheese over and place in the air fryer.

Cook for 15 minutes. Remove the baking dish and garnish with fresh chives.

339. Nutty Pumpkin with Blue Cheese

Total Time: 30 min | **Serve**: 1 | **Per serving**: Calories: 495; Carbs: 29g; Fat: 27g; Protein: 9g

INGREDIENTS

½ small pumpkin
2 oz blue cheese, cubed
2 tbsp pine nuts

1 tbsp olive oil
½ cup baby spinach, packed
1 spring onion, sliced

1 radish, thinly sliced
1 tsp vinegar

DIRECTIONS

Preheat the air fryer to 170 C, and place the pine nuts in a baking dish to toast them for 5 minutes; set aside. Peel the pumpkin and chop it into small pieces. Place in the baking dish and toss with the olive oil. Increase the temperature to 195 C and cook the pumpkin for 20 minutes.

Place the pumpkin in a serving bowl. Add baby spinach, radish and spring onion; toss with the vinegar. Stir in the cubed blue cheese and top with the toasted pine nuts, to serve.

340. Chili Bean Burritos

Total Time: 30 min | **Serves**: 6 | **Per serving**: Calories: 248; Carbs: 25g; Fat: 8.7g; Protein: 9g

INGREDIENTS

6 tortillas
120g grated Cheddar cheese

1 can (8 oz) beans
1 tsp seasoning, any kind

DIRECTIONS

Preheat the air fryer to 175 C, and mix the beans with the seasoning. Divide the bean mixture between the tortillas and top with cheddar cheese. Roll the burritos and arrange them on a lined baking dish.

Place in the air fryer and cook for 5 minutes, or to your liking.

341. Veggie Meatballs

Total Time: 30 min | **Serves**: 3 | **Per serving**: Calories: 288; Carbs: 32g; Fat: 21g; Protein: 6g

INGREDIENTS

2 tbsp olive oil
2 tbsp soy sauce
1 tbsp flax meal
340g cooked chickpeas

30g sweet onion, diced
50g grated carrots
80g roasted cashews
Juice of 1 lemon

½ tsp turmeric
1 tsp cumin
1 tsp garlic powder
100g rolled oats

DIRECTIONS

Combine the oil, onions, and carrots into a baking dish and cook them in the air fryer for 6 minutes at 175 C.

Meanwhile, ground the oats and cashews in a food processor. Place them in a large bowl. Process the chickpeas with the lemon juice and soy sauce, until smooth. Add them to the bowl as well.

Add onions and carrots to the bowl with chickpeas. Stir in the remaining ingredients; mix until fully incorporated. Make meatballs out of the mixture. Increase the temperature to 185 C and cook for 12 minutes.

342. Eggplant Cheeseburger

Total Time: 10 min | **Serve**: 1 | **Per serving**: Calories: 399: Carbs: 21g; Fat: 17g; Protein: 8g

INGREDIENTS

- 1 hamburger bun
- 2-inch aubergine slice, cut along the round axis
- 1 mozzarella slice
- 1 red onion cut into 3 rings
- 1 lettuce leaf
- ½ tbsp tomato sauce
- 1 pickle, sliced

DIRECTIONS

Preheat the air fryer to 170 C, and place the eggplant slice to roast for 6 minutes. Place the mozzarella slice on top of the eggplant and cook for 30 more seconds. Spread the tomato sauce on one half of the bun.

Place the lettuce leaf on top of the sauce. Place the cheesy eggplant on top of the lettuce. Top with onion rings and pickles, and then with the other bun half and enjoy.

343. Cheesy Broccoli with Eggs

Total Time: 15 min | **Serves**: 4 | **Per serving**: Calories: 265: Carbs: 19g; Fat: 23g; Protein: 26g

INGREDIENTS

- 1 lb broccoli
- 4 eggs
- 90g cheese, shredded
- 240g cream
- 1 pinch nutmeg
- 1 tsp ginger powder
- salt and pepper to taste

DIRECTIONS

Steam the broccoli for 5 minutes. Then drain them and add 1 egg, cream, nutmeg, ginger, salt and pepper. Butter small ramekins and spread the mixture. Sprinkle the shredded cheese on top. Cook for 10 minutes at 140 C.

344. Air-Fried Sweet Potato

Total Time: 30min | **Serves**: 4 | **Per serving**: Calories: 111; Carbs: 12.3g; Fat: 3.8g; Protein: 8.9g

INGREDIENTS

- ½ tsp garlic powder
- ½ tsp cayenne pepper
- ¼ tsp cumin
- 3 tbsp olive oil
- 3 sweet potatoes, cut into ½-inch thick wedges
- A handful of chopped fresh parsley
- Sea salt

DIRECTIONS

In a bowl, mix salt, garlic powder, chili powder, and cumin. Whisk in oil, and coat the potatoes. Arrange in the air fryer, without overcrowding, and cook for 20 minutes at 190 C; toss regularly to get the crispy on all sides. Sprinkle with parsley and sea salt, and serve!

345. Crunchy Parmesan Zucchini

Total Time: 40 min | **Serves**: 4 | **Per serving**: Calories: 369: Carbs: 14g; Fat: 12g; Protein: 9.5g

INGREDIENTS

4 small courgatte cut lengthwise
50g grated Parmesan cheese
60g breadcrumbs
60g melted butter
20g chopped parsley
4 garlic cloves, minced
Salt and pepper, to taste

DIRECTIONS

Preheat the air fryer to 175 C, and in a bowl, mix the breadcrumbs, Parmesan cheese, garlic, and parsley. Season with salt and pepper, to taste; stir in the melted butter. Arrange the zucchinis with the cut side up.

Spread the mixture onto the zucchini evenly. Place half of the zucchinis in the air fryer and cook for 13 minutes.

Increase the temperature to 185 C, and cook for 3 more minutes for extra crunchiness. Repeat, and serve hot.

346. Spinach and Feta Crescent Triangles

Total Time: 20 min | **Serves**: 4 | **Per serving**: Calories: 178; Carbs: 10.8g; Fat: 11.9g; Protein: 8g

INGREDIENTS

14 oz store-bought crescent dough
220g steamed spinach
150g crumbled Feta cheese
¼ tsp garlic powder
1 tsp chopped oregano
¼ tsp salt

DIRECTIONS

Preheat the air fryer to 175 C, and roll the dough onto a lightly floured flat surface. Combine the feta, spinach, oregano, salt, and garlic powder together in a bowl. Cut the dough into 4 equal pieces.

Divide the spinach/feta mixture between the dough pieces. Make sure to place the filling in the center. Fold the dough and secure with a fork. Place onto a lined baking dish, and then in the air fryer. Cook for 12 minutes, until lightly browned.

347. Feta Cheese Triangles

Total Time: 20 min | **Serves**: 4 | **Per serving**: Calories: 254; Carbs: 21g; Fat: 19g; Protein: 21g

INGREDIENTS

4 oz feta cheese
2 sheets filo pastry
1 egg yolk
2 tbsp parsley, finely chopped
1 scallion, finely chopped
2 tbsp olive oil
Salt and black pepper to taste

DIRECTIONS

In a large bowl, beat the yolk and mix with the cheese, the chopped parsley and scallion. Season with salt and black pepper. Cut each filo sheet in three parts or strips. Put a teaspoon of the feta mixture on the bottom.

Roll the strip in a spinning spiral way until the filling of the inside mixture is completely wrapped in a triangle. Preheat the air fryer to 180 C, and brush the surface of the filo with oil. Place up to 5 triangles in the Air frier's basket and cook for 5 minutes. Lower the temperature to 170 C, cook for 3 more minutes or until golden brown.

348. Eggplant Caviar

Total Time: 20 min | **Serves**: 3 | **Per serving**: Calories: 125; Carbs: 12g; Fat: 3g; Protein: 2g

INGREDIENTS

3 medium aubergine
½ red onion, chopped and blended
2 tbsp balsamic vinegar
1 tbsp olive oil
Salt to taste

DIRECTIONS

Arrange the eggplants in the basket and cook them for 15 minutes at 190 C. Remove them and let them cool. Then cut the eggplants in half, lengthwise, and empty their insides with a spoon.

Blend the onion in a blender. Put the inside of the eggplants in the blender and process everything. Add the vinegar, olive oil and salt, then blend again. Serve cool with bread and tomato sauce or ketchup.

349. Ratatouille

Total Time: 30 min | Serves: 2 | Per serving: Calories: 171; Carbs: 25.8g; Fat: 7.8g; Protein: 4.2g

INGREDIENTS

1 tbsp olive oil
3 Roma tomatoes, thinly sliced
2 garlic cloves, minced
1 courgatte, thinly sliced
2 yellow bell peppers, sliced
1 tbsp vinegar
2 tbsp herbs de Provence
Salt and pepper, to taste

DIRECTIONS

Preheat the air fryer to 195 C, and place all ingredients in a bowl. Season with salt and pepper, and stir until the veggies are well coated. Arrange the vegetable in a round baking dish and place in the air fryer. Cook for 15 minutes, shaking occasionally. Let sit for 5 more minutes after the timer goes off.

350. Cheesy Spinach Enchiladas

Total Time: 20 min | Serves: 4 | Per serving: Calories: 356; Carbs: 43g; Fat: 27g; Protein: 21g

INGREDIENTS

8 corn tortillas
180g shredded cheese
220g Ricotta cheese
1 package frozen spinach
1 garlic clove, minced
60g sliced onions
120g sour cream
1 tbsp butter
1 can enchilada sauce

DIRECTIONS

In a saucepan, heat oil and sauté garlic and onion, until brown. Stir in the frozen spinach and cook for 5 more minutes. Remove from the heat and stir in the ricotta cheese, sour cream and the shredded cheese.

Warm the tortillas on low heat for 15 seconds in the air fryer. Spoon ¼ cup of spinach mixture in the middle of a tortilla. Roll up and place seam side down in the air fryer's basket. Pour the enchilada sauce over the tortillas and sprinkle with the remaining cheese. Cook for 15 minutes at 190 C.

351. Chile Relleno

Total Time: 35 min | Serves: 4 | Per serving: Calories: 269; Carbs: 35.3g; Fat: 15.5g; Protein: 23.8g

INGREDIENTS

2 cans green chili peppers
120g Cheddar cheese, shredded
120g Monterey Jack cheese.
2 tbsp all-purpose flour
2 large eggs, beaten
120 ml milk
1 can tomato sauce

DIRECTIONS

Preheat the air fryer to 190 C, and spray a baking dish with cooking spray. Take half of the chilies and arrange them in the baking dish. Top with half of the cheese and cover with the other half of the chilies.

In a medium bowl, combine the eggs, the milk, the flour and pour the mixture over the chilies. Cook for 20 minutes. Remove the chilies from the air fryer and pour the tomato sauce over them; cook for more 15 minutes.

Remove from the air fryer and top with the remaining cheese.

352. Cabbage Steaks

Total Time: 25 min | **Serves**: 3 | **Per serving**: Calories: 161; Carbs: 17.5g; Fat: 10g; Protein: 4.6g

INGREDIENTS

1 cabbage head
1 tbsp garlic stir-in paste
1 tsp salt
2 tbsp olive oil
½ tsp black pepper
2 tsp fennel seeds

DIRECTIONS

Preheat the air fryer to 175 C, and slice the cabbage into 1 ½-inch slice. In a small bowl, combine all the other ingredients; brush cabbage with the mixture. Arrange the cabbage steaks in the air fryer and cook for 15 minutes.

353. Cauliflower Rice with Tofu

Total Time: 30 min | **Serves**: 4 | **Per serving**: Calories: 137; Carbs: 19.7g; Fat: 4g; Protein: 10.2g

INGREDIENTS

Tofu:
½ block tofu
30g diced onion
2 tbsp soy sauce
1 tsp turmeric
100g diced carrot

Cauliflower:
200g cauliflower rice (pulsed in a food processor)
2 tbsp soy sauce
100g chopped broccoli
2 garlic cloves, minced
1 ½ tsp toasted sesame oil
1 tbsp minced ginger
70g frozen peas
1 tbsp rice vinegar

DIRECTIONS

Preheat the air fryer to 185 C, crumble the tofu and combine it with all tofu ingredients. Place in a baking dish and air fry for 10 minutes. Place all cauliflower ingredients in a large bowl; mix to combine well.

Add the cauliflower mixture to the tofu and stir to combine; cook for 12 minutes. Serve and enjoy.

354. Vegetable Spring Rolls

Total Time: 15 min | **Serves**: 4 | **Per serving**: Calories: 169; Carbs: 32.3g; Fat: 2.3g; Protein: 5.5g

INGREDIENTS

½ cabbage, grated
2 carrots, grated
1 tsp minced ginger
1 tsp minced garlic
1 tsp sesame oil
1 tsp soy sauce
1 tsp sesame seeds
½ tsp salt
1 tsp olive oil
1 package spring roll wrappers

DIRECTIONS

Preheat the air fryer to 185 C, and combine all ingredients in a large bowl. Divide the mixture between the spring roll sheets, and roll them up. Arrange them on the greased frying basket and cook for 5-7 minutes until crispy.

355. Crispy Ham Rolls

Total Time: 20 min | Serves: 3 | Per serving: Calories: 246; Carbs: 41.7g; Fat: 21.5g; Protein: 18.7g

INGREDIENTS

1 lb chopped ham
3 packages Pepperidge farm rolls
1 tbsp softened butter
1 tsp mustard seeds
1 tsp poppy seeds
1 small chopped onion

DIRECTIONS

Mix butter, mustard, onion and poppy seeds. Spread the mixture on top of the rolls. Cover the bottom halves with the chopped ham. Arrange the rolls in the basket of the air fryer and cook at 175 C for 15 minutes.

356. Pineapple Appetizer Ribs

Total Time: 30 min | Serves: 4 | Per serving: Calories: 386; Carbs: 54.7g; Fat: 17.5g; Protein: 32.7g

INGREDIENTS

2 lb cut spareribs
7 oz salad dressing
5 oz can pineapple juice
450 ml water
Garlic salt
Salt and black pepper to taste

DIRECTIONS

Sprinkle the ribs with salt and pepper, and place them in a saucepan. Pour water and cook the ribs for 12 minutes on high heat. Drain the ribs and arrange them in the fryer; sprinkle with garlic salt. Bake for 15 minutes at 195 C.

Prepare the sauce by combining the salad dressing and the pineapple juice. Serve the ribs drizzled with the sauce.

357. Pasta with Roasted Veggies

Total Time: 25 min | Serves: 6 | Per serving: Calories: 391; Carbs: 64.4g; Fat: 14.4g; Protein: 9.5g

INGREDIENTS

1 lb penne, cooked
1 courgatte, sliced
1 pepper, sliced
1 acorn squash, sliced
4 oz mushrooms, sliced
90g kalamata olives, pitted and halved
60 ml olive oil
1 tsp Italian seasoning
200g grape tomatoes, halved
3 tbsp balsamic vinegar
2 tbsp chopped basil
Salt and pepper, to taste

DIRECTIONS

Preheat the air fryer to 190 C, and combine pepper, zucchini, squash, mushrooms, and olive oil, in a large bowl.

Season with salt and pepper. Air fry the veggies for 15 minutes. In a large bowl, combine penne, roasted vegetables, olives, tomatoes, Italian seasoning, and vinegar. Sprinkle basil and serve.

358. Parsley-Loaded Mushrooms

Total Time: 15 min | Serves: 2 | Per serving: Calories: 116; Carbs: 19g; Fat: 11g; Protein: 5g

INGREDIENTS

200g small mushrooms
2 slices white bread
1 garlic clove, crushed
2 tsp olive oil
2 tbsp parsley, finely chopped
Salt and black pepper

DIRECTIONS

Preheat the air fryer to 180 C, and in a food processor, grind the bread into very fine crumbs. Add garlic, parsley and pepper; mix and stir in the olive oil. Cut off the mushroom stalks and fill the caps with the breadcrumbs.

Pat the crumbs inside the caps to ensure there are no loose crumbs. Place the mushroom caps, one by one, inside the cooking basket and carefully slide them in the air fryer. Cook for 10 minutes or until golden and crispy.

359. Stuffed Mushrooms with Vegetables

Total Time: 15 min | **Serves**: 3 | **Per serving**: Calories: 111; Carbs: 12.3g; Fat: 3.8g; Protein: 8.9g

INGREDIENTS

3 portobello mushrooms
1 tomato, diced
1 small red onion, diced
1 green bell pepper, diced
120g grated mozzarella cheese
½ tsp garlic powder
¼ tsp pepper
¼ tsp salt

DIRECTIONS

Preheat the air fryer to 170 C, wash the mushrooms, remove the stems, and pat them dry. Coat with the olive oil.

Combine all remaining ingredients, except mozzarella, in a small bowl. Divide the filling between the mushrooms. Top the mushrooms with mozzarella. Place in the air fryer and cook for 8 minutes.

360. Air Fried Vegetables with Garlic

Total Time: 25 min | **Serves**: 6 | **Per serving**: Calories: 176; Carbs: 21.7g; Fat: 9g; Protein: 12.2g

INGREDIENTS

¾ lb green pepper
¾ lb tomatoes
1 medium onion
1 tbsp lemon juice
1 tbsp olive oil
½ tbsp salt
1 tbsp coriander powder

DIRECTIONS

Preheat the air fryer to 180 C, and line the peppers, the tomatoes and the onion in the basket. Cook for 5 minutes, then flip and cook for 5 more minutes. Remove them from the fryer and peel the skin. Place the vegetables in a blender and sprinkle with the salt and coriander powder. Blend to smooth and season with salt and olive oil.

361. Poblano and Tomato Stuffed Squash

Total Time: 50 min | **Serves**: 3 | **Per serving**: Calories: 98; Carbs: 8.2g; Fat: 5.3g; Protein: 4.3g

INGREDIENTS

½ butternut squash
6 grape tomatoes, halved
1 poblano pepper, cut into strips
120g grated mozzarella, optional
2 tsp olive oil divided
Salt and pepper, to taste

DIRECTIONS

Preheat the air fryer to 175 C, trim the ends and cut the squash lengthwise. You will only need one half for this recipe Scoop the flash out, so you make room for the filling. Brush 1 tsp. oil over the squash.

Place in the air fryer and roast for 30 minutes. Combine the other teaspoon of olive oil with the tomatoes and poblanos, season with salt and pepper, to taste. Place the peppers and tomatoes into the squash. Cook for 15 more minutes. If using mozzarella, add it on top of the squash, two minutes before the end.

362. Spicy Pepper, Sweet Potato Skewers

Total Time: 20 min | Serve: 1 | **Per serving**: Calories: 335; Carbs: 49.6g; Fat: 14.3g; Protein: 4.9g

INGREDIENTS

- 1 large sweet potato
- 1 beetroot
- 1 green bell pepper
- 1 tsp chili flakes
- ¼ tsp black pepper
- ½ tsp turmeric
- ¼ tsp garlic powder
- ¼ tsp paprika
- 1 tbsp olive oil

DIRECTIONS

Soak 3 to 4 skewers until ready to use. Preheat the air fryer to 175 C, peel the veggies and cut them into bite-sized chunks. Place the chunks in a bowl, along with the remaining ingredients; mix until fully coated.

Thread the veggies in this order: potato, pepper, beetroot. Place in the air fryer and cook for 15 minutes.

363. Grilled Tofu Sandwich

Total Time: 20 min | Serve: 1 | **Per serving**: Calories: 225; Carbs: 21.5g; Fat: 30.5g; Protein: 12.3g

INGREDIENTS

- 2 slices of bread
- 1-inch thick Tofu slice
- 30g red cabbage, shredded
- 2 tsp olive oil divided
- ¼ tsp vinegar
- Salt and pepper, to taste

DIRECTIONS

Preheat the air fryer to 175 C, add in the bread slices and toast for 3 minutes; set aside. Brush the tofu with 1 tsp. oil and place in the air fryer; grill for 5 minutes on each side. Combine the cabbage, remaining oil, and vinegar, and season with salt and pepper. Place the tofu on top of one bread slice, place the cabbage over, and top with the other bread slice. Serve and enjoy.

364. Quinoa and Veggie Stuffed Peppers

Total Time: 16 min | Serve: 1 | **Per serving**: Calories: 190; Carbs: 29.6g; Fat: 6.6g; Protein: 5.7g

INGREDIENTS

- 50g cooked quinoa
- 1 bell pepper
- ½ tbsp diced onion
- ½ diced tomato, plus one tomato slice
- ¼ tsp smoked paprika
- Salt and pepper, to taste
- 1 tsp olive oil
- ¼ tsp dried basil

DIRECTIONS

Preheat the air fryer to 175 C, core and clean the bell pepper to prepare it for stuffing. Brush the pepper with half of the olive oil on the outside. In a small bowl, combine all of the other ingredients, except the tomato slice and reserved half-teaspoon of olive oil.

Stuff the pepper with the filling and top with the tomato slice. Brush the tomato slice with the remaining half-teaspoon of olive oil and sprinkle with basil. Air fry for 10 minutes, until thoroughly cooked.

365. Tasty Baby Porcupine

Total Time: 30 min | **Serves**: 4 | **Per serving**: Calories: 255; Carbs: 31g; Fat: 15.5g; Protein: 19.5g

INGREDIENTS

70g rice
1 lb ground beef
1 tbsp minced onion
2 tbsp green bell peppers, finely chopped
1 tsp celery salt
2 tbsp Worcestershire sauce
1 clove garlic
450g tomato juice
1 tsp oregano

DIRECTIONS

Combine the rice, ground beef, onion, celery salt, green peppers and garlic. Shape into balls of 1-inch each.

Arrange the balls in the basket of the air fryer and cook for 25 minutes at 160 C. Heat the tomato juice, the cloves, the oregano and the Worcestershire sauce. Serve the balls warm with the sauce.

366. Avocado Rolls

Total Time: 15 min | Serves: 5 | Per serving: Calories: 270; Carbs: 24.7g; Fat: 18.7g; Protein: 5.8g

INGREDIENTS

3 ripe avocados, pitted and peeled
10 egg roll wrappers
1 tomato, diced
¼ tsp pepper
½ tsp salt

DIRECTIONS

Place all filling ingredients in a bowl; mash with a fork until somewhat smooth. There should be chunks left.

Divide the feeling between the egg wrappers. Wet your finger and brush along the edges, so the wrappers can seal well. Roll and seal the wrappers. Arrange them on a baking sheet lined dish, and place in the air fryer. Cook at 175 C, for 5 minutes. Serve with sweet chili dipping and enjoy.

367. Vegetable Tortilla Pizza

Total Time: 15 min | Serve: 1 | Per serving: Calories: 385; Carbs: 50.2g; Fat: 12.4g; Protein: 21.7g

INGREDIENTS

1 ½ tbsp tomato paste
60g grated Cheddar cheese
60g grated Mozzarella cheese
1 tbsp cooked sweet corn
4 courgatte slices
4 aubergine slices
4 red onion rings
½ green bell pepper, chopped
3 cherry tomatoes, quartered
1 tortilla
¼ tsp basil
¼ tsp oregano

DIRECTIONS

Preheat the air fryer to 175 C, and spread the tomato paste on the tortilla. Arrange the zucchini and eggplant slices first, then green peppers, and onion rings. Arrange the cherry tomatoes and sprinkle the sweet corn over.

Sprinkle with oregano and basil and top with cheddar and mozzarella. Place in the fryer and cook for 10 minutes.

368. Veggie Skewers

Total Time: 20 min | Serves: 4 | Per serving: Calories: 211; Carbs: 25g; Fat: 11.4g; Protein: 8g

INGREDIENTS

2 tbsp cornflour
180g canned beans
30g grated carrots
2 boiled and mashed potatoes
10g chopped fresh mint leaves
½ tsp garam masala powder
80g paneer
1 green chili
1-inch piece of fresh ginger
3 garlic cloves
Salt to taste

DIRECTIONS

Soak 12 skewers until ready to use. Preheat the air fryer to 195 C, and place the beans, carrots, garlic, ginger, chili, paneer, and mint, in a food processor; process until smooth, then transfer to a bowl.

Add the mashed potatoes, cornflour, some salt, and garam masala powder to the bowl; mix until fully incorporated. Divide the mixture into 12 equal pieces. Shape each of the pieces around a skewer. Cook skewers for 10 minutes.

369. Paneer Cutlet

Total Time: 15 min | Serve: 1 | **Per serving**: Calories: 567; Carbs: 21g; Fat: 23g; Protein: 19g

INGREDIENTS

330g grated paneer
120g grated cheese
½ tsp chai masala
1 tsp butter
½ tsp garlic powder
1 small onion, finely chopped
½ tsp oregano
½ tsp salt

DIRECTIONS

Preheat the air fryer to 175 C, and grease a baking dish. Mix all ingredients in a bowl, until well incorporated.

Make cutlets out of the mixture and place them on the greased baking dish. Place the baking dish in the air fryer and cook the cutlets for 10 minutes, until crispy.

370. Simple Air Fried Ravioli

Total Time: 15 min | **Serves**: 6 | **Per serving**: Calories: 298.8; Carbs: 42.1g; Fat: 8.7g; Protein: 13.4g

INGREDIENTS

1 package cheese ravioli
240g Italian breadcrumbs
30g Parmesan cheese
230g buttermilk
1 tsp olive oil
¼ tsp garlic powder

DIRECTIONS

Preheat the air fryer to 195 C, and in a small bowl, combine the breadcrumbs, Parmesan cheese, garlic powder, and olive oil. Dip the ravioli in the buttermilk and then coat them with the breadcrumb mixture.

Line a baking sheet with parchment paper and arrange the ravioli on it. Place in the air fryer and cook for 5 minutes. Serve the air-fried ravioli with marinara jar sauce.

371. Crispy Nachos

Total Time: 20 min | **Serves**: 2 | **Per serving**: Calories: 251; Carbs: 25g; Fat: 11.4g; Protein: 8g

INGREDIENTS

170g sweet corn
120g all-purpose flour
1 tbsp butter
½ tsp chili powder
3 tbsp water
salt

DIRECTIONS

Add a small amount of water to the sweet corn and grind until you obtain a very fine paste. In a large bowl, add the flour, salt, chili powder, butter and mix very well; add corn and stir well.

Start to knead with your palm until you obtain a stiff dough. Preheat the air fryer to 175 C.

Meanwhile, dust a little bit of flour and spread the dough with a rolling pin. Make it around ½ inch thick. Cut it in any shape you want and fry the shapes in the air fryer for around 10 minutes. Serve with guacamole salsa.

372. Cheesy Muffins

Total Time: 8 min | **Serves**: 3 | **Per serving**: Calories: 276; Carbs: 31g; Fat: 17g; Protein: 19g

INGREDIENTS

3 split english muffins, toasted
230g Cheddar cheese, smoked and shredded
1 mashed avocado
60g ranch-style salad dressing
180g alfalfa sprouts
1 tomato, chopped
1 sweet onion, chopped
40g sesame seeds, toasted

DIRECTIONS

Arrange the muffins open-faced in the air fryer's basket. Spread the mashed avocado on each half of the muffin. Place the halves close to each other. Cover the muffins with the sprouts, tomatoes, onion, dressing, sesame seeds and the cheese. Cook for 7-8 minutes at 175 C.

373. Roasted Vegetable Salad

Total Time: 25 min | **Serve**: 1 | **Per serving**: Calories: 263; Carbs: 21.4g; Fat: 12g; Protein: 10.7g

INGREDIENTS

1 potato, peeled and chopped
¼ onion, sliced
1 carrot, sliced diagonally
½ small beetroot, sliced
150g cherry tomatoes
Juice of 1 lemon
A handful of rocket salad
A handful of baby spinach
3 tbsp canned chickpeas
½ tsp cumin
½ tsp turmeric
¼ tsp sea salt
2 tbsp olive oil
Parmesan shavings

DIRECTIONS

Preheat the air fryer to 185 C, and combine the onion, potato, cherry tomatoes, carrot, beetroot, cumin, sea salt, turmeric, and 1 tbsp. olive oil, in a bowl. Place in the fryer and cook for 20 minutes; let cool for 2 minutes.

Place the rocket, salad, spinach, lemon juice, and 1 tbsp. olive oil, into a serving bowl; mix to combine. Stir in the roasted veggies. Top with chickpeas and Parmesan shavings.

374. Quick Crispy Cheese Lings

Total Time: 15 min | **Serves**: 4 | **Per serving**: Calories: 155; Carbs: 23.5g; Fat: 17.3g; Protein: 11.6g

INGREDIENTS

340g grated cheese, any
130g all-purpose flour
1 tbsp butter
1 tbsp baking powder
¼ tsp chili powder
¼ tsp salt, to taste
2 tbsp water

DIRECTIONS

In a bowl, mix the flour and the baking powder. Add the chili powder, salt, butter, cheese and 2 tbsp of water to the mixture. Make a stiff dough. Knead the dough for a while and sprinkle about 1 tbsp of flour on the table.

With a rolling pin, roll the dough into ½-inch thickness. Cut into any shape and cook for 6 minutes at 185 C.

375. Paneer Cheese Balls

Total Time: 12 min | **Serves**: 2 | **Per serving**: Calories: 257; Carbs: 31g; Fat: 22g; Protein: 16g

INGREDIENTS

2 oz paneer cheese
2 tbsp flour
2 medium onions, chopped
1 tbsp cornflour
1 green chili, chopped
1-inch ginger piece, chopped
1 tsp red chili powder
A few leaves of coriander, chopped
oil and salt

DIRECTIONS

Mix all ingredients, except the oil and cheese. Take a small part of the mixture, roll it up and slowly press it to flatten. Stuff in 1 cube of cheese and seal the edges. Repeat with the rest of the mixture. Fry the balls in the fryer for 12 minutes and at 185 C. Serve hot with ketchup!

376. Potato Filled Bread Rolls

Total Time: 25 min | Serves: 4 | Per serving: Calories: 451; Carbs: 93.5g; Fat: 5.2g; Protein: 14.2g

INGREDIENTS

8 bread slices
5 large potatoes, boiled and mashed
½ tsp turmeric
2 green chilies, deseeded and chopped
1 medium onion, finely chopped
½ tsp mustard seeds
1 tbsp olive oil
2 sprigs curry leaf
Salt, to taste

DIRECTIONS

Preheat the air fryer to 175 C, and combine the olive oil, onion, curry leaves, and mustard seed, in a baking dish. Air fry for 5 minutes. Mix the onion mixture with the mashed potatoes, chilies, turmeric, and some salt.

Divide the mixture into 8 equal pieces. Trim the sides of the bread, and wet with some water. Make sure to get rid of the excess water. Take one wet bread slice in your palm and place one of the potato pieces in the center. Roll the bread over the filling, sealing the edges. Place the rolls onto a prepared baking dish, and air fry for 12 minutes.

377. Delicious Potato Pancakes

Total Time: 15 min | Serves: 4 | Per serving: Calories: 255; Carbs: 42g; Fat: 8g; Protein: 7g

INGREDIENTS

4 potatoes, sauce and shredded
1 medium onion, chopped
1 beaten egg
60 ml milk
2 tbsp unsalted butter
½ tsp garlic powder
¼ tsp salt and black pepper
3 tbsp flour

DIRECTIONS

Preheat your air fryer to 195 C, and in a medium bowl, mix egg, potatoes, onion, milk, butter, black pepper, garlic powder and salt; add flour and form batter. Forms cakes about ¼ cup of batter. Place the cakes in the fryer's cooking basket and cook for 12 minutes. Serve and enjoy!

378. Drizzling Blooming Onion

Total Time: 20 min | Serves: 4 | Per serving: Calories: 324; Carbs: 20g; Fat: 26g; Protein: 3g

INGREDIENTS

2 lb cipollini onions, cut into flowers
olive oil as needed
1 tsp cayenne pepper
1 tsp garlic powder
270g flour
½ tsp pepper
1 tbsp paprika
½ tsp salt
1 tbsp ketchup
70g mayonnaise
60g sour cream

DIRECTIONS

In a bowl, mix salt, pepper, paprika, flour, garlic powder, and cayenne pepper. Add mayonnaise, ketchup, sour cream to the mixture and stir. Coat the onions with prepared mixture and spray with oil. Preheat your air fryer to 180 C. Add the coated onions to the basket and cook for 15 minutes.

379. Chickpeas & Spinach With Coconut

Total Time: 20 min | Serves: 4 | Per serving: Calories: 228; Carbs: 32g; Fat: 9g; Protein: 8g

INGREDIENTS

2 tbsp olive oil
1 tbsp pepper
1 onion, chopped
1 tsp salt

4 garlic cloves, minced
1 can coconut milk
1 tbsp ginger, minced
1 pound spinach

50g dried tomatoes, chopped
1 can chickpeas
1 lemon, juiced
1 hot pepper

DIRECTIONS

Preheat your air fryer to 185 C, and in a bowl, mix lemon juice, tomatoes, pepper, ginger, coconut milk, garlic, salt, hot pepper and onion. Rinse chickpeas under running water to get rid of all the gunk. Put them in a large bowl. Cover with spinach. Pour the sauce over, and stir in oil. Cook in the air fryer for 15 minutes. Serve warm.

380. Low-Calorie Beets Dish

Total Time: 20 min | Serves: 2 | Per serving: Calories: 149; Carbs: 5g; Fat: 1g; Protein: 30g

INGREDIENTS

4 beets, sauce and cubed
80 ml balsamic vinegar

1 tbsp olive oil
1 tbsp honey

Salt and pepper to taste
2 springs rosemary

DIRECTIONS

In a bowl, mix rosemary, pepper, salt, vinegar and honey. Cover beets with the prepared sauce and then coat with oil. Preheat your air fryer to 200 C, and cook the beets for 10 minutes. Pour the balsamic vinegar in a pan over medium heat; bring to a boil and cook until reduced by half. Drizzle the beets with balsamic glaze, to serve.

381. Parsnip & Potato Bake

Total Time: 30 min | Serves: 8 | Per serving: Calories: 103; Carbs: 18g; Fat: 2.6g; Protein: 2.7g

INGREDIENTS

28 oz potato, cubed
3 tbsp pine nuts
28 oz parsnips, chopped

2 oz Parmesan cheese, chopped
6 ¾ oz crème fraiche
1 slice bread

2 tbsp sage
4 tbsp butter
4 tsp mustard

DIRECTIONS

Preheat the air fryer to 180 C, and boil salted water in a pot over medium heat. Add potatoes and parsnips. Bring to a boil. In a bowl, mix mustard, crème fraiche, sage, salt and pepper. Drain the potatoes and parsnips and mash them with butter using a potato masher. Add mustard mixture, bread, cheese, and nuts to the mash and mix.

Add the batter to your air fryer's basket and cook for 25 minutes. Serve and enjoy!

382. Cool Mini Zucchini's

Total Time: 25 min | **Serves**: 4 | **Per serving**: Calories: 201; Carbs: 13g; Fat: 12g; Protein: 11g

INGREDIENTS
- 12 oz thawed puff pastry
- 4 large eggs, beaten
- 1 medium courgatte, sliced
- 4 oz feta cheese, crumbled
- 2 tbsp fresh dill, chopped
- Salt and pepper as needed

DIRECTIONS
Preheat the air fryer to 180 C, and un a bowl, add the beaten eggs and season with salt and pepper.

Stir in zucchini, dill and feta cheese. Grease 8 muffin tins with cooking spray. Roll pastry and arrange them to cover the sides of the muffin tins. Divide the egg mixture evenly between the holes. Place the prepared tins in your air fryer and cook for 15 minutes. Serve and enjoy!

383. Roasted Brussels Sprouts & Pine Nuts

Total Time: 20 min | **Serves**: 6 | **Per serving**: Calories: 260; Carbs: 14g; Fat: 20g; Protein: 7g

INGREDIENTS
- 15 oz brussels sprouts, stems cut off and cut in half
- 1 tbsp olive oil
- 1 ¾ oz raisins, drained
- Juice of 1 orange
- 1 ¾ oz toasted pine nuts

DIRECTIONS
Take raisins and soak in orange juice for 20 minutes. In a bowl, pop the sprouts with oil and salt and stir to combine well. Preheat your air fryer to 185 C.

Add the sprouts to the air fryer and roast for 15 minutes. Check often and remove brussel sprouts from the air fryer. Mix with toasted pine nuts and soaked raisins. Drizzle with remaining orange juice, to serve.

384. Baked Mediterranean Veggies

Total Time: 10 min | **Serves**: 8 | **Per serving**: Calories: 279; Carbs: 27g; Fat: 13g; Protein: 10g

INGREDIENTS
- 4 tbsp olive oil
- 18 oz aubergine, cubed
- 4 garlic cloves, minced
- 18 oz courgatte, sliced
- A bunch of thyme sprig
- 18 ounces mixed bell peppers, sliced and deseeded
- Salt and pepper to taste
- 4 whole onions, chopped
- 18 oz tomatoes, sliced
- Breadcrumbs as needed

DIRECTIONS
Preheat your air fryer to 190 C and in a bowl, mix eggplant, garlic, oil, spices, and transfer the mix to the cooking basket; cook for 4 minutes. Add zucchini, tomatoes, bell pepper, onion, and bake for 6 minutes. Serve and enjoy!

385. Indian Aloo Tikka

Total Time: 20 min | **Serves**: 2 | **Per serving**: Calories: 144; Carbs: 24g; Fat: 5g; Protein: 3g

INGREDIENTS
- 4 potatoes, cubed
- 3 tbsp lemon juice
- 1 bell pepper, sliced
- 2 onions, chopped
- 4 tbsp fennel
- 5 tbsp flour

2 tbsp ginger-garlic paste   20g mint leaves, chopped   40g coriander, chopped

DIRECTIONS

Preheat your air fryer to 180 C, and in a bowl, mix coriander, mint, fennel, ginger garlic paste, flour, salt and lemon juice. Blend to form a paste and add potato cubes. In another bowl, mix capsicum, onions and fennel mixture. Blend the mixture until you have a thick mix. Divide the mixture evenly into 5-6 cakes.

Add the prepared potato cakes into your air fryer and cook for 15 minutes. Serve with ketchup and enjoy.

386.   Extreme Zucchini Fries

Total Time: 25 min | **Serves**: 4 | **Per serving**: Calories: 367; Carbs: 5g; Fat: 28g; Protein: 4g

INGREDIENTS

3 medium courgatte, sliced
2 egg whites
120g seasoned breadcrumbs
2 tbsp grated Parmesan cheese
Cooking spray as needed
¼ tsp garlic powder
Salt and pepper to taste

DIRECTIONS

Preheat your air fryer to 210 C, and coat cooling rack with cooking spray; place it in the fryer's basket. In a bowl, beat the egg whites and season with salt and pepper. In another bowl, mix garlic powder, cheese and breadcrumbs.

Take zucchini slices and dredge them in eggs, followed by breadcrumbs. Add zucchini to the rack (in the cooking basket) and spray more oil. cook for 20 minutes. Serve and enjoy!

387.   Easy Fried Tomatoes

Total Time: 15 min | **Serves**: 3 | **Per serving**: Calories: 166; Carbs: 11g; Fat: 12g; Protein: 3g

INGREDIENTS

1 green tomato, sliced
¼ tbsp creole seasoning
Salt and pepper to taste
40g flour
120g buttermilk
breadcrumbs as needed

DIRECTIONS

Add flour to one bowl and buttermilk to another. Season the tomatoes with salt and pepper. Make a mix of creole seasoning and breadcrumbs. Cover tomato slices with flour, dip in buttermilk and then into the breadcrumbs.

Do the same for all the slices. Cook the tomato slices in your air fryer for 5 minutes at 200 C. Serve and enjoy!

388.   Zesty Pepper Bites

Total Time: 20 min | **Serves**: 4 | **Per serving**: Calories: 148; Carbs: 17g; Fat: 7g; Protein: 5g

INGREDIENTS

3 mixed bell peppers, sliced
3 tbsp balsamic vinegar
2 tbsp olive oil
1 tbsp garlic, minced
½ tsp dried basil
½ tsp dried parsley
Salt and pepper to taste
70g garlic mayo to serve

DIRECTIONS

In a bowl, mix peppers, oil, garlic, balsamic vinegar, basil, and parsley; season with salt and black pepper. Preheat your air fryer to 195 C and place the pepper mixture inside; cook for 10-15 minutes, tossing once or twice. Serve with garlic mayo and enjoy.

389. Cottage Cheese And Potatoes

Total Time: 30 min | **Serves**: 5 | **Per serving**: Calories: 293; Carbs: 17g; Fat: 18g; Protein: 16g

INGREDIENTS

4 potatoes, cubed, shells reserved
1 bunch asparagus, trimmed
60g fresh cream
40g Cottage cheese, cubed
1 tbsp whole-grain mustard

DIRECTIONS

Preheat the air fryer to 200 C and place the potatoes in the basket; cook for 25 minutes. Boil salted water in a pot over medium heat. Add asparagus and cook for 3 minutes until tender.

In a bowl, mix cooked potatoes, cottage cheese, cream, asparagus and mustard. Toss well and season with salt and black pepper. Transfer the mixture to the potato skin shells and serve.

390. Crispy & Tasty Tofu

Total Time: 25 min | **Serves**: 4 | **Per serving**: Calories: 130; Carbs: 15g; Fat: 6g; Protein: 9g

INGREDIENTS

1 block firm tofu, cubed
1 tbsp potato starch
Salt and pepper to taste
2 tsp rice vinegar
2 tsp soy sauce
2 tsp sesame oil
1 green onion, chopped
A bunch of basil, chopped

DIRECTIONS

Preheat your air fryer to 185 C, open your tofu pack and transfer to a plate. In a bowl, make a marinade of sesame oil, soy sauce and rice vinegar. Add spices to the marinade and pour the marinade over the tofu block. Set aside for 10 minutes to get tasty.

Toss the marinated tofu with the potato starch; place into the fryer's basket and cook for 20 minutes, shaking after 10 minutes. Serve with a topping of chopped onion and basil.

391. Spiced Up Potato Wedges

Total Time: 30 min | **Serves**: 6 | **Per serving**: Calories: 123; Fat: 2g; Carbs: 5g; Protein: 2.7g

INGREDIENTS

26 oz large waxy potatoes, sauce and cut into wedges
2 tbsp olive oil
2 tsp smoked paprika
2 tbsp sriracha hot chili sauce
150g Greek yogurt

DIRECTIONS

Soak potatoes under cold water for 30 minutes; pat dry with a towel. Preheat your air fryer to 175 C, and coat potatoes with oil and paprika. Cook them for 20 minutes, shaking once halfway through.

Remove to a paper to let them dry; season with salt and pepper. Serve with the yogurt and chili sauce on the side.

392. Prawn Toast

Total Time: 12 min | **Serves**: 2 | **Per serving**: Calories: 158; Carbs: 21g; Fat:14g; Protein: 25g

INGREDIENTS

6 large prawns, shells removed
1 large spring onion, finely sliced
3 white bread slices

80g sweet corn

1 egg white, whisked

1 tbsp black sesame seeds

DIRECTIONS

In a bowl, place the chopped prawns, corn, spring onion and the black sesame seeds. Add the whisked egg and mix the ingredients. Spread the mixture over the bread slices. Place in the prawns in the air fryer's basket and sprinkle oil. Fry the prawns until golden, for 8-10 minutes at 185 C. Serve with ketchup or chili sauce.

393. Hearty Carrots

Total Time: 25 min | **Serves**: 4 | **Per serving**: Calories: 130; Carbs: 23g; Fat: 0.6g; Protein: 8g

INGREDIENTS

2 tsp olive oil
2 shallots, chopped
3 carrots, sliced

Salt to taste
60g yogurt
2 garlic cloves, minced

3 tbsp parsley, chopped

DIRECTIONS

Preheat your air fryer to 185 C, and in a bowl, mix sliced carrots, salt, garlic, shallots, parsley and yogurt. Sprinkle with oil. Place the veggies in your air fryer basket and cook for 15 minutes. Serve with basil and garlic mayo.

394. Surprising Quinoa Eggplant Rolls

Total Time: 15 min | **Serves**: 3 | **Per serving**: Calories: 101; Carbs: 15g; Fat: 2g; Protein: 3g

INGREDIENTS

1 whole aubergine, sauce and sliced
Marinara sauce for dipping

50g cheese, grated
2 tbsp milk

1 whole egg, beaten
240g breadcrumbs

DIRECTIONS

Preheat your air fryer to 200 C, and in a bowl, mix beaten egg and milk. In another bowl, mix crumbs and cheese until crumbly. Place eggplant slices in the egg mixture, followed by a dip in the crumb mixture. Place the eggplant slices in the cooking basket and cook for 5 minutes. Serve with marinara sauce.

395. Healthy Avocado Fries

Total Time: 20 min | **Serves**: 2 | **Per serving**: Calories: 251; Carbs: 10g; Fat: 15g; Protein: 6g

INGREDIENTS

60g breadcrumbs
Salt as needed

1 avocado, cubed
40g aquafaba

DIRECTIONS

In a bowl, mix crumbs, aquafaba and salt. Preheat your air fryer to 195 C, and roll the avocado cubes in the crumbs mixture to coat evenly. Place the prepared cubes in your air fryer's cooking basket and cook for 10 minutes.

396. Broccoli And Parmesan Dish

Total Time: 25 min | **Serves**: 4 | **Per serving**: Calories: 114; Carbs: 10g; Fat: 6g; Protein: 7g

INGREDIENTS

1 head broccoli, cut into florets
1 tbsp olive oil
1 lemon, juiced
Salt and pepper to taste
1-ounce Parmesan cheese, grated

DIRECTIONS

In a bowl, mix all ingredients. Add the mixture to your air fryer and cook for 20 minutes at 180 C. Serve warm.

397. Quick Beetroot Chips

Total Time: 9 min | Serves: 2 | Per serving: Calories: 107; Carbs: 18g; Fat: 18.4g; Protein: 5.2g

INGREDIENTS

550g golden beetroot, sliced
2 tbsp olive oil
1 tbsp yeast flakes
1 tsp vegan seasoning
Salt to taste

DIRECTIONS

In a bowl, add the oil, beetroot, the vegan seasoning, and the yeast and mix well. Dump the coated chips in the basket. Set the heat to 185 C and fry for a total of 6 minutes, shaking once halfway through cooking.

398. Curly Vegan Fries

Total Time: 20 min | Serves: 2 | Per serving: Calories: 349; Carbs: 49g; Fat: 13g; Protein: 5g

INGREDIENTS

2 potatoes
1 tbsp tomato ketchup
2 tbsp olive oil
Salt and pepper to taste
2 tbsp coconut oil

DIRECTIONS

Preheat your air fryer to 180 C and use a spiralizer to spiralize the potatoes. In a bowl, mix oil, coconut oil, salt and pepper. Cover the potatoes with the oil mixture. Place the potatoes in the cooking basket and cook for 15 minutes. Serve with ketchup and enjoy!

399. Traditional Jacket Potatoes

Total Time: 30 min | Serves: 4 | Per serving: Calories: 140; Carbs: 26g; Fat: 0.5g; Protein: 4g

INGREDIENTS

17 oz potatoes
2 garlic cloves, minced
Salt and pepper to taste
1 tsp rosemary
1 tsp butter

DIRECTIONS

Wash the potatoes thoroughly under water. Preheat your air fryer to 180 C, and prick the potatoes with a fork. Place them into your air fryer's cooking basket and cook for 25 minutes. Cut the potatoes in half and top with butter and rosemary; season with salt and pepper. Serve immediately.

400. Baked Green Beans

Total Time: 20 min | Serves: 6 | Per serving: Calories: 134; Carbs: 8g; Fat: 6.7g; Protein: 22g

INGREDIENTS

120g panko
2 whole eggs, beaten
50g Parmesan cheese, grated

60g flour
1 tsp cayenne pepper

1 ½ pounds green beans
Salt to taste

DIRECTIONS

Preheat your air fryer to 200 C, and in a bowl, mix panko, Parmesan cheese, cayenne pepper, season with salt and pepper. Cover the green beans in flour and dip in eggs. Dredge beans in the Parmesan-panko mix. Place the prepared beans in your air fryer's cooking basket and cook for 15 minutes. Serve and enjoy!

401. Feisty Baby Carrots

Total Time: 20 min | Serves: 4 | Per serving: Calories: 367; Carbs: 5g; Fat: 28g; Protein: 4g

INGREDIENTS

1 pound baby carrots
1 tsp dried dill

1 tbsp olive oil
1 tbsp honey

Salt and pepper to taste

DIRECTIONS

Preheat your air fryer to 175 C, and in a bowl, mix oil, carrots and honey; gently stir to coat the carrots. Season with dill, pepper and salt. Place the prepared carrots in your air fryer's cooking basket and cook for 12 minutes.

402. Elegant Garlic Mushroom

Total Time: 20 min | Serves: 3 | Per serving: Calories: 130; Carbs: 2g; Fat: 7g; Protein: 1g

INGREDIENTS

2 lb portobello mushrooms, sliced
2 tbsp vermouth

½ tsp garlic powder
1 tbsp olive oil

2 tsp herbs
1 tbsp duck fat

DIRECTIONS

Preheat your air fryer to 175 C, add duck fat, garlic powder and herbs in a blender, and process. Pour the mixture over the mushrooms and cover with vermouth. Place the mushrooms in the cooking basket and cook for 10 minutes. Top with more vermouth and cook for 5 more minutes.

403. Mozzarella Cabbage with Blue cheese

Total Time: 25 min | Serves: 4 | Per serving: Calories: 108; Carbs: 11g; Fat: 7g; Protein: 2g

INGREDIENTS

½ head cabbage, cut into wedges
180g Parmesan cheese, chopped

4 tbsp melted butter
Salt and pepper to taste

120g Blue cheese sauce

DIRECTIONS

Preheat your air fryer to 190 C, and cover cabbage wedges with melted butter; coat with mozzarella. Place the coated cabbage in the cooking basket and cook for 20 minutes. Serve with blue cheese.

404. Simple Brown Carrot Roast With Cumin

Total Time: 15 min | Serves: 6 | Per serving: Calories: 135; Carbs: 17 g; Fat: 6g; Protein: 1g

INGREDIENTS

20 oz carrots, sauce
1 tbsp olive oil
1 tsp cumin seeds
A handful of fresh coriander

DIRECTIONS

Preheat the fryer to 175 C, and in a bowl, mix oil, carrots, and cumin seeds. Gently stir to coat the carrots well. Place the carrots in your air fryer basket and cook for 12 minutes. Scatter fresh coriander over the carrots.

SWEETS AND DESSERTS

405. Air Fried Snickerdoodle Poppers

Total Time: 30 min | **Serves**: 6 | **Per serving**: Calories: 278; Carbs: 75g; Fat: 2.4g; Protein: 4g

INGREDIENTS

1 box instant vanilla Jell-O

1 can of Pillsbury Grands Flaky Layers Biscuits

300g cinnamon sugar

melted butter, for brushing

DIRECTIONS

Preheat the air fryer to 175 C, and unroll the flaky biscuits; cut them into fourths. Roll each ¼ into a ball. Arrange the balls on a lined baking sheet, and cook in the air fryer for 7 minutes, or until golden.

Meanwhile, prepare the Jell-O following the package's instructions. Using an injector, inject some of the vanilla pudding into each ball. Brush the balls with melted butter and then coat them with cinnamon sugar.

406. Moon Pie

Total Time: 10 min | **Serves**: 4 | **Per serving**: Calories: 305; Carbs: 44g; Fat: 13.4g; Protein: 4g

INGREDIENTS

4 graham cracker sheets, snapped in half

8 large marshmallows

8 squares each of dark, milk and white chocolate

DIRECTIONS

Arrange the cracker halves on a cutting board. Put 2 marshmallows onto half of the graham cracker halves. Place 2 squares of chocolate onto the cracker with the marshmallows. Put the remaining crackers on top to create 4 sandwiches. Wrap each one in the baking paper so it resembles a parcel. Cook in the fryer for 5 minutes at 175 C.

407. Lemony Cheesecake

Total Time: 80 min + chilling time | **Serves**: 8 | **Per serving**: Calories: 487; Carbs: 23g; Fat: 38g; Protein: 9.3g

INGREDIENTS

8 oz graham crackers, crushed
4 oz butter, melted
16 oz plain cream cheese

3 eggs
3 tbsp sugar
1 tbsp vanilla extract

Zest of 2 lemons

DIRECTIONS

Line a cake tin, that fits in your air fryer, with baking paper. Mix together the crackers and butter, and press at the bottom of the tin. In a bowl, add cream cheese, eggs, sugar, vanilla and lemon zest and beat with a hand mixer until well combined and smooth. Pour the mixture into the tin, on top of the cracker's base. Cook for 40-45 minutes at 175 C, checking it to ensure it's set but still a bit wobbly. Let cool, then refrigerate overnight.

408. Baked Apples

Total Time: 35 min | **Serves**: 2 | **Per serving**: Calories: 322; Carbs: 37g; Fat: 19g; Protein: 3.8g

INGREDIENTS

2 granny smith apples, cored, bottom intact
2 tbsp butter, cold
3 tbsp sugar
3 tbsp crushed walnuts
2 tbsp raisins
1 tsp cinnamon

DIRECTIONS

In a bowl, add butter, sugar, walnuts, raisins and cinnamon; mix with fingers until you obtain a crumble. Arrange the apples in the air fryer. Stuff the apples with the filling mixture. Cook for 30 minutes at 200 C.

409. Dark Chocolate Brownies

Total Time: 35 min | **Serves**: 10 | **Per serving**: Calories: 513; Carbs: 32g; Fat: 55g; Protein: 7g

INGREDIENTS

6 oz dark chocolate
6 oz butter
50g white sugar
3 eggs
2 tsp vanilla extract
100g flour
30g cocoa powder
120g chopped walnuts
170g white chocolate chips

DIRECTIONS

Line a pan inside your air fryer with baking paper. In a saucepan, melt chocolate and butter over low heat. Do not stop stirring until you obtain a smooth mixture. Let cool slightly, whisk in eggs and vanilla. Sift flour and cocoa and stir to mix well. Sprinkle the walnuts over and add the white chocolate into the batter. Pour the batter into the pan and cook for 20 minutes at 175 C. Serve with raspberry syrup and ice cream.

410. Chocolate and Raspberry Cake

Total Time: 40 min | **Serves**: 8 | **Per serving**: Calories: 486; Carbs: 63g; Fat: 23.6g; Protein: 8.1g

INGREDIENTS

200g flour
40g cocoa powder
2 tsp baking powder
150g white sugar
50g brown sugar
180g butter
2 tsp vanilla extract
250ml milk
1 tsp baking soda
2 eggs
20g freeze-dried raspberries
170g chocolate chips

DIRECTIONS

Line a cake tin with baking powder. In a bowl, sift flour, cocoa and baking powder. Place the sugars, butter, vanilla, milk and baking soda into a microwave-safe bowl and heat for 60 seconds until the butter melts and the ingredients incorporate; let cool slightly. Whisk the eggs into the mixture.

Pour the wet ingredients into the dry ones, and fold to combine. Add in the raspberries and chocolate chips into the batter. Pour the batter into the tin and cook for 30 minutes at 175 C.

411. Apple Caramel Relish

Total Time: 40 min | **Serves**: 4 | **Per serving**: Calories: 382; Carbs: 56g; Fat: 18g; Protein: 3.4g

INGREDIENTS

1 vanilla box cake
2 apples, peeled, sliced
3 oz butter, melted
110g brown sugar
1 tsp cinnamon
70g flour
340g caramel sauce

DIRECTIONS

Line a cake tin with baking paper. In a bowl, mix butter, sugar, cinnamon and flour until you obtain a crumbly texture. Prepare the cake mix according to the instructions (no baking). Pour the batter into the tin and arrange the apple slices on top. Spoon the caramel over the apples and add the crumble over the sauce. Cook in the air fryer for 35 minutes at 180 C; make sure to check it halfway through, so it's not overcooked.

412. Chocolate and Peanut Butter Fondants

Total Time: 25 minutes | **Serves**: 4 | Calories: 157; Carbs: 4g; Fat: 4g; Protein: 0.9g

INGREDIENTS

120g dark chocolate
70g peanut butter, crunchy
2 tbsp butter, diced
50g + 50g sugar
4 eggs, room temperature
20g flour, sieved
1 tsp salt
60ml water
Cooking spray

DIRECTIONS

Make a salted praline to top the chocolate fondant. Add ¼ cup of sugar, 1 tsp of salt and water into a saucepan. Stir and bring it to a boil over low heat on a stovetop. Simmer until the desired color is achieved and reduced.

Pour it into a baking tray and leave to cool and harden. Preheat the air fryer to 150 C. Place a pot of water over medium heat and place a heatproof bowl over it. Add the chocolate, butter, and peanut butter to the bowl.

Stir continuously until fully melted, combined, and smooth. Remove the bowl from the heat and allow to cool slightly. Add the eggs to the chocolate and whisk. Add the flour and remaining sugar; mix well.

Grease 4 small loaf pans with cooking spray and divide the chocolate mixture between them. Place 2 pans at a time in the basket and cook for 7 minutes. Remove them and serve the fondants with a piece of salted praline.

413. White chocolate Pudding

Total Time: 40 min | **Serves**: 2 | **Per serving**: Calories : 320; Carbs: 3.06g; Fat: 25g; Protein: 11g

INGREDIENTS

3 oz white chocolate
4 large egg whites
2 egg yolks, at room temperature
50g sugar + more for garnishing
1 tbsp melted butter
1 tbsp unmelted butter
¼ tsp vanilla extract
1 ½ tbsp flour

DIRECTIONS

Coat two 6-oz ramekins with melted butter. Add the sugar and swirl it in the ramekins to coat the butter. Pour out the remaining sugar and keep it. Melt the unmelted butter with the chocolate in a microwave; set aside.

In another bowl, beat the egg yolks vigorously. Add the vanilla and kept sugar; beat to incorporate fully. Add the chocolate mixture and mix well. Add the flour and mix it with no lumps.

Preheat the air fryer to 170 C, and whisk the egg whites in another bowl till it holds stiff peaks. Add ⅓ of the egg whites into the chocolate mixture; fold in gently and evenly. Share the mixture into the ramekins with ½ inch space left at the top. Place the ramekins in the fryer basket, close the air fryer and cook for 14 minutes.

Dust with the remaining sugar and serve.

414. Lemon Curd

Total Time: 30 min | **Serves**: 2 | **Per serving**: Calories : 60; Carbs: 0g; Fat: 6g; Protein: 2g

INGREDIENTS

3 tbsp butter
3 tbsp sugar
1 egg
1 egg yolk
¾ lemon, juiced

DIRECTIONS

Add sugar and butter in a medium ramekin and beat evenly. Add egg and yolk slowly while still whisking the fresh yellow color will be attained. Add the lemon juice and mix. Place the bowl in the fryer basket and cook at 125 C for 6 minutes. Increase the temperature again to 160 C and cook for 15 minutes.

Remove the bowl onto a flat surface; use a spoon to check for any lumps and remove. Cover the ramekin with a plastic wrap and refrigerate overnight or serve immediately.

415. Almond Meringue Cookies

Total Time: 145 min | **Serves**: 4 | **Per serving**: Calories : 215; Carbs: 35g; Fat: 1.6g; Protein: 7.6g

INGREDIENTS

8 egg whites
½ tsp almond extract
270g sugar
¼ tsp salt
2 tsp lemon juice
1 ½ tsp vanilla extract
Melted dark chocolate to drizzle

DIRECTIONS

In a mixing bowl, add egg whites, salt, and lemon juice. Beat using an electric mixer until foamy. Slowly add the sugar and continue beating until completely combined; add the almond and vanilla extracts. Beat until stiff peaks form and glossy.

Line a round baking sheet with parchment paper. Fill a piping bag with the meringue mixture and pipe as many mounds on the baking sheet as you can leaving 2-inch spaces between each mound.

Place the baking sheet in the fryer basket and bake at 125 C for 5 minutes. Reduce the temperature to 110 C and bake for 15 more minutes. Then, reduce the temperature once more to 100 C and cook for 15 minutes. Remove the baking sheet and let the meringues cool for 2 hours. Drizzle with the dark chocolate before serving.

416. Chocolate Banana Sandwiches

Total Time: 30 min | **Serves**: 2 | **Per serving**: Calories: 240; Carbs: 26g; Fat: 9.1g; Protein: 12.3g

INGREDIENTS

4 slices of brioche
1 tbsp butter, melted
6 oz milk chocolate, broken into chunks
1 banana, sliced

DIRECTIONS

Brush the brioche slices with butter. Spread chocolate and banana on 2 brioche slices. Top with the remaining 2 slices to create 2 sandwiches. Arrange the sandwiches into your air fryer and cook for 14 minutes at 200 C, turning once halfway through. Slice in half and serve with vanilla ice cream.

417. Crème Brulee

Total Time: 60 min | **Serves**: 3 | **Per serving**: Calories : 402; Carbs: 9.5g; Fat: 32.5g; Protein: 13.6g

INGREDIENTS

240g whipped cream
250ml milk
2 vanilla pods

10 egg yolks

4 tbsp sugar + extra for topping

DIRECTIONS

In a pan, add the milk and cream. Cut the vanilla pods open and scrape the seeds into the pan with the vanilla pods also. Place the pan over medium heat on a stovetop until almost boiled while stirring regularly. Turn off the heat. Add the egg yolks to a bowl and beat it. Add the sugar and mix well but not too bubbly.

Remove the vanilla pods from the milk mixture; pour the mixture onto the eggs mixture while stirring constantly.

Let it sit for 25 minutes. Fill 2 to 3 ramekins with the mixture. Place the ramekins in the fryer basket and cook them at 160 C for 25 minutes. Once ready, remove the ramekins and let sit to cool. Sprinkle the remaining sugar over and use a torch to melt the sugar, so it browns at the top.

418. The Most Chocolaty Fudge

Total Time: 55 min | **Serves**: 8 | **Per serving**: Calories: 494; Carbs: 65.7g; Fat: 25.1g; Protein: 5.6g

INGREDIENTS

200g sugar
7 oz flour
1 tbsp honey

60ml milk
1 tsp vanilla extract
1 oz cocoa powder

2 eggs
4 oz butter
1 orange, juice and zest

Icing:
1 oz butter, melted
4 oz powdered sugar

1 tbsp brown sugar
1 tbsp milk

2 tsp honey

DIRECTIONS

Preheat the air fryer to 175 C, and in a bowl, mix the dry ingredients for the fudge. Mix the wet ingredients separately; combine the two mixtures gently. Transfer the batter to a prepared cake pan. Cook for 35 minutes.

Meanwhile, whisk together all icing ingredients. When the cake cools, coat with the icing. Let set before slicing.

419. White Chocolate Chip Cookies

Total Time: 30 min | **Serves**: 8 | **Per serving**: Calories: 167; Carbs: 21.3g; Fat: 11.3g; Protein: 0.7g

INGREDIENTS

6 oz self-rising flour
3 oz brown sugar

2 oz white chocolate chips
1 tbsp honey

1 ½ tbsp milk
4 oz butter

DIRECTIONS

Preheat the air fryer to 175 C, and beat the butter and sugar until fluffy. Beat in the honey, milk, and flour. Gently fold in the chocolate cookies. Drop spoonfuls of the mixture onto a prepared cookie sheet. Cook for 18 minutes.

420. White Filling Coconut and Oat Cookies

Total Time: 30 min | **Serves**: 4 | **Per serving**: Calories: 477; Carbs: 73.8g; Fat: 16.8g; Protein: 7.4g

INGREDIENTS

5 ½ oz flour
1 tsp vanilla extract

3 oz sugar
50g oats

1 small egg, beaten
30g coconut flakes

Filling:
1 oz white chocolate, melted

2 oz butter

4 oz powdered sugar

1 tsp vanilla extract

DIRECTIONS

Beat all the cookie ingredients, with an electric mixer, except the flour. When smooth, fold in the flour. Drop spoonfuls of the batter onto a prepared cookie sheet. Cook in the air fryer at 175 C for 18 minutes; then let cool.

Meanwhile, prepare the filling by beating all ingredients together; spread the filling on half of the cookies. Top with the other halves to make cookie sandwiches.

421. No Flour Lime Muffins

Total Time: 30 min | **Serves**: 6 | **Per serving**: Calories: 207; Carbs: 14.1g; Fat: 11g; Protein: 11.8g

INGREDIENTS

2 eggs plus 1 yolk
Juice and zest of 2 limes
250g yogurt
50g superfine sugar
8 oz cream cheese
1 tsp vanilla extract

DIRECTIONS

Preheat the air fryer to 170 C, and with a spatula, gently combine the yogurt and cheese. In another bowl, beat together the rest of the ingredients. Gently fold the lime with the cheese mixture. Divide the batter between 6 lined muffin tins. Cook in the air fryer for 10 minutes.

422. Mock Cherry Pie

Total Time: 30 min | **Serves**: 8 | **Per serving**: Calories: 325; Carbs: 49.8g; Fat: 13.8g; Protein: 2.5g

INGREDIENTS

2 store-bought pie crusts
21 oz cherry pie filling
1 egg yolk
1 tbsp milk

DIRECTIONS

Preheat the air fryer to 160 C, and place one pie crust in a pie pan; poke holes into the crust. Cook for 5 minutes. Spread the pie filling over. Cut the other pie crust into strips and arrange the pie-style over the baked crust. Whisk milk and egg yolk, and brush the mixture over the pie. Return the pie to the fryer and cook for 15 minutes.

423. Blueberry Muffins

Total Time: 30 min | **Serve**: 10 | **Per serving**: Calories: 178; Carbs: 26g; Fat: 7.6g; Protein: 2.9g

INGREDIENTS

180g flour
½ tsp salt
100g sugar
60ml vegetable oil
2 tsp vanilla extract
150g blueberries
1 egg
2 tsp baking powder
Yogurt, as needed

DIRECTIONS

Preheat the air fryer to 175 C, and combine flour, salt and baking powder, in a bowl. In another bowl, add the oil, vanilla extract, and egg. Fill the rest of the bowl with yogurt, and whisk the mixture until fully incorporated.

Combine the wet and dry ingredients; gently fold in the blueberries. Divide the mixture between 10 muffin cups. You may need to work in batches. Cook for 10 minutes.

424. Pineapple Cake

Total Time: 50 min | **Serves**: 4 | **Per serving**: Calories: 411; Carbs: 42g; Fat: 5.1g; Protein: 4g

INGREDIENTS

- 2 oz dark chocolate, grated
- 8 oz self-rising flour
- 4 oz butter
- 7 oz pineapple chunks
- 120 ml pineapple juice
- 1 egg
- 2 tbsp milk
- 100g sugar

DIRECTIONS

Preheat the air fryer to 195 C, place the butter and flour into a bowl, and rub the mixture with your fingers until crumbed. Stir in pineapple, sugar, chocolate, and juice. Beat eggs and milk separately, and then add to the batter.

Transfer the batter to a previously prepared (greased or lined) cake pan, and cook for 40 minutes. Let cool for at least 10 minutes before serving.

425. Lemon Glazed Muffins

Total Time: 30 min | **Serves**: 6 | **Per serving**: Calories: 235; Carbs: 43g; Fat: 6g; Protein: 3.7g

INGREDIENTS

- 120g flour
- 100g sugar
- 1 small egg
- 1 tsp lemon zest

Glaze:
- 70g powdered sugar
- ¾ tsp baking powder
- ¼ tsp baking soda
- ½ tsp salt
- 2 tbsp vegetable oil

- 2 tsp lemon juice
- 120ml milk
- ½ tsp vanilla extract

DIRECTIONS

Preheat the air fryer to 175 C, and combine all dry muffin ingredients, in a bowl. In another bowl, whisk together the wet ingredients. Gently combine the two mixtures. Divide the batter between 6 greased muffin tins.

Place the muffin tins in the air fryer and cook for 12 to 14 minutes. Whisk the powdered sugar with the lemon juice. Spread the glaze over the muffins.

426. Molten Lava Cake

Total Time: 20 min | **Serves**: 4 | **Per serving**: Calories: 785; Carbs: 31.6g; Fat: 60.2g; Protein: 30.7g

INGREDIENTS

- 3 ½ oz butter, melted
- 3 ½ tbsp sugar
- 1 ½ tbsp self-rising flour
- 3 ½ oz dark chocolate, melted
- 2 eggs

DIRECTIONS

Grease 4 ramekins with butter. Preheat the air fryer to 185 C and beat the eggs and sugar until frothy. Stir in the butter and chocolate; gently fold in the flour. Divide the mixture between the ramekins and bake in the air fryer for 10 minutes. Let cool for 2 minutes before turning the lava cakes upside down onto serving plates.

427. Air Fried Doughnuts

Total Time: 25 min | **Serves**: 4 | **Per serving**: Calories: 253; Carbs: 42.5g; Fat: 9.4g; Protein: 5.6g

INGREDIENTS

8 oz self-rising flour
1 tsp baking powder
120ml milk
2 ½ tbsp butter
1 egg
2 oz brown sugar

DIRECTIONS

Preheat the air fryer to 175 C, and beat the butter with the sugar, until smooth. Beat in eggs, and milk. In a bowl, combine the flour with the baking powder. Gently fold the flour into the butter mixture.

Form donut shapes and cut off the center with cookie cutters. Arrange on a lined baking sheet and cook in the fryer for 15 minutes. Serve with whipped cream or icing.

428. Chocolate Soufflé

Total Time: 25 min | Serves: 2 | Per serving: Calories: 598; Carbs: 50.9g; Fat: 41.3g; Protein: 10.3g

INGREDIENTS

2 eggs, whites and yolks separated
60g butter, melted
2 tbsp flour
3 tbsp sugar
3 oz chocolate, melted
½ tsp vanilla extract

DIRECTIONS

Beat the yolks along with the sugar and vanilla extract; stir in butter, chocolate, and flour. Preheat the air fryer to 170 C and whisk the whites until a stiff peak forms. Working in batches, gently combine the egg whites with the chocolate mixture. Divide the batter between two greased ramekins. Cook for 14 minutes.

429. Cheat Apple Pie

Total Time: 30 min | Serves: 9 | Per serving: Calories: 296; Carbs: 42.5g; Fat: 13.8g; Protein: 2.4g

INGREDIENTS

4 apples, diced
2 oz butter, melted
2 oz sugar
1 oz brown sugar
2 tsp cinnamon
1 egg, beaten
3 large puff pastry sheets
¼ tsp salt

DIRECTIONS

Whisk white sugar, brown sugar, cinnamon, salt, and butter, together. Place the apples in a baking dish and coat them with the mixture. Place the baking dish in the air fryer, and cook for 10 minutes at 175 C.

Meanwhile, roll out the pastry on a floured flat surface, and cut each sheet into 6 equal pieces. Divide the apple filling between the pieces. Brush the edges of the pastry squares with the egg.

Fold them and seal the edges with a fork. Place on a lined baking sheet and cook in the fryer for 8 minutes. Flip over, increase the temperature to 195 C, and cook for 2 more minutes.

430. Soft Buttermilk Biscuits

Total Time: 25 min | Serves: 4 | Per serving: Calories: 319; Carbs: 47.2g; Fat: 11.9g; Protein: 6.4g

INGREDIENTS

200g all-purpose flour, plus some for dusting
½ tsp baking soda
70g cake flour
¾ tsp salt
½ tsp baking powder
4 tbsp butter, chopped
1 tsp sugar
180g buttermilk

DIRECTIONS

Preheat the air fryer to 200 C and combine all dry ingredients, in a bowl. Place the chopped butter in the bowl, and rub it into the flour mixture, until crumbed. Stir in the buttermilk.

Flour a flat and dry surface and roll out until half-inch thick. Cut out 10 rounds with a small cookie cutter. Arrange the biscuits on a lined baking sheet. Cook for 8 minutes.

431. Orange Sponge Cake

Total Time: 50 min | **Serves**: 6 | **Per serving**: Calories: 187; Carbs: 36.4g; Fat: 2.7g; Protein: 4.6g

INGREDIENTS

- 9 oz sugar
- 9 oz self-rising flour
- 9 oz butter
- 3 eggs
- 1 tsp baking powder
- 1 tsp vanilla extract
- fzest of 1 orange

Frosting:
- 4 egg whites
- Juice of 1 orange
- 1 tsp orange food coloring
- zest of 1 orange
- 7 oz superfine sugar

DIRECTIONS

Preheat the air fryer to 160 C and place all cake ingredients, in a bowl and beat with an electric mixer. Transfer half of the batter into a prepared cake pan; bake for 15 minutes. Repeat the process for the other half of the batter.

Meanwhile, prepare the frosting by beating all frosting ingredients together. Spread the frosting mixture on top of one cake. Top with the other cake.

432. Simple Coffee Cake

Total Time: 30 min | **Serves**: 2 | **Per serving**: Calories: 418; Carbs: 44.8g; Fat: 25.5g; Protein: 5.1g

INGREDIENTS

- 60g butter
- ½ tsp instant coffee
- 1 tbsp black coffee, brewed
- 1 egg
- 50g sugar
- 40g flour
- 1 tsp cocoa powder
- A pinch of salt
- Powdered sugar, for icing

DIRECTIONS

Preheat the air fryer to 170 C and grease a small ring cake pan. Beat the sugar and egg together in a bowl. Beat in cocoa, instant and black coffee; stir in salt and flour. Transfer the batter to the prepared pan. Cook for 15 minutes.

433. Banana Fritters

Total Time: 15 min | **Serves**: 8 | **Per serving**: Calories: 203; Carbs: 36.5g; Fat: 6.3g; Protein: 3.4g

INGREDIENTS

- 8 bananas
- 3 tbsp vegetable oil
- 3 tbsp cornflour
- 1 egg white
- 90g breadcrumbs

DIRECTIONS

Preheat the air fryer to 175 C, and combine the oil and breadcrumbs, in a small bowl. Coat the bananas with the cornflour first, brush them with egg white, and dip them in the breadcrumb mixture. Arrange on a lined baking sheet and cook for 8 minutes.

434. Berry Crumble

Total Time: 30 min | **Serves**: 6 | **Per serving**: Calories: 261; Carbs: 42.7g; Fat: 9.6g; Protein: 2.6g

INGREDIENTS

12 oz fresh strawberries
7 oz fresh raspberries
5 oz fresh blueberries

5 tbsp cold butter
2 tbsp lemon juice
120g flour

100g sugar
1 tbsp water
A pinch of salt

DIRECTIONS

Gently mass the berries, but make sure there are chunks left. Mix with the lemon juice and 2 tbsp. of the sugar.

Place the berry mixture at the bottom of a prepared round cake. Combine the flour with the salt and sugar, in a bowl. Add the water and rub the butter with your fingers until the mixture becomes crumbled.

Arrange the crisp batter over the berries. Cook in the air fryer at 195 C for 20 minutes. Serve chilled.

435. Baked Apples with Nuts

Total Time: 13 min | **Serves**: 2 | **Per serving**: Calories: 483; Carbs: 76.5g; Fat: 21.8g; Protein: 8.1g

INGREDIENTS

4 apples
1 oz butter
2 oz breadcrumbs

Zest of 1 orange
2 tbsp chopped hazelnuts
2 oz mixed seeds

1 tsp cinnamon
2 tbsp brown sugar

DIRECTIONS

Preheat the air fryer to 175 C and core the apples. Make sure to also score their skin to prevent from splitting. Combine the remaining ingredients in a bowl; stuff the apples with the mixture and cook for 10 minutes. Serve topped with chopped hazelnuts.

436. Pecan Pie

Total Time: 1 hr 10 min | **Serves**: 4 | **Per serving**: Calories: 410; Carbs: 53g; Fat: 21.6g; Protein: 6.1g

INGREDIENTS

180g maple syrup
2 eggs
½ tsp salt
¼ tsp nutmeg

½ tsp cinnamon
2 tbsp almond butter
2 tbsp brown sugar
70g chopped pecans

1 tbsp butter, melted
1 8-inch pie dough
¾ tsp vanilla extract

DIRECTIONS

Preheat the air fryer to 185 C, and coat the pecans with the melted butter. Place the pecans in the air fryer and toast them for 10 minutes. Place the pie crust into an 8-inch round pie pan, and place the pecans over.

Whisk together all remaining ingredients, in a bowl. Pour the maple mixture over the pecans. Set the air fryer to 160 C and cook the pie for 25 minutes.

437. Delicious Apple Pie

Total Time: 25 min | **Serves**: 9 | **Per serving**: Calories: 223; Carbs: 37g; Fat: 8g; Protein: 2g

INGREDIENTS

2 ¾ oz flour
5 tbsp sugar

1 ¼ oz butter
3 tbsp cinnamon

2 whole apple, sliced

DIRECTIONS

Preheat the air fryer to 180 C and in a bowl, mix 3 tbsp sugar, butter and flour; form pastry using the batter. Roll out the pastry on a floured surface and transfer it to the fryer's basket. Arrange the apple slices atop.

Cover apples with sugar and cinnamon; cook for 20 minutes. Sprinkle with powdered sugar and mint, to serve.

438. Black & White Brownies

Total Time: 25 min | **Serves**: 2 | **Per serving**: Calories: 470; Carbs: 30g; Fat: 13g; Protein: 2g

INGREDIENTS

1 whole egg, beaten
50g chocolate chips
2 tbsp white sugar

40g flour
2 tbsp safflower oil
1 tsp vanilla

30g cocoa powder

DIRECTIONS

Preheat the air fryer to 160 C and in a bowl, mix the beaten egg, sugar, oil, and vanilla. In another bowl, mix cocoa powder and flour. Add the flour mixture to the vanilla mixture and stir until fully incorporated.

Prepare a baking form for your air fryer and pour the mixture into the form; sprinkle chocolate chips on top. Add the baking form in the cooking basket and cook for 20 minutes.

439. Hearty Apricot Crumbles

Total Time: 30 min | **Serves**: 4 | **Per serving**: Calories: 807; Carbs: 89g; Fat: 37g; Protein: 13g

INGREDIENTS

550g fresh apricot, de-stoned and cubed
150g fresh blackberries

100g sugar
2 tbsp lemon Juice
120g flour

Salt as needed
5 tbsp butter

DIRECTIONS

Add the apricot cubes to a bowl and mix with lemon juice, 2 tbsp sugar, and blackberries. Scoop the mixture into a greased dish and spread it evenly. In another bowl, mix flour and remaining sugar.

Add 1 tbsp of cold water and butter and keep mixing until you have a crumbly mixture. Preheat the air fryer to 195 C and place the fruit mixture in the cooking basket. Top with crumb mixture and cook for 20 minutes.

440. Hearty Banana Pastry

Total Time: 15 min | **Serves**: 2 | **Per serving**: Calories: 205; Carbs: 10g; Fat: 13g; Protein: 12g

INGREDIENTS

3 bananas, sauce and sliced
3 tbsp honey

2 puff pastry sheets, cut into strips
Fresh berries to serve

DIRECTIONS

Preheat your air fryer up to 175 C and place the banana slices into the cooking basket. Cover with the pastry strips and top with honey. Cook for 10 minutes. Serve with fresh berries.

441. All-Star Banana Fritters

Total Time: 15 min | **Serves**: 5 | **Per serving**: Calories: 242; Carbs: 38g; Fat: 9g; Protein: 5g

INGREDIENTS

- 200g flour
- 5 bananas, sauce and sliced
- 1 tsp salt
- 3 tbsp sesame seeds
- 250ml water
- 2 eggs, beaten
- 1 tsp baking powder
- ½ tbsp sugar

DIRECTIONS

Preheat the air fryer to 175 C, in a bowl, mix salt, sesame seeds, flour, baking powder, eggs, sugar, and water. Coat sliced bananas with the flour mixture; place the prepared slices in the air fryer basket; cook for 8 minutes.

442. Almond Apples Treat

Total Time: 15 min | **Serves**: 4 | **Per serving**: Calories: 383; Carbs: 33g; Fat: 24g; Protein: 5g

INGREDIENTS

- 4 apples, cored
- 1 ½ oz almonds
- ¾ oz raisins
- 2 tbsp sugar

DIRECTIONS

Preheat the air fryer to 180 C and in a bowl, mix sugar, almonds, raisins. Blend the mixture using a hand mixer. Fill cored apples with the almond mixture. Place the prepared apples in your air fryer's cooking basket and cook for 10 minutes. Serve with a sprinkle of powdered sugar.

MORE AIR FRYER FAVORITES

443. Orange-Flavored Cupcakes

Total Time: 25 min | Serves: 5 | Per serving: Calories : 412; Carbs: 2g; Fat: 25g; Protein: 4.6g

INGREDIENTS

Lemon Frosting:

- 250g natural yogurt
- Sugar to taste
- 1 orange, juiced
- 1 tbsp orange zest
- 7 oz cream cheese

Cake:

- 2 lemons, quartered
- 70g flour + extra for basing
- ¼ tsp salt
- 2 tbsp sugar
- 1 tsp baking powder
- 1 tsp vanilla extract
- 2 eggs
- 120g softened butter
- 2 tbsp milk

DIRECTIONS

In a bowl, add the yogurt and cream cheese. Mix until smooth. Add the orange juice and zest; mix well. Gradually add the sweetener to your taste while stirring until smooth. Make sure the frost is not runny. Set aside.

For cupcakes: Place the lemon quarters in a food processor and process it until pureed. Add the baking powder, softened butter, milk, eggs, vanilla extract, sugar, and salt. Process again until smooth.

Preheat the air fryer to 200 C. Flour the bottom of 10 cupcake cases and spoon the batter into the cases ¾ way up. Place them in the air fryer and bake for 7 minutes. Once ready, remove and let cool. Design the cupcakes with the frosting.

444. Blueberry Oat Bars

Total Time: 40 min | Serves: 10 | Per serving: Calories: 276; Carbs: 32g; Fat: 16g; Protein: 8g

INGREDIENTS

- 270g rolled oats
- 50g ground almonds
- 60g flour
- 1 tsp baking powder
- 1 tsp ground cinnamon
- 3 eggs, lightly beaten
- 120ml canola oil
- 80ml milk
- 2 tsp vanilla extract
- 380g blueberries

DIRECTIONS

Spray a baking pan that fits in your air fryer with cooking spray.

In a bowl, add oats, almonds, flour, baking powder and cinnamon into and stir well. In another bowl, whisk eggs, oil, milk, and vanilla.

Stir the wet ingredients gently into the oat mixture. Fold in the blueberries. Pour the mixture in the pan and place it in the fryer. Cook for 30 minutes at 165 C. When ready, check if the bars are nice and soft.

445. Potato and Spinach Omelet

Total Time: 35 min | Serves: 4 | Per serving: Calories: 242; Carbs: 23g; Fat: 8g; Protein: 19g

INGREDIENTS

- 450g potato cubes, boiled
- 60g spinach, chopped
- 5 eggs, lightly beaten

60g heavy cream
220g grated mozzarella cheese
30g parsley, chopped
Fresh thyme, chopped
Salt and pepper to taste

DIRECTIONS

Spray the air fryer's basket with oil. Arrange the potatoes inside.

In a bowl, whisk eggs, cream, spinach, mozzarella, parsley, thyme, salt and pepper, and pour over the potatoes. Cook for 16 minutes at 200 C, until nice and golden.

446. Air-Fried Sourdough Sandwiches

Total Time: 25 min | **Serves**: 2 | **Per serving**: Calories: 315; Carbs: 32g; Fat: 12.1g; Protein: 20.4g

INGREDIENTS

4 slices sourdough bread
2 tbsp mayonnaise
2 slices ham
2 lettuce leaves
1 tomato, sliced
2 slices mozzarella cheese
Salt and pepper to taste
Cooking spray

DIRECTIONS

On a clean board, lay the sourdough slices and spread with mayonnaise. Top 2 of the slices with ham, lettuce, tomato, and mozzarella cheese. Season with salt and pepper.

Top with the remaining two slices to form two sandwiches. Spray with oil and transfer to the air fryer. Cook for 14 minutes at 170 C, flipping once halfway through cooking. Serve hot!

447. Mango Bread

Total Time: 60 min | **Serves**: 8 | **Per serving**: Calories: 332; Carbs: 51g; Fat: 13g; Protein: 4g

INGREDIENTS

120g melted butter
1 egg, lightly beaten
100g brown sugar
1 tsp vanilla extract
3 ripe mango, mashed
200g plain flour
1 tsp baking powder
½ tsp grated nutmeg
½ tsp ground cinnamon

DIRECTIONS

Spray a loaf tin that fits in the air fryer, with cooking spray and line with baking paper. In a bowl, whisk melted butter, egg, sugar, vanilla, and mango. Sift in flour, baking powder, nutmeg, and cinnamon; stir without overmixing.

Pour the batter into the tin and place it in the air fryer. Cook for 35 minutes at 150 C. Make sure to check at the 20-25-minute mark. When ready, let cool before slicing it.

448. Greek-Style Frittata

Total Time: 10 min | **Serves**: 2 | **Per serving**: Calories: 387; Carbs: 13.2g; Fat: 32.1g; Protein: 21.4g

INGREDIENTS

4 eggs, lightly beaten
2 tbsp heavy cream
60g spinach, chopped
100g chopped mushrooms
3 oz Feta cheese, crumbled
A handful of fresh parsley, chopped
Salt and black pepper

DIRECTIONS

Spray your air fryer basket with cooking spray. In a bowl, whisk eggs and until combined. Stir in spinach, mushrooms, feta, parsley, salt, and black pepper.

Pour into the basket and cook for 6 minutes at 175 C. Serve immediately with a touch of tangy tomato relish.

449. Cheddar Hash Browns

Total Time: 25 min | **Serves**: 4 | **Per serving**: Calories: 404; Carbs: 73.2g; Fat: 15.1g; Protein: 8g

INGREDIENTS

4 russet potatoes, peeled, grated
1 brown onion, chopped
3 garlic cloves, chopped

50g grated Cheddar cheese
1 egg, lightly beaten
Salt and black pepper

3 tbsp finely thyme sprigs
Cooking spray

DIRECTIONS

In a bowl, mix with hands potatoes, onion, garlic, cheese, egg, salt, black pepper, and thyme. Spray the fryer with cooking spray.

Press the hash brown mixture into the basket and cook for 9 minutes at 200 C, shaking once halfway through cooking. When ready, ensure the hash browns are golden and crispy.

450. Cherry and Almond Scones

Total Time: 30 min | **Serves**: 4 | **Per serving**: Calories: 433; Carbs: 62g; Fat: 15g; Protein: 10.4g

INGREDIENTS

250g flour
70g sugar
2 tsp baking powder

50g sliced almonds
100g chopped cherries, dried
60g cold butter, cut into cubes

120ml milk
1 egg
1 tsp vanilla extract

DIRECTIONS

Line air fryer basket with baking paper. Mix together flour, sugar, baking powder, almonds, and dried cherries. Rub the butter into the dry ingredients with hands to form a sandy, crumbly texture.

Whisk together egg, milk, and vanilla extract. Pour into the dry ingredients and stir to combine. Sprinkle a working board with flour, lay the dough onto the board and give it a few kneads. Shape into a rectangle and cut into 9 squares. Arrange the squares in the air fryer's basket and cook for 14 minutes at 200 C. Serve immediately.

451. French Toast with Vanilla Filling

Total Time: 15 min | **Serves**: 3 | **Per serving**: Calories: 266; Carbs: 27g; Fat: 12.1g; Protein: 11g

INGREDIENTS

6 slices white bread
2 eggs
60g heavy cream

70g sugar mixed with
1 tsp ground cinnamon
6 tbsp caramel

1 tsp vanilla extract
Cooking spray

DIRECTIONS

In a bowl, whisk eggs and cream. Dip each piece of bread into the egg and cream. Dip the bread into the sugar and cinnamon mixture until well-coated. On a clean board, lay the coated slices and spread three of the slices with about 2 tbsp of caramel each, around the center.

Place the remaining three slices on top to form three sandwiches. Spray the air fryer basket with oil. Arrange the sandwiches into the fryer and cook for 10 minutes at 170 C, turning once halfway through cooking.

452. Bacon & Egg Muffins

Total Time: 30 min | **Serves**: 10 | **Per serving**: Calories: 302; Carbs: 3.2g; Fat: 27.1g; Protein: 10g

INGREDIENTS

10 eggs, lightly beaten
10 bacon rashers, cut into small pieces
30g chopped chives
1 brown onion, chopped
80g grated Cheddar cheese
Salt and black pepper
Cooking spray

DIRECTIONS

Spray a 10-hole muffin pan with cooking spray. In a bowl, add eggs, bacon, chives, onion, cheese, salt, and pepper, and stir to combine. Pour into muffin pans and place inside the fryer. Cook for 12 minutes at 170 C, until nice and set.

453. Banana and Hazelnut Muffins

Total Time: 40 min | **Serves**: 6 | **Per serving**: Calories: 559; Carbs: 80g; Fat: 23.1g; Protein: 12g

INGREDIENTS

120g melted butter
170g honey
2 eggs, lightly beaten
4 ripe bananas, mashed
1 tsp vanilla extract
250g flour
1 tsp baking powder
½ tsp baking soda
1 tsp ground cinnamon
80g chopped hazelnuts
180g dark chocolate chips

DIRECTIONS

Spray 10-hole muffin with oil spray. In a bowl, whisk butter, honey, eggs, bananas, and vanilla, until well-combine. Sift in flour, baking powder, baking soda, and cinnamon without overmixing.

Stir in the hazelnuts and chocolate into the mixture. Pour the mixture into the muffin holes and place in the air fryer. Cook for 30 minutes at 175 C, checking them at the around 20-minute mark.

454. Broccoli Cheese Quiche

Total Time: 50 min | **Serves**: 2 | **Per serving**: Calories : 316; Carbs: 5g; Fat: 23.8g; Protein: 9.9g

INGREDIENTS

4 eggs
250ml whole milk
2 medium broccoli, cut into florets
2 medium tomatoes, diced
4 medium carrots, diced
50g Feta cheese, crumbled
80g grated Cheddar cheese
Salt and pepper to taste
1 tsp chopped parsley
1 tsp dried thyme

DIRECTIONS

Put the broccoli and carrots in a food steamer and cook until soft, about 10 minutes. In a jug, crack in the eggs, add the parsley, salt, pepper, and thyme. Using a whisk, beat the eggs while adding the milk gradually until a pale mixture is attained.

Once the broccoli and carrots are ready, strain them through a sieve and set aside. In a 3 X 3 inches quiche dish, add the carrots and broccoli. Put the tomatoes on top, then the feta and cheddar cheese following. Leave a little bit of cheddar cheese. Pour the egg mixture over the layering and top with the remaining cheddar cheese.

Place the dish in the air fryer and cook at 175 C for 20 minutes.

455. Cinnamon French Toast Sticks

Total Time: 15 min | **Serves**: 3 | **Per serving**: Calories : 276; Carbs: 34g; Fat: 14.3g; Protein: 6.2g

INGREDIENTS

5 slices bread
3 eggs
Salt and pepper to taste
1 ½ tbsp butter
⅛ tsp cinnamon powder
A pinch nutmeg powder
A pinch clove powder
Cooking spray

DIRECTIONS

Preheat the air fryer to 175 C. In a bowl, add clove powder, eggs, nutmeg powder, and cinnamon powder. Beat well using a whisk. Season with salt and pepper. Use a bread knife to apply butter on both sides of the bread slices and cut them into 3 or 4 strips.

Dip each strip in the egg mixture and arrange them in one layer in the fryer's basket. Cook for 2 minutes. Once ready, pull out the fryer basket and spray the toasts with cooking spray. Flip the toasts and spray the other side with cooking spray.

Slide the basket back to the fryer and cook for 4 minutes. Check regularly to prevent them from burning. Once the toasts are golden brown, remove them onto a serving platter. Dust with cinnamon and serve with syrup.

456. Sausage and Egg Casserole

Total Time: 20 min | **Serves**: 6 | **Per serving**: Calories : 494; Carbs: 9.1g; Fat: 41g; Protein: 26g

INGREDIENTS

1 lb minced breakfast sausage
6 eggs
1 red pepper, diced
1 green pepper, diced
1 yellow pepper, diced
1 sweet onion, diced
180g Cheddar cheese, shredded
Salt and pepper to taste
fresh parsley to garnish

DIRECTIONS

Place a skillet over medium heat on a stovetop, add the sausage and cook until brown, stirring occasionally. Once done, drain any excess fat derived from cooking and set aside.

Grease a casserole dish that fits into the fryer basket with cooking spray, and arrange the sausage on the bottom. Top with onion, red pepper, green pepper, and yellow pepper. Spread the cheese on top.

In a bowl, beat the eggs and season with salt and black pepper. Pour the mixture over the casserole. Place the casserole dish in the air basket, and bake at 180 C for 13-15 minutes. Serve warm garnished with fresh parsley.

457. Chili Hash Browns

Total Time: 50 min | **Serves**: 3 | **Per serving**: Calories : 312; Carbs: 4g; Fat: 15g; Protein: 16g

INGREDIENTS

1 lb potatoes, peeled and shredded
Salt and pepper to taste
1 tsp garlic powder
1 tsp chili flakes
1 tsp onion powder
1 egg, beaten
1 tbsp olive oil
Cooking spray

DIRECTIONS

Place a skillet over medium heat on a stovetop, add the olive oil and potatoes. Sauté until evenly golden, about 10 minutes. Transfer to a bowl and let cool completely. After they have cooled, add in the egg, pepper, salt, chili flakes, onion powder, and garlic powder; mix well.

In a flat plate, spread the mixture and pat firmly with your fingers. Refrigerate for 20 minutes and preheat the air fryer to 175 C. Remove from the fridge and divide into equal sizes. Grease the fryer basket with cooking spray and add in the patties. Cook for 15 minutes, then flip and cook for 6 more minutes. Serve with sunshine eggs.

458. Buttered Eggs in Hole

Total Time: 11 min | **Serves:** 2 | **Per serving:** Calories : 220; Carbs: 10g; Fat: 16g; Protein: 8g

INGREDIENTS

2 slices bread
2 eggs
Salt and pepper to taste
2 tbsp butter

DIRECTIONS

Place a 3 X 3 inches heatproof bowl in the fryer's basket and brush with butter. Make a hole in the middle of the bread slices with a bread knife and place in the heatproof bowl in 2 batches.

Break an egg into the center of each hole. Season with salt and pepper. Close the air fryer and cook for 4 minutes at 170 C. Turn the bread with a spatula and cook for another 4 minutes. Serve as a breakfast accompaniment.

459. Breakfast Muffins with Walnuts

Total Time: 20 min | **Serves:** 4 | **Per serving:** Calories: 214; Carbs: 24.3 g; Fat: 12.7 g; Protein: 2.7 g

INGREDIENTS

120g flour
80g mashed banana
50g powdered sugar
1 tsp milk
1 tsp chopped walnuts
½ tsp baking powder
30g oats
50g butter, room temperature

DIRECTIONS

Preheat the air fryer to 160 C. Place the sugar, walnuts, banana, and butter in a bowl and mix to combine. In another bowl, combine the flour, baking powder and oats. Combine the two mixtures and stir in the milk.

Grease a muffin tin and pour the batter in. Bake for 10-12 minutes until golden brown.

460. Paprika Rarebit

Total Time: 15 min | **Serves:** 2 | **Per serving:** Calories: 401; Carbs: 15.4 g; Fat: 27.2 g; Protein: 26.9 g

INGREDIENTS

3 slices bread
1 tsp smoked paprika
2 eggs
1 tsp dijon mustard
4 ½ oz cheddar cheese, grated
Salt and pepper, to taste

DIRECTIONS

Toast the bread in the air fryer to your liking. In a bowl, whisk the eggs, stir in the mustard, cheddar and paprika. Season with salt and pepper. Spread the mixture on the toasts. Cook the slices for 10 minutes at 180 C.

461. Breakfast Banana Bread

Total Time: 50 minute | **Serves:** 2 | **Per serving:** Calories: 438; Carbs: 58 g; Fat: 21 g; Protein: 7.6 g

INGREDIENTS

120 g plus
1 tbsp flour
¼ tsp baking soda
1 tsp baking powder
70g sugar

2 mashed bananas
60 ml vegetable oil
1 egg, beaten
1 tsp vanilla extract
120g chopped walnuts

¼ tsp salt
2 tbsp peanut butter
2 tbsp sour cream
Cooking spray for greasing

DIRECTIONS

Preheat the air fryer to 165 C. Spray a small baking dish, that fits inside, with cooking spray or grease with butter. Combine the flour, salt, baking powder, and baking soda, in a bowl.

In another bowl, combine bananas, oil, egg, peanut butter, vanilla, sugar, and sour cream. Combine both mixtures gently. Stir in the chopped walnuts. Pour the batter into the dish. Cook for 40 minutes and serve chill.

462. Ham and Cheese Mini Quiche

Total Time: 30 min | **Serves**: 8 | **Per serving**: Calories: 365; Carbs: 21.4 g; Fat: 20.4 g; Protein: 8.9 g

INGREDIENTS

1 shortcrust pastry
3 oz chopped ham
50g grated cheese

4 eggs, beaten
3 tbsp Greek yogurt
¼ tsp garlic powder

¼ tsp salt
¼ tsp black pepper

DIRECTIONS

Preheat the air fryer to 165 C. Take 8 ramekins and sprinkle them with flour to avoid sticking. Cut the shortcrust pastry into 8 equal pieces to make 8 mini quiches. Line the ramekins with the pastry. Combine all of the other ingredients in a bowl. Divide the filling between the ramekins and cook for 20 minutes in the air fryer.

463. Chorizo Spanish Frittata

Total Time: 12 min | **Serves**: 2 | **Per serving**: Calories: 438; Carbs: 39.4 g; Fat: 22.9 g; Protein: 20.4 g

INGREDIENTS

3 eggs
1 large potato, boiled and cubed
80g frozen corn

80g Feta cheese, crumbled
1 tbsp chopped parsley
½ chorizo, sliced

3 tbsp olive oil
Salt and pepper, to taste

DIRECTIONS

Pour the olive oil into the air fryer and preheat it to 165 C. Cook the chorizo until slightly browned. Beat the eggs with some salt and pepper in a bowl. Stir in all of the remaining ingredients. Pour the mixture into the air fryer, give it a stir, and cook for 6 minutes.

464. Zucchini Muffins

Total Time: 20 min | **Serves**: 4 | **Per serving**: Calories: 357; Carbs: 47.6 g; Fat: 13 g; Protein: 12.6 g

INGREDIENTS

190g flour
1 tsp cinnamon
3 eggs
2 tsp baking powder
2 tbsp sugar

240ml milk
2 tbsp butter, melted
1 tbsp yogurt
60g shredded courgatte
A pinch of salt

2 tbsp cream cheese

DIRECTIONS

Preheat the air fryer to 180 C. In a bowl, whisk the eggs along with the sugar, salt, cinnamon, cream cheese, flour, and baking powder. In another bowl, combine all of the liquid ingredients.

Gently combine the dry and liquid mixtures. Stir in zucchini. Line the muffin tins with baking paper, and pour the batter inside them. Arrange in the air fryer and cook for 15 minutes. Check with a toothpick.

465. Onion and Cheese Omelet

Total Time: 15 min | Serve: 1 | **Per serving**: Calories: 347; Carbs: 6 g; Fat: 23.2 g; Protein: 13.6 g

INGREDIENTS

2 eggs
2 tbsp grated Cheddar cheese
1 tsp soy sauce
½ onion, sliced
¼ tsp pepper
1 tbsp olive oil

DIRECTIONS

Whisk the eggs along with the pepper and soy sauce. Preheat the air fryer to 180 C. Heat the olive oil and add the egg mixture and the onion. Cook for 8 to 10 minutes. Top with the grated cheddar cheese.

466. The Simplest Grilled Cheese

Total Time: 10 min | Serve: 1 | **Per serving**: Calories: 452; Carbs: 23 g; Fat: 32.3 g; Protein: 17 g

INGREDIENTS

2 tbsp butter
2 slices bread
3 slices American cheese

DIRECTIONS

Preheat the air fryer to 180 C. Spread one tsp of butter on the outside of each of the bread slices. Place the cheese on the inside of one bread slice. Top with the other slice. Cook in the air fryer for 4 minutes. Flip the sandwich over and cook for an additional 4 minutes. Serve cut diagonally.

467. Air Fried Shirred Eggs

Total Time: 20 min | **Serves**: 2 | **Per serving**: Calories: 279; Carbs: 1.8 g; Fat: 20 g; Protein: 20.8 g

INGREDIENTS

2 tsp butter, for greasing
4 eggs, divided
2 tbsp heavy cream
4 slices of ham
3 tbsp Parmesan cheese
¼ tsp paprika
¾ tsp salt
¼ tsp pepper
2 tsp chopped chives

DIRECTIONS

Preheat the air fryer to 160 C. Grease a pie pan with the butter. Arrange the ham slices on the bottom of the pan to cover it completely. Whisk one egg along with the heavy cream, salt and pepper, in a small bowl.

Pour the mixture over the ham slices. Crack the other eggs over the ham. Sprinkle with Parmesan cheese. Cook for 14 minutes. Season with paprika, garnish with chives and serve with bread.

468. Crustless Mediterranean Quiche

Total Time: 40 min | **Serves**: 2 | **Per serving**: Calories: 540; Carbs: 10.8 g; Fat: 43.9g; Protein: 25.8 g

INGREDIENTS

4 eggs
100g chopped tomatoes
150g crumbled Feta cheese
1 tbsp chopped basil

1 tbsp chopped oregano
50g chopped kalamata olives
20g chopped onion
2 tbsp olive oil

120ml milk
Salt and pepper to taste

DIRECTIONS

Preheat the air fryer to 170 C. Brush a pie pan with olive oil. Beat the eggs along with the milk and some salt and pepper. Stir in all of the remaining ingredients. Pour the egg mixture into the pan. Cook for 30 minutes.

469. Prosciutto, Mozzarella and Egg in a Cup

Total Time: 20 min | Serves: 2 | Per serving: Calories: 291; Carbs: 12.9 g; Fat: 20.5 g; Protein: 13 g

INGREDIENTS

2 slices bread
2 prosciutto slices, chopped
2 eggs
4 tomato slices

¼ tsp balsamic vinegar
2 tbsp grated mozzarella
¼ tsp maple syrup
2 tbsp mayonnaise

Salt and pepper, to taste
Cooking spray for greasing

DIRECTIONS

Preheat the air fryer to 160 C. Grease two large ramekins. Place one bread slice on the bottom of each ramekin. Arrange 2 tomato slices on top of each bread slice. Divide the mozzarella between the ramekins.

Crack the eggs over the mozzarella. Drizzle with maple syrup and balsamic vinegar. Season with some salt and pepper. Cook for 10 minutes, or until desired. Top with mayonnaise.

470. Three Meat Cheesy Omelet

Total Time: 20 min | Serves: 2 | Per serving: Calories: 590; Carbs: 6.1 g; Fat: 42.5 g; Protein: 44 g

INGREDIENTS

1 beef sausage, chopped
4 slices prosciutto, chopped
3 oz salami, chopped

220g grated Mozzarella cheese
4 eggs
1 tbsp chopped onion

1 tbsp ketchup

DIRECTIONS

Preheat the air fryer to 175 C. Whisk the eggs with the ketchup in a bowl. Stir in the onion. Brown the sausage in the air fryer for 2 minutes. Combine the egg mixture, mozzarella cheese, salami and prosciutto. Pour the egg mixture over the sausage and give it a stir. Cook for 10 minutes.

471. Raspberry and Vanilla Pancakes

Total Time: 15 min | Serves: 4 | Per serving: Calories: 483; Carbs: 108 g; Fat: 4.8 g; Protein: 13.5 g

INGREDIENTS

250g all-purpose flour
250ml milk
3 eggs, beaten
1 tsp baking powder
220g brown sugar

1 ½ tsp vanilla extract
60g frozen raspberries, thawed
2 tbsp maple syrup
A pinch of salt
Cooking spray for greasing

DIRECTIONS

Preheat the air fryer to 190 C. In a bowl, mix the flour, baking powder, salt, milk, eggs, vanilla extract, sugar, and maple syrup, until smooth. Stir in the raspberries. Do it gently to avoid coloring the batter.

Grease a baking dish or spray it with cooking spray. Drop the batter onto the recipe. Just make sure to leave some space between the pancakes. If there is some batter left, repeat the process. Cook for 10 minutes.

472. Very Berry Breakfast Puffs

Total Time: 20 min | Serves: 3 | Per serving: Calories: 255; Carbs: 24.5 g; Fat: 15.7 g; Protein: 4.3 g

INGREDIENTS

- 3 pastry dough sheets
- 2 tbsp mashed strawberries
- 2 tbsp mashed raspberries
- ¼ tsp vanilla extract
- 450g cream cheese
- 1 tbsp honey

DIRECTIONS

Preheat the air fryer to 190 C. Divide the cream cheese between the dough sheets and spread it evenly. In a small bowl, combine the berries, honey and vanilla.

Divide the mixture between the pastry sheets. Pinch the ends of the sheets, to form puff. Place the puffs on a lined baking dish. Place the dish in the air fryer and cook for 15 minutes.

473. Sweet Bread Pudding with Raisins

Total Time: 45 min | Serves: 3 | Per serving: Calories: 529; Carbs: 77 g; Fat: 20 g; Protein: 13 g

INGREDIENTS

- 8 slices of bread
- 120g buttermilk
- 80g honey
- 250ml milk
- 2 eggs
- ½ tsp vanilla extract
- 2 tbsp butter, softened
- 50g sugar
- 4 tbsp raisins
- 2 tbsp chopped hazelnuts
- Cinnamon for garnish

DIRECTIONS

Preheat the air fryer to 160 C. Beat the eggs along with the buttermilk, honey, milk, vanilla, sugar and butter. Stir in raisins and hazelnuts. Cut the bread into cubes and place them, in a bowl. Pour the milk mixture over the bread. Let soak for 10 minutes. Cook the bread pudding for 30 minutes and garnish with cinnamon.

474. Easy Air Fried Egg

Total Time: 15 minute | Serves: 6 | Per serving: Calories: 63; Carbs: 1g; Fat: 4g; Protein: 6g

INGREDIENTS

6 large eggs

DIRECTIONS

Preheat your air fryer 150 C. Lay the eggs in your air fryer's basket and bake for at least 8 minutes for a slightly runny yolk or 12 to 15 minutes for a firmer yolk. Using tongs, place the eggs in a bowl with icy water. Allow to cool in cold water for 5 minutes before cracking the shell underwater. Peel and serve.

475. Vanilla Toast

Total Time: 10 min | **Serves**: 6 | **Per serving**: Calories: 342; Carbs: 39.2 g; Fat: 19.3 g; Protein: 3.2 g

INGREDIENTS

12 slices bread
100g sugar
1 ½ tsp cinnamon
1 stick of butter, softened
1 tsp vanilla extract

DIRECTIONS

Preheat the air fryer to 200 C. Combine all ingredients, except the bread, in a bowl. Spread the buttery cinnamon mixture onto the bread slices. Place the bread slices in the air fryer. Cook for 5 minutes.

476. Flaxseed Porridge

Total Time: 5 min | **Serves**: 4 | **Per serving**: Calories: 450; Carbs: 67 g; Fat: 18.9 g; Protein: 20.2 g

INGREDIENTS

340g steel cut oats
130g flax seeds
1 tbsp peanut butter
1 tbsp butter
1000ml milk
4 tbsp honey

DIRECTIONS

Preheat the air fryer to 200 C. Combine all of the ingredients in an ovenproof bowl. Place in the air fryer and cook for 5 minutes. Stir and serve.

477. Breakfast Sandwich

Total Time: 10 min | **Serve**: 1 | **Per serving**: Calories: 240; Carbs: 25.5 g; Fat: 8.8 g; Protein: 13.3 g

INGREDIENTS

1 egg
1 English muffin
2 slices of bacon
Salt and pepper, to taste

DIRECTIONS

Preheat the air fryer to 200 C. Crack the egg into a ramekin. Place the muffin, egg and bacon in the air fryer. Cook for 6 minutes. Let cool slightly so you can assemble the sandwich. Cut the muffin in half. Place the egg on one half and season with salt and pepper. Arrange the bacon on top. Top with the other muffin half.

478. Sausage Frittata with Parmesan

Total Time: 15 min | **Serve**: 1 | **Per serving**: Calories: 491; Carbs: 11g; Fat: 33g; Protein: 35g

INGREDIENTS

½ sausage, chopped
Salt and pepper to taste
A bunch of parsley, chopped
3 whole eggs
1 tbsp olive oil
1 slice bread
4 cherry tomatoes, halved
1 slice bread
2 tbsp Parmesan cheese, shredded for garnish

DIRECTIONS

Preheat your air fryer to 180 C. Place tomatoes and sausages in your air fryer's cooking basket and cook for 5 minutes. In a bowl, mix baked tomatoes, sausages, eggs, salt, parsley, Parmesan cheese, oil, and pepper.

Add the bread to the air fryer cooking basket and cook for 5 minutes. Add the frittata mixture over baked bread and top with Parmesan cheese. Serve and enjoy!

479. Cinnamon Flavored Grilled Pineapples

Total Time: 15 min | **Serves**: 2 | **Per serving**: Calories: 480; Carbs: 71g; Fat: 18g; Protein: 13g

INGREDIENTS

1 tsp cinnamon
5 pineapple slices
100g brown sugar
1 tbsp basil, chopped for garnish
1 tbsp honey, for garnish

DIRECTIONS

Preheat your air fryer to 170 C. In a small bowl, mix brown sugar and cinnamon. Drizzle the sugar mixture over your pineapple slices and set aside for 20 minutes.

Place the pineapple rings in the air fryer cooking basket and cook for 10 minutes. Flip the pineapples and cook for 10 minutes more. Serve with basil and a drizzle of honey.

480. Great Japanese Omelette

Total Time: 20 min | Serve: 1 | **Per serving**: Calories: 305; Carbs: 19g; Fat: 40g; Protein: 72g

INGREDIENTS

1 small Japanese tofu, cubed
3 whole eggs
Pepper to taste
1 tsp coriander
1 tsp cumin
2 tbsp soy sauce
2 tbsp green onion, chopped
Olive oil
1 whole onion, chopped

DIRECTIONS

In a bowl, mix eggs, soy sauce, cumin, pepper, oil, and salt. Add cubed tofu to baking forms and pour the egg mixture on top. Place the prepared forms in the air fryer cooking basket and cook for 10 minutes at 200 C. Serve with a sprinkle of coriander and green onion.

481. Blueberry Cream Cheese with French Toast

Total Time: 15 min | **Serves**: 4 | **Per serving**: Calories: 428; Carbs: 53.7g; Fat: 11.3g; Protein: 23.4g

INGREDIENTS

2 eggs, beaten
4 slices bread
3 tbsp sugar
50g corn flakes
80ml milk
¼ tsp nutmeg
4 tbsp berry-flavored cheese
¼ tsp salt

DIRECTIONS

Preheat your air fryer to 200 C. In a bowl, mix sugar, eggs, nutmeg, salt and milk. In a separate bowl, mix blueberries and cheese. Take 2 bread slices and pour the blueberry mixture over the slices.

Top with the milk mixture. Cover with the remaining two slices to make sandwiches. Dredge the sandwiches over cornflakes to coat thoroughly. Lay the sandwiches in your air fryer's cooking basket and cook for 8 minutes. Serve with berries and syrup.

482. Clean Breakfast Sandwich

Total Time: 10 min | Serve: 1 | **Per serving**: Calories: 320; Carbs: 33g; Fat: 13g; Protein: 17g

INGREDIENTS

1 whole egg, cracked
1 slice English bacon

Salt and pepper to taste
1 slice bread

100g butter

DIRECTIONS

Preheat your air fryer to 200 C. Spread butter on one side of the bread slice. Add the cracked egg on top and season with salt and pepper. Place bacon on top. Arrange the bread slice in your air fryer's cooking basket and cook for 3-5 minutes. Serve and enjoy!

483. Bread Cups Omelette

Total Time: 25 min | **Serves**: 4 | **Per serving**: Calories: 499; Carbs: 46g; Fat: 24g; Protein: 26g

INGREDIENTS

4 crusty rolls
5 eggs, beaten
A pinch of salt

½ tsp thyme, dried
3 strips precooked bacon, chopped
2 tbsp heavy cream

4 Gouda cheese mini wedges, thin slices

DIRECTIONS

Preheat your air fryer 165 C. Cut the tops off the rolls and remove the inside with your fingers. Line the rolls with a slice of cheese and press down, so the cheese conforms to the inside of the roll. In a bowl, mix eggs with heavy cream, bacon, thyme, salt and pepper.

Stuff the rolls with the egg mixture. Lay the rolls in your air fryer's cooking basket and bake for 8 to 12 minutes or until the eggs become puffy and the roll shows a golden brown texture.

484. Air Fried Turkey Calzone

Total Time: 20 min | **Serves**: 4 | **Per serving**: Calories: 339; Carbs: 10.6 g; Fat: 17.3 g; Protein: 33.6 g

INGREDIENTS

Pizza dough
4 oz cheddar cheese, grated
1 oz mozzarella cheese
1 oz bacon, diced

500g cooked and shredded turkey
1 egg, beaten
1 tsp thyme
4 tbsp tomato paste

1 tsp basil
1 tsp oregano
Salt and pepper, to taste

DIRECTIONS

Preheat the air fryer to 175 C. Divide the pizza dough into 4 equal pieces so you have the dough for 4 small pizza crusts. Combine the tomato paste, basil, oregano, and thyme, in a small bowl.

Brush the mixture onto the crusts; just make sure not to go all the way and avoid brushing near the edges on one half of each crust, place ½ turkey, and season the meat with some salt and pepper.

Top the meat with some bacon. Combine the cheddar and mozzarella and divide it between the pizzas, making sure that you layer only one half of the dough. Brush the edges of the crust with the beaten egg. Fold the crust and seal with a fork. Cook for 10 minutes.

485. Parsnip Hash Browns

Total Time: 20 min | **Serves**: 2 | **Per serving**: Calories: 507; Carbs: 74.2 g; Fat: 14.8 g; Protein: 18.3 g

INGREDIENTS

1 large parsnip, grated

3 eggs, beaten

½ tsp garlic powder

¼ tsp nutmeg
1 tbsp olive oil

120g flour
Salt and pepper, to taste

DIRECTIONS

Heat olive oil in the air fryer at 195 C. In a bowl, combine flour, eggs, parsnip, nutmeg, and garlic powder. Season with salt and pepper. Form patties out of the mixture. Arrange in the air fryer and cook for 15 minutes.

486. Spicy Egg and Bacon Wraps

Total Time: 15 min | **Serves**: 3 | **Per serving**: Calories: 385; Carbs: 20.1 g; Fat: 25.3 g; Protein: 17.1 g

INGREDIENTS

3 tortillas
2 previously scrambled eggs

3 slices bacon, cut into strips
3 tbsp salsa

3 tbsp cream cheese, divided
120g grated pepper Jack cheese

DIRECTIONS

Preheat the air fryer to 195 C. Spread one tbsp. of cream cheese onto each tortilla. Divide the eggs and bacon between the tortillas evenly. Top with salsa. Sprinkle some grated cheese over. Roll up the tortillas. Cook for 10 minutes.

487. Mock Stir Fry

Total Time: 25 min | **Serves**: 4 | **Per serving**: Calories: 277; Carbs: 15.6 g; Fat: 4.4 g; Protein: 43.1 g

INGREDIENTS

4 boneless and skinless chicken breasts cut into cubes
2 carrots, sliced

1 red bell pepper, cut into strips
1 yellow bell pepper, cut into strips
100g snow peas

15 oz broccoli florets
1 scallion, sliced

SAUCE:

3 tbsp soy sauce
2 tbsp oyster sauce
1 tbsp brown sugar

1 tsp sesame oil
1 tsp cornstarch
1 tsp sriracha

2 garlic cloves, minced
1 tbsp grated ginger
1 tbsp rice wine vinegar

DIRECTIONS

Preheat the air fryer to 185 C. Place the chicken, bell peppers, and carrot, in a bowl. In another bowl, combine the sauce ingredients. Coat the chicken mixture with the sauce.

Place on a lined baking sheet and cook for 5 minutes. Add snow peas and broccoli and cook for an additional 8 to 10 minutes. Serve garnished with scallion.

488. Exquisite German Pancake

Total Time: 30 min | **Serves**: 4 | **Per serving**: Calories: 196; Carbs: 19g; Fat: 9g; Protein: 16g

INGREDIENTS

3 eggs, beaten
2 tbsp unsalted butter

60g flour
2 tbsp sugar, powdered

120ml milk
300g fresh strawberries, sliced

DIRECTIONS

Preheat your air fryer to 170 C. Add butter to a pan and melt over low heat. In a bowl, mix flour, milk, eggs and vanilla until fully incorporated. Add the mixture to the pan with melted butter.

Place the pan in your air fryer's cooking basket and cook for 12-16 minutes until the pancake is fluffy and golden brown. Drizzle powdered sugar and toss sliced strawberries on top.

489. Grilled Apple and Brie Sandwich

Total Time: 8 - 10 min | Serve: 1 | **Per serving**: Calories: 391; Carbs: 27.8 g; Fat: 25.9 g; Protein: 18 g

INGREDIENTS

2 bread slices
½ apple, thinly sliced
2 tsp butter
2 oz brie cheese, thinly sliced

DIRECTIONS

Spread butter on the outside of the bread slices. Arrange apple slices on the inside of one bread slice. Place brie slices on top of the apple. Top with the other slice of bread. Cook for 5 minutes at 175 C. Serve cut diagonally.

490. Turkey and Mushroom Sandwich

Total Time: 15 min | Serve: 1 | **Per serving**: Calories: 315; Carbs: 25.6 g; Fat: 16.4 g; Protein: 18.4 g

INGREDIENTS

100g shredded leftover turkey
40g sliced mushrooms
1 tbsp butter, divided
2 tomato slices
½ tsp red pepper flakes
¼ tsp salt
¼ tsp black pepper
1 hamburger bun

DIRECTIONS

Melt half of the butter and add the mushrooms in a saucepan over medium heat. Stir-fry for 4 minutes. Cut the bun in half and spread the remaining butter on the outside of the bun. Place the turkey on one half of the bun.

Arrange the mushroom slices on top of the turkey. Place the tomato slices on top of the mushrooms. Sprinkle with salt pepper and red pepper flakes. Top with the other bun half. Bake the sandwich in the preheated air fryer for 5 minutes at 175 C, until crunchy.

491. Garlicky Chicken on Green Bed

Total Time: 20 min | Serve: 1 | **Per serving**: Calories: 551; Carbs: 10.7 g; Fat: 45 g; Protein: 28.7 g

INGREDIENTS

30g baby spinach leaves
50g shredded romaine
3 large kale leaves, chopped
4 oz chicken breasts, cut into cubes
3 tbsp olive oil, divided
1 tsp balsamic vinegar
1 garlic clove, minced
Salt and pepper, to taste

DIRECTIONS

Place the chicken, 1 tbsp. olive oil and garlic, in a bowl. Season with salt and pepper and toss to combine.

Put on a lined baking dish and cook for 14 minutes at 195 C. Place the greens in a large bowl. Add the remaining olive oil and balsamic vinegar. Season with salt and pepper and toss to combine. Top with the chicken.

492. Baked Kale Omelet

Total Time: 15 min | Serve: 1 | **Per serving**: Calories: 294; Carbs: 3.9 g; Fat: 19.5 g; Protein: 24.7 g

INGREDIENTS

3 eggs
3 tbsp cottage cheese
3 tbsp chopped kale
½ tbsp chopped basil
½ tbsp chopped parsley
Salt and pepper, to taste
1 tsp olive oil

DIRECTIONS

Preheat the air fryer to 170 C. Beat the eggs with salt and pepper, in a bowl. Stir in the rest of the ingredients. Pour the mixture into the greased with olive oil air fryer and cook for 10 minutes, until slightly golden and set.

493. Craving Cinnamon Toast

Total Time: 15 minute | **Serves**: 6 | **Per serving**: Calories: 281; Carbs: 18g; Fat: 5g; Protein: 3g

INGREDIENTS

12 slices bread
Pepper to taste
100g sugar
1 stick butter
1½ tbsp vanilla extract
1½ tbsp cinnamon

DIRECTIONS

In a microwave-proof bowl, mix butter, pepper, sugar and vanilla extract. Warm and stir the mixture for 30 seconds until everything melts. Pour the mixture over bread slices. Lay the bread slices in your air fryer's cooking basket and cook for 5 minutes at 200 C. Serve with fresh banana and berry sauce.

494. Toasted Herb and Garlic Bagel

Total Time: 10 min | **Serve**: 1 | **Per serving**: Calories: 432; Carbs: 40.4 g; Fat: 25.7 g; Protein: 10.4 g

INGREDIENTS

2 tbsp butter, softened
1 tsp dried basil
1 tsp dried parsley
1 tsp garlic powder
1 tbsp Parmesan cheese
Salt and pepper, to taste
1 bagel

DIRECTIONS

Preheat the air fryer to 185 C. Cut the bagel in half. Place in the air fryer and cook for 3 minutes. Combine the butter, Parmesan cheese, garlic, basil, and parsley in a small bowl. Season with salt and pepper, to taste. Spread the mixture onto the toasted bagel. Return the bagel to the air fryer and cook for an additional 3 minutes.

495. Feta Breakfast

Total Time: 30 min | **Serves**: 3 | **Per serving**: Calories: 426; Carbs: 65g; Fat: 14g; Protein: 9g

INGREDIENTS

3½ pounds Feta cheese
pepper to taste
1 whole onion, chopped
2 tbsp parsley, chopped
1 egg yolk
Olive oil for drizzling
5 sheets frozen filo pastry

DIRECTIONS

Cut each of the 5 filo sheets into three equal-sized strips. Cover the strips with oil. In a bowl, mix onion, pepper, feta, salt, egg yolk, and parsley.

Make triangles using the cut strips and add a little bit of the feta mixture on top of each triangle. Place the triangles in fryer's basket and cook for 3 minutes at 200 C. Serve with a drizzle of oil and green onions.

496. Cheesy Omelet

Total Time: 15 min | Serve: 1 | **Per serving**: Calories: 396; Carbs: 1g; Fat: 32g; Protein: 27g

INGREDIENTS

2 eggs, beaten
pepper to taste
240g cheddar cheese, shredded
1 whole onion, chopped
2 tbsp soy sauce

DIRECTIONS

Preheat your air fryer to 175 C. Drizzle soy sauce over the chopped onions. Place the onions in your air fryer's cooking basket and cook for 8 minutes. In a bowl, mix the beaten eggs with salt and pepper.

Pour the egg mixture over onions (in the cooking basket) and cook for 3 minutes. Add cheddar cheese over eggs and bake for 2 more minutes. Serve with fresh basil and enjoy!

497. Caprese on Toast

Total Time: 10 min | Serve: 1 | **Per serving**: Calories: 514; Carbs: 24.8 g; Fat: 33.3 g; Protein: 34.2 g

INGREDIENTS

2 slices of bread
4 tomato slices
4 mozzarella slices
1 tbsp olive oil
1 tbsp chopped basil
Salt and pepper, to taste

DIRECTIONS

Preheat the air fryer to 185 C. Place the bread slices in the air fryer and toast for 3 minutes. Arrange two tomato slices on each bread slice. Season with salt and pepper.

Top each slice with 2 mozzarella slices. Return to the air fryer and cook for 1 minute more. Drizzle the caprese toasts with olive oil and top with chopped basil.

498. Italian Sausage Patties

Total Time: 20 min | **Serves**: 4 | **Per serving**: Calories: 332; Carbs: 6.2 g; Fat: 24.6 g; Protein: 18.6 g

INGREDIENTS

1 lb ground Italian sausage
30g breadcrumbs
1 tsp dried parsley
1 tsp red pepper flakes
½ tsp salt
¼ tsp black pepper
¼ tsp garlic powder
1 egg, beaten

DIRECTIONS

Preheat the air fryer to 175 C. Combine all of the ingredients in a large bowl. Line a baking sheet with parchment paper. Make patties out of the sausage mixture and arrange them on the baking sheet. Cook for 15 minutes, flipping once halfway through cooking.

499. Mac and Cheese

Total Time: 15 min | **Serves**: 2 | **Per serving**: Calories: 375; Carbs: 23 g; Fat: 1.8 g; Protein: 6.4 g

INGREDIENTS

200g cooked macaroni
240g grated cheddar cheese
120ml warm milk
1 tbsp Parmesan cheese
Salt and pepper, to taste

DIRECTIONS

Preheat the air fryer to 175 C. Add the macaroni to an ovenproof baking dish. Stir in the cheddar and milk. Season with salt and pepper, to taste. Place the dish in the air fryer and cook for 10 minutes. Sprinkle with Parmesan cheese, to serve.

500. Prosciutto and Mozzarella Bruschetta

Total Time: 7 min | Serve: 1 | **Per serving**: Calories: 674; Carbs: 41.6 g; Fat: 38.8 g; Protein: 38.4 g

INGREDIENTS

100g finely chopped tomatoes
3 oz chopped mozzarella
3 prosciutto slices, chopped
1 tbsp olive oil
1 tsp dried basil
6 small slices of French bread

DIRECTIONS

Preheat the air fryer to 175 C. Place the bread slices and toast for 3 minutes. Top the bread with tomatoes, prosciutto and mozzarella. Sprinkle the basil over the mozzarella. Drizzle with olive oil. Return to the air fryer and cook for 1 more minute, enough to become melty and warm.

Printed in Great Britain
by Amazon